Guide to North Carolina Highway Historical Markers

Ninth Edition
Edited by Michael Hill

Raleigh
Division of Archives and History
Department of Cultural Resources
2001

Preface

An Overview of North Carolina's Historic Places by Region

North Carolina, site of the first English colonies in the New World and one of the thirteen original colonies, offers a variety of public attractions for Tar Heel and out-of-state travelers. Each of the state's three geographic regions has its own distinctive history, natural scenery, and recreational opportunities. This volume introduces the traveler to 1,434 sites where history happened, each spot commemorated by an official state highway historical marker. Further information on the state's history may be obtained by writing to the Research Branch, North Carolina Division of Archives and History, 4611 Mail Service Center, Raleigh, North Carolina 27699-4611. Information about scenic attractions and recreation is available from the North Carolina Division of Tourism, Film, and Sports Development, 4324 Mail Service Center, Raleigh, North Carolina 27699-4324.

The Coastal Plain

Extending from the Outer Banks to the fall line of the rivers of eastern North Carolina, the Coastal Plain is a region of tobacco farms, flat terrain, and tidal rivers and sounds. For two centuries, beginning in the late 1500s, these waterways were avenues of exploration and settlement. Sir Walter Raleigh's ships found their way through the sounds to Roanoke Island from 1584 to 1587 and established there the first English colonies in America. Across Roanoke Sound and within sight of Roanoke Island is Kill Devil Hill, where Orville and Wilbur Wright three centuries later, in 1903, made the first successful flight of a power-driven airplane.

Albemarle Sound leads into the heart of northeastern North Carolina, where permanent settlement of the colony was first made in the 1650s by emigrants from neighboring Virginia. The town of Edenton, with its many well-preserved old homes and public buildings, has retained a sense of the eighteenth century. Within easy driving distance of Edenton are a number of plantation houses, such as Somerset Place on Lake Phelps in Washington County. To the west of the Albemarle section is the town of Halifax, steeped in Revolutionary history, where North Carolina in 1776 endorsed the first formal sanction of American independence.

To the south, Pamlico Sound opens to two river systems, the Tar-Pamlico and the Neuse, which were also routes of early exploration and settlement. Bath, the oldest incorporated town in North Carolina, is located on the Pamlico River and boasts the state's oldest church building, in continuous use since 1734. New Bern, founded on the Neuse River in 1710 by Baron Christoph de Graffenried and his Swiss colonists, is the site of reconstructed Tryon Palace, colonial capitol and residence of the royal governor. Up the river is the town of Kinston, home to Richard Caswell, the state's first governor. In Kinston, scene of several Civil War actions, rest the remains of the ironclad CSS *Neuse*.

In the southeastern corner of the state, the Cape Fear River region attracted settlers as early as 1664. The ruins of Brunswick Town (a flourishing colonial port), Orton Plantation, the Confederate Fort Fisher, the World War II battleship USS *North Carolina*, and the many historic sites of downtown Wilmington are among the attractions of the Cape Fear area.

Up the river from Wilmington is Fayetteville, center of the area settled by Scottish Highlanders in the eighteenth century and seat of the state convention that ratified the United States Constitution in 1789. Within driving distance are two battlefields: Moores Creek, scene in 1776 of an early conflict of the American Revolution, and Bentonville, site in 1865 of the last major battle of the Civil War. In nearby Wayne County is the birthplace of Charles B. Aycock, twentieth-century governor noted for his education reforms.

The Piedmont

The central area of North Carolina, the Piedmont, is a land of rolling terrain and traditionally has been the state's industrial and commercial focus. The region was populated in the 1700s by successive waves of migration, principally settlers from coastal North Carolina and Virginia, joined by Scotch-Irish and German groups from Pennsylvania entering by way of the Great Wagon Road.

Raleigh, the state capital since 1792, stands at the eastern extremity of the Piedmont. The State Capitol, the birthplace of Andrew Johnson, the North Carolina Museum of Natural Sciences, and the North Carolina Museum of History are among its attractions. Raleigh, Durham, and Chapel Hill, with their respective campuses of North Carolina State University, Duke University, and the University of North Carolina, constitute the nationally acclaimed Research Triangle. The reconstructed farmhouse known as the Bennett Place, where Confederate General Joseph E. Johnston surrendered to Union General William T. Sherman, is in Durham. Nearby stands the Duke Homestead, where that family's tobacco manufacturing empire was born.

Just to the west, Hillsborough was an early outpost in the westward settlement and the center of the Regulators' uprising against colonial authorities. That movement was crushed at the Battle of Alamance, near present-day Burlington. A bit farther west, at Sedalia in Guilford County, is the Charlotte Hawkins Brown State Historic Site, devoted to African American history and culture. Guilford Courthouse National Military Park at Greensboro was the scene of a major Revolutionary conflict between the forces of Nathanael Greene and Lord Cornwallis. Historic Old Salem in downtown Winston-Salem is a restored community founded by Moravians in the late eighteenth century. North of the city are several sites worth visiting, among them the campus of Wake Forest University and Reynolda House.

Salisbury, in the Yadkin River valley, was an important outpost for trade and migration into the backcountry. The site of Fort Dobbs, located just north of Statesville, was the scene of a Cherokee attack during the French and Indian War. Town Creek Indian Mound near Mount Gilead is the site of an archaeological project and restored Indian village. The House in the Horseshoe, located nearby, still bears evidence of a Tory raid during the Revolution. The North Carolina Zoological Park at Asheboro is an increasingly popular destination for travelers.

In and around Charlotte, the state's largest city, are sites that illustrate the diversity of North Carolina history. Downtown Charlotte was the scene of a Revolutionary War battle and the location of the first branch of the United States Mint. (The structure, relocated and enlarged, is today the Mint Museum of Art.) In 1799 gold was discovered twenty miles to the northeast at the Reed Gold Mine near Concord, giving rise to the nation's first gold rush. Southeast of Charlotte are the birthplaces of Presidents James K.

Polk and Andrew Jackson. To the north in Rowan County, Spencer Shops, once Southern Railway's main staging and repair facility, has been converted into the North Carolina Transportation Museum.

The Mountains

Mountainous western North Carolina was the last region in the state to be settled and long remained virtually inaccessible. Yet, owing to their climate and scenic beauty, the Mountains have hosted a steady tourist trade since antebellum times. Before the Civil War, Flat Rock and Warm Springs were popular summer resorts. In the late-nineteenth and early-twentieth centuries, economic vitality and an influx of outside wealth produced an eclectic mix of architectural showplaces in Asheville, most notably Biltmore House, constructed for George W. Vanderbilt from 1890 to 1895.

The relative isolation of the mountain region helped preserve cultural traditions that might have soon faded in more accessible areas. From the earliest times the Cherokee Indians dominated the mountains, setting the stage for a series of dramatic encounters between Indians and white settlers. Today in Cherokee their native culture is displayed at Oconaluftee Village and in the Cherokee Museum. The Blue Ridge Parkway and the Great Smoky Mountains National Park were created, in part, to preserve and promote both the scenic beauty and native culture of the southern Appalachians. Folk traditions are also preserved in street fairs, annual festivals, curb markets, and craft exhibits, such as those at the Folk Art Center near Asheville. North of that city, on Reems Creek, is the restored birthplace of Zebulon B. Vance, North Carolina's popular Civil War governor. The Asheville home of Thomas Wolfe is open to the public, as is the home of Carl Sandburg in Flat Rock.

Scores of historic sites, operated by the state, the federal government, and local private organizations await the Tar Heel traveler willing to forsake the interstates. Hundreds of other spots where history happened are recorded in the pages that follow. As an inventory of the people, places, and events that have shaped North Carolina, the marker guide is a handbook to the state's past.

Introduction

History on a stick. Tombstones on posts. "Lyin' by the road." History by the spoonful. From academics to cartoonists to wisecracking backseat drivers, observers have taken note of the proliferation of historical markers in the state of North Carolina. During the latter two-thirds of the twentieth century, the Tar Heel State placed cast aluminum signs dedicated to selected subjects next to its roads. These ubiquitous roadside markers commemorate the formative events, people, and sites in the state's history. Each marker topic, the location of the sign, and inscription is selected only after much consideration and review. As these signs constitute, in a manner of speaking, the common heritage or the public memory of North Carolinians, it is only fitting that the history of the program and the process by which the decisions are made be laid plain. Viewed with the perspective of sixty-five-plus years, the marker program also can provide insight into the evolving conception of what is "historic."

The North Carolina General Assembly in 1935 established a program "to provide for the erection of markers at points of historic interest along the public highways" (*Public Laws of North Carolina*, 1935, c. 197). The North Carolina Highway Historical Marker Program is one of the oldest such programs in continuous operation in the United States. Over the years it has been administered cooperatively by state agencies, initially the North Carolina Historical Commission, the Highway Commission, and the Department of Conservation and Development. The program today is the joint responsibility of the Research Branch, Division of Archives and History, Department of Cultural Resources, and the Traffic Engineering Branch, Division of Highways, Department of Transportation.

Individuals active in the North Carolina Literary and Historical Association (founded in 1900) had long recognized the need to mark historic sites in the state. In 1917, R. D. W. Connor, first secretary of the state Historical Commission (the agency founded in 1903 which today is known as the Division of Archives and History), drew up a seven-page list of potential sites. In the prospectus Connor noted that "a visitor traveling through North Carolina will look in vain for any statue or monument, stone, bronze or marble tablet, with a very few striking exceptions, commemorating the services of eminent sons of the State, or marking the sites of historic events." To that date marker efforts in other states had been mostly scattershot private or local initiatives, from "Washington slept here" signs on New England inns to directional plaques placed along roadways by the American Automobile Association.

Between 1917 and 1935, the Historical Commission and private organizations, such as the Daughters of the American Revolution and the United Daughters of the Confederacy, together sponsored a small number of historical markers and plaques. For the most part these early monuments denoted "shrines" associated with military leaders, statesmen, early settlers, or battlefields. The 1935 state program, modeled after one begun in Virginia in 1926, was an effort to standardize the practice of marking broader categories of sites of statewide historical significance.

Speaking to the Raleigh Lions Club in November 1934, Albert Ray Newsome, then secretary of the Historical Commission, stressed the educational, cultural, and commercial value of a standardized state marker program. "Such markers would emphasize the high spots of the construction of the civilization which we have inherited," Newsome told the group. Four legislators—Senators Dudley Bagley of Currituck County and Lee Graveley of Pitt County plus Representatives David L. Ward of Craven County and Harry R. Lindsay of Rockingham County—took the lead in guiding the legislation, which authorized an annual appropriation of five thousand dollars for the purpose, through the General Assembly. The legislative largesse was remarkably progressive and farsighted, coming in the midst of the Great Depression.

Christopher C. Crittenden, who replaced Newsome as Historical Commission secretary in 1935, pressed forward the program with typical enthusiasm. He circulated a twenty-seven-page list of potential topics among historians, writers, newspaper editors, leaders of patriotic organizations, and others, inviting their suggestions. A general call for topics was pub-

Between 1903 and 1935 the North Carolina Historical Commission, in cooperation with local organizations, erected a number of bronze plaques. This sign in Warren County, erected in 1919, is typical of those memorials.

licized through the state's newspapers. Jeb Stuart Hinckey of Roanoke Rapids suggested a tree behind which Confederate general Matt Ransom jumped to avoid being shot, but this went unmarked.

The legislation establishing the program also provided for the creation of the North Carolina Highway Historical Marker Advisory Committee. That initial group was made up of Albert Ray Newsome, then affiliated with the University of North Carolina; William K. Boyd of Duke University; Forrest Clonts of Wake Forest College; Thomas W. Lingle of Davidson College; and Hugh T. Lefler, who had recently moved from North Carolina State College to take a teaching post at Chapel Hill. That group today is composed of ten four-year college and university faculty members who are experts in North Carolina history. Members are appointed by the secretary of cultural resources and serve five-year terms. The committee advises the Department of Cultural Resources on the historical authenticity, the comparative merit, and the appropriateness of proposed markers; approves or disapproves any proposed marker; fixes the wording of inscriptions; and establishes criteria for carrying out these responsibilities. No official state marker can be erected without the committee's review and approval.

During the fall of 1935, the advisory committee held several meetings in Raleigh and Chapel Hill. The first five topics approved for markers were the Roanoke colonies in Dare County, Green Hill Place in Franklin County, the homeplace of John Penn in Granville County, Calvary Episcopal Church in Henderson County, and the birthplace of Zebulon B. Vance in Buncombe County. The committee gave considerable thought to the design and materials for the signs. Marker program administrators in Virginia loaned two signs for examination and comparison. Professor Boyd of Duke University suggested the scroll or open book pattern and the raised State Seal emblem. Consideration also was given to use of the State Capitol dome in place of the seal. Two professors from State College, experts in casting and design, sat in on the planning meetings. Representatives from four manufacturers made presentations to the committee. Before settling on the use of cast aluminum, wrought iron and porcelain enamel were also considered as materials.

On January 10, 1936, a group of state officials, several members of the local chapter of the Daughters of the American Revolution, and others gathered in the Stovall community of Granville County for the dedication of the first marker erected under the state program. Among the officials present were Christopher Crittenden and Mattie Erma Edwards, collector for the North Carolina Hall of History (today the North Carolina Museum of History) and the marker program's first researcher. That first marker identified the homesite of John Penn, one of the state's three signers of the Declaration of Independence. (To commemorate the marker program's fiftieth anniversary, the original sign was retrieved in 1985 for safekeeping and display, and a replacement was ordered for the Stovall site.) Other staff members associated with the program over its history include Marybelle Delamar, William S. Powell, Edwin A. Miles, William S. Tarlton, Elizabeth Wall Wilborn, and Jerry C. Cashion.

The silver-and-black markers have become a familiar part of the landscape since 1935. To date, 1,434 markers have been erected across North Carolina, with at least one in each of the state's one hundred counties. Wake County with seventy-two markers has the most; New Hanover and Guilford follow, with fifty-nine and fifty-one, respectively. Efforts have been made over the years to avoid slighting any area, but the fact remains that topics of statewide historical significance can be commemorated by markers only at or near associated sites.

The first edition of the *Guide to North Carolina Highway Historical Markers* was published in 1939 and listed the inscriptions for 218 markers. As the program expanded, subsequent editions were published in 1940, 1949, 1956, 1961, 1964, 1979, and 1990. The present edition, the ninth, incorporates 136 new markers erected between 1990 and

North Carolina's first highway historical marker was dedicated at the Stovall community in Granville County on January 10, 1936. Among those present were Christopher Crittenden, secretary of the North Carolina Historical Commission (fourth from left), and Mattie Erma Edwards, marker program researcher (second from right).

2001. The reader should note that all inscriptions are reproduced exactly as they appear on the markers. No attempt has been made to edit the discrepancies of punctuation and style that have appeared over the years. An effort has been made to check the marker locations against recent maps and to be as specific as possible regarding the sites.

From the outset the marker program has divided the state into seventeen districts, listed A through Q (see the map on the inside front cover). On the face of each marker the district letter and that marker's number appear. Several changes effective with this edition of the *Guide* are designed to make it simpler to use and more informative. First, the markers, listed in past *Guides* by district, here are grouped by county and arranged Alamance-Yancey. Second, the year the marker was approved appears in the listing following its location. With the county-by-county arrangement, it has been necessary to key the subject index to page numbers rather than to individual marker numbers. Finally, to accompany the text and photos, detailed county-level highway maps have been prepared by the Geographic Information Systems Office of the Department of Transportation.

In January 1986, Mattie Erma Edwards Parker took part in a brief ceremony to retire the first marker. Also present were Jerry C. Cashion, research supervisor of Archives and History (left), and Michael Hill, marker program researcher (center).

In the 1990s, the concept of public memory received attention from historians. In a 1992 study, John Bodnar wrote, "The shaping of a past worthy of public commemoration in the present is contested and involves a struggle for supremacy between advocates of various political ideas and sentiments." James W. Loewen in 1999 published a critical examination of markers and monuments. He was particularly critical of those with outdated interpretations or "politically incorrect" wording. The professors who have volunteered their time to serve on the Marker Advisory Committee in North Carolina over the years, in their deliberations, have established high standards of historical accuracy and have refused to authorize markers without sufficient documentary historical evidence. Their concern has been that the decisions stand the test of time and, to the extent possible, that contemporary opinion not intrude upon committee decision-making.

One check upon this intrusion has been the "twenty-five-year rule," the prohibition against the consideration of a subject until twenty-five years (or the rough equivalent of a generation) has passed. Early in the development of the North Carolina marker program, exceptions to this rule were allowed for former governors and U.S. senators. Applied consistently today to all individuals, the rule permits the review committee members to assess the importance of people and events with the perspective of time. Commemorative fever generally peaks around fifty years after an event as the participants and witnesses age. In many cases it is not those who were involved in an event who take the lead in commemorations but rather their sons and daughters, literal or figurative. This, it is generally acknowledged, was the case after the Civil War. The appearance of statues on courthouse greens accelerated early in the twentieth century. In our own time more attention has been given to veterans of World War II and the civil rights movement.

To be eligible for a state marker, a subject must be judged to be of statewide historical significance. Markers cannot be approved for subjects of only regional or local importance. Local organizations, church congregations, or individuals may purchase privately or locally financed markers or plaques. Such private or local markers are not considered part of the official state program, cannot bear the State Seal, must be erected

The local chapter of the Daughters of the American Revolution in Bladen County sponsored a dedication ceremony for the Thomas Robeson marker (I 37) in 1952.

outside the highway right-of-way, and must differ from state signs in design and color.

State historical markers are placed only on state or federal numbered highways but cannot be located on interstates or limited-access routes. The signs erected by North Carolina contain shorter blocks of text than those found in other states so that they can be read by passing motorists. Wherever possible, the marker is located at a turn-off or at an intersection where traffic slows. The inscriptions are limited to five or six lines of about twenty-four letters and spaces each.

Exceptions to this general rule are larger map markers that illustrate battles or historic events that occurred within a region. (These non-standard-size markers are designated in the text with double-letter prefixes, such as BB 1.) Smaller signs have been used to mark driving tours or to designate points of interest over wide areas such as the Bentonville and Averasboro battlefields. (The designations for these markers use triple-letter prefixes, such as BBB 1.) A number of signs of both types were approved and erected during the Civil War centennial in the 1960s. As these special markers have been replaced in recent years, they have been incorporated into the regular marker numbering scheme.

The overall design and appearance of the signs has changed little over the years. During World War II the program was suspended because of a shortage of materials necessary for casting the signs. Signs cast before 1947 bear all capital letters. A change in manufacturers in that year led to the present style, made of cast aluminum and bearing the title in capital letters with the text in upper√ and lowercase. Since 1947 the state's supplier has been Sewah Studios of Marietta, Ohio, the supplier of such signs to more than thirty states. In 1996, the foundry cast for the North Carolina Museum of Art in Raleigh one-third size replicas of sixty-one state highway historical markers. These were installed on the grounds as part of the Museum Park Theater.

Anyone can submit a proposal for a new marker. A full listing of the criteria and an application form are available upon request. After a marker is approved, its location is subject to review by the Department of Transportation and the local governing body, that is, the board of county commissioners or the municipal government. The requesting party may wish to schedule a dedication and unveiling ceremony. In that event, the Division of Archives and History can assist with the planning and, in most cases, send a representative and cloth cover for unveiling purposes.

Many of the state highway historical markers have now been in service for more than sixty years. The marker materials and design were selected in part for their permanence.

In February 1999 several hundred members of the North Carolina Bar Association gathered on Edenton Street, just north of the State Capitol, to witness the unveiling of a marker (H 106) dedicated to that organization's founding in Raleigh one hundred years earlier.

Still, regular maintenance, such as painting, straightening, or post replacement, is required from time to time. Individuals wishing to report missing or damaged markers or to propose a subject for a new marker should address correspondence to: Research Supervisor, Research Branch, North Carolina Division of Archives and History, 4611 Mail Service Center, Raleigh, North Carolina 27699-4611.

Over the years the North Carolina Highway Historical Marker Program has spurred interest in state and local history. The distinctive signs are now in place in practically every city and town (as well as at many crossroads) across the state. For young people, the markers may spark a curiosity that leads to further study of and appreciation for the historical development of the region. The signs may be visitors' only exposure to the history of the Tar Heel State. For resident North Carolinians, a state marker can be a familiar landmark, serving as a reminder that an event of historical significance took place close to home. The Department of Cultural Resources and the Department of Transportation remain committed to the program as it nears its eighth decade.

All illustrations in this guide are from the files of the North Carolina Division of Archives and History with the following exceptions: John and Ruth Lanning, Asheville (marker photos on front cover and title page); North Carolina Collection, University of North Carolina Library at Chapel Hill (p. 50); Rare Book, Manuscript, and Special Collections Library, Duke University (p. 78); North Carolina Bar Association, Cary (p. 11); *Greensboro News and Record*, Greensboro (p. 12, 99); *Wilmington Star-News*, Wilmington (p. 154); Trawick Ward, Research Labs of Anthropology (p. 157); and Richard Hunter, Warrenton (p. 205). For assistance with the editing and production of this volume I wish to acknowledge the contributions of Jerry C. Cashion, Lisa Kay Keenum, and Dennis F. Daniels of the Research Branch of the Division of Archives and History; Lang Baradell and Joe A. Mobley of the division's Historical Publications Section; and Terry Norris, Lori Mann, and Beverly Hunter of the North Carolina Department of Transportation.

The North Carolina Highway Historical Marker Program, now in its eighth decade, in that time has touched all corners of the state. These two photographs illustrate the range of subjects and settings, from an early eighteenth-century writer/explorer to mid-twentieth-century civil rights protests, from rural to urban locales. The John Lawson marker, cast in 1936, was formerly located on NC 58 west of Snow Hill and was relocated in 1961 to its present location on NC 118 in Grifton. Note the use of the post to support the barbed wire fence in this 1949 photograph. In the second image, taken almost forty years later, demonstrators move past the marker commemorating the Woolworth sit-ins, erected at the junction of Elm Street and Friendly Avenue in Greensboro in 1980.

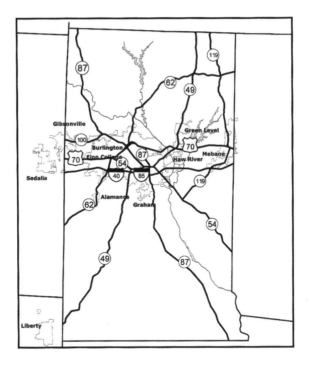

ALAMANCE COUNTY

G-2　BATTLE OF ALAMANCE
Militia under Governor William Tryon defeated Regulators on May 16, 1771. Six miles S.W.

NC 62 at I-85 south of Burlington / 1936

G-13　EARLY RAILROADS
First public meeting to promote railroads in North Carolina, Aug. 1, 1828, was at Wm. Albright's home, which stood 4 mi. S.E.

NC 49 southwest of Rock Creek / 1938

G-21　LINDLEY'S MILL
In a battle, September 13, 1781, four miles southwest, Butler's Whigs failed to rescue Governor Burke from Fanning's Tories.

NC 87 at SR 1003 (Sutphin Mill Road) west of Saxapahaw / 1939

G-22　PYLE'S DEFEAT
A body of Tories, going to join Cornwallis' Army at Hillsborough, was destroyed by a Whig force, Feb. 23, 1781. 3/4 mile southwest.

NC 49 southwest of Graham / 1939

G-24　BATTLE OF ALAMANCE
The militia under royal Governor Tryon defeated the Regulators at this point, May 16, 1771.

NC 62 at Alamance Battleground southwest of Burlington / 1939

G-30　HAWFIELDS CHURCH
Presbyterian, founded about 1755, three miles N.E. Henry Patillo the first pastor. Present building erected 1852.

NC 119 southwest of Mebane / 1941

G-34　TRADING PATH
Colonial trading route, dating from 17th century, from Petersburg, Virginia, to Catawba and Waxhaw Indians in Carolina, passed nearby.

US 70 (North Center Street) in Mebane / 1941

G-35　TRADING PATH
Colonial trading route, dating from 17th century, from Petersburg, Virginia, to Catawba and Waxhaw Indians in Carolina, passed nearby.

NC 62 in Alamance / 1941

**Alamance Cotton Mill and its founder, Edwin M. Holt (G 82),
shown here in a postcard view**

G-36   BINGHAM SCHOOL
Founded (1812?) by Wm. Bingham, noted teacher. Stood 1.5 miles north. Moved in 1826 by Wm. J. Bingham to Hillsboro.
NC 119 north of Mebane / 1948

G-52   ELON COLLEGE
Established in 1889 by the Christian Church. Coeducational. Burned 1923; rebuilt 1923-26.
NC 100 (Hoggard Avenue) in Elon College / 1949

G-54   ALEXANDER MEBANE
Brigadier general of North Carolina militia, member House of Commons, conventions 1788, 1789, and U.S. Congress. His home stood nearby.
US 70 in Mebane / 1951

G-55   ALEXANDER WILSON
Teacher in Piedmont area from 1819 to 1867; operated own school in Alamance County, 1851-67. Home is 1 mile, grave is 3fi miles northeast.
NC 54 at NC 119 northeast of Swepsonville / 1951

**G-58   HENRY JEROME
        STOCKARD**
Poet, author of "Fugitive Lines" and other works; lifelong educator; president of Peace Institute, 1907-12. Home stood here.
US 70 (South Church Street) in Burlington / 1952

G-59   THOMAS M. HOLT
Governor, 1891-93; cotton mill owner. Sponsor of railroad development and state aid to education. Home stood 350 yards S.
NC 49 at SR 1941 (Holt Street) in Haw River / 1953

G-60   TRYON'S CAMP
Before and after the Battle of Alamance, the Militia of Governor William Tryon camped nearby, along Alamance Creek, May 13-19, 1771.
NC 62 in Alamance / 1954

**G-69   CANE CREEK
        MEETING**
First Monthly Meeting of Friends in central North Carolina, 1751. Present building is on the original site.
SR 1004 (Snow Camp Road) at Snow Camp / 1957

G-76   SNOW CAMP
Settled by Quakers in 1749. Cornwallis camped in area after Battle of Guilford Courthouse and used home of Simon Dixon as headquarters.

SR 1004 (Snow Camp Road)
at Snow Camp / 1960

G-81   W. KERR SCOTT
Governor, 1949-1953; United States Senator, 1954-1958; N.C. Commissioner of Agriculture, 1937-1948. Birthplace is nearby.

NC 119 northeast of Swepsonville / 1963

G-82   ALAMANCE COTTON
MILL
Built 1837 by E. M. Holt. Produced Alamance Plaid, the first factory-dyed cotton cloth south of the Potomac. Stood here.

NC 62 at Great Alamance Creek bridge in
Alamance / 1965

G-89   NORTH CAROLINA
RAILROAD
Company Shops built here in 1857 for maintenance and repair of the N.C. Railroad. Closed in 1866.

US 70 (Church Street) in Burlington / 1972

G-91   SPRING FRIENDS
MEETING
Meeting house by 1761; Meeting recognized, 1773; Preparative Meeting, 1779; & Monthly Meeting, 1793.

SR 1005 (Kimesville Road) west of
Eli Whitney / 1973

G-95   B. EVERETT JORDAN
1896-1974
United States Senator, 1958-1973, and textile executive. Home stands one mile northeast.

NC 87 at SR 2171 (Saxapahaw School
Road) southwest of Saxapahaw / 1976

G-96   GRAHAM COLLEGE
Est. by the Christian Church, 1851, as Graham Institute; forerunner of Elon College. Burned in 1892. Stood 1 blk. west.

NC 87 (South Main Street) at West McAden
Street in Graham / 1979

G-111   BATTLE OF
CLAPP'S MILL
Troops led by Henry Lee ambushed British cavalry of Banastre Tarleton one mile north, Mar. 2, 1781. Americans retreated under heavy British fire.

NC 62 at SR 1135 (Porter Sharpe Road)
southwest of Alamance / 1992

GG-1   BATTLE OF ALAMANCE
Here was fought on May 16, 1771, the Battle of Alamance. Opposing forces were Colonial Militia, mainly from the eastern part of the province, commanded by Governor William Tryon, and a band of frontier dwellers known as Regulators, who had risen in arms against corrupt practices in local government.

On May 14 Tryon's force of 1,100 men, arriving in the heart of Regulator country to subdue these uprisings, made camp on Alamance Creek. Already some 2,000 Regulators, armed with old muskets and makeshift weapons, had come together five miles southwest of Tryon's position. Messages were exchanged between the camps, the Governor demanding immediate and complete surrender of the Regulators and the Regulators petitioning the Governor for reforms. Nothing came of the negotiations and on the morning of May 16 Tryon ordered his force to march. His route led along the old Hillsboro-Salisbury road which connected the two camps.

After marching about three miles, Tryon halted the militia and ordered a practice battle formation. After this maneuver the force re-formed in marching column and continued down the road. At ten o'clock Tryon's men arrived within half a mile of the Regulators where they formed battle lines. Tryon sent ahead messages offering surrender terms while his militia marched slowly forward. When three hundred yards from the Regulators, they halted. The messengers returned to say that the Regulators had scornfully rejected surrender. Much time was then consumed in an attempt to exchange prisoners taken by both sides, but this effort failed.

Tryon feared that the Regulators were stalling for time to improve their battle position and ordered his troops to draw closer. He then sent a final warning that he was ready to open fire. To this message the Regulators replied, "Fire, fire and be damned." A barrage from the Governor's artillery, consisting of six swivel guns and two brass field pieces, began the engagement and was the signal for concentrated musket fire from the militia ranks.

The Regulators responded with volley after volley from their nondescript weapons. For half an hour they held their position in the open, then retreated to the protective covering of the woods at the edge of the clearing. For another hour and a half the battle raged, then the Regulator fire slackened. Tryon immediately ordered a charge and soon drove the Regulators from their positions. The fleeing frontiersmen were pursued half a mile. There Tryon halted his men and turned back toward the camp on Alamance Creek.

Two wounded militiamen, as well as many of the wounded Regulators, were brought into camp and treated by the Governor's physicians. Regulator losses were nine killed, upward of two hundred wounded and between twenty and thirty taken prisoner. Nine of Tryon's men were killed and sixty-one wounded. On May 17 James Few, one of the

captured Regulators, was hanged as an outlaw after refusing to take an oath of allegiance to the king.

With the Battle of Alamance the Regulators were decisively crushed, but the effect of their campaign for reforms was embodied in the North Carolina Constitution. Newspapers throughout the colonies gave the battle wide publicity. In Boston and Philadelphia they cited the Regulators as martyrs and used their example to encourage the American cause on the eve of the Revolution.

*State Historic Site Visitor Center
at Alamance Battleground* / 1956

**GG-2   THE BATTLE
OF ALAMANCE**
On May 16, 1771, North Carolina militia, commanded by Royal Governor William Tryon, defeated the Regulators on this site. The pennants represent the second, or decisive, positions of the two armies and the Regulator camp.

*State Historic Site Visitor Center
at Alamance Battleground* / 1971

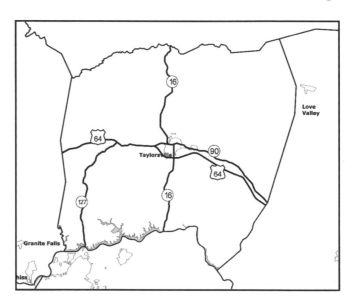

ALEXANDER COUNTY

M-29   HIDDENITE
A gem found only in N.C., named for W. E. Hidden, mineralogist of N.Y., who prospected in this area about 1880. Mines were nearby.

NC 90/US 64 northwest of Hiddenite / 1954

M-32   BRANTLEY YORK
Noted educator and minister. Founded York Collegiate Institute & numerous academies. Professor at Rutherford College. Grave 5 mi. N.

NC 90/US 64 northwest of Hiddenite / 1959

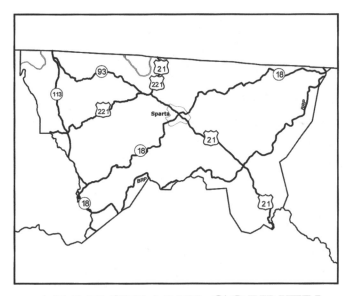

ALLEGHANY COUNTY

M-14 NORTH CAROLINA-VIRGINIA
NORTH CAROLINA
Colonized, 1585-87, by first English settlers in America; permanently settled c. 1650; first to vote readiness for independence, Apr. 12, 1776.
(Reverse)   VIRGINIA
First permanent English colony in America, 1607, one of thirteen original states. Richmond, the capital, was seat of Confederate government.

*NC 93 northwest of Piney Creek at NC/VA
boundary / 1941*

M-34   ROBERT L. DOUGHTON
1863-1954
Congressman, 1911-1953. Chairman, House Ways and Means Committee, 1933-1947, 1949-1953. Home 2/10 mi. S.E.

NC 88 and NC 18 at Laurel Springs / 1963

M-37   RUFUS A. DOUGHTON
Legislator, 14 terms. Lt. Governor, 1893-1897. Headed Revenue & Highway Commissions. Was U.N.C. Trustee for 56 yrs. Office was 30 feet W.

US 21 (North Main Street) in Sparta / 1966

M-49   BLUE RIDGE PARKWAY
First rural national parkway. Construction began near here on September 11, 1935.

*Blue Ridge Parkway and NC 18
at Cumberland Knob / 1987*

Rufus A. Doughton (M 37)

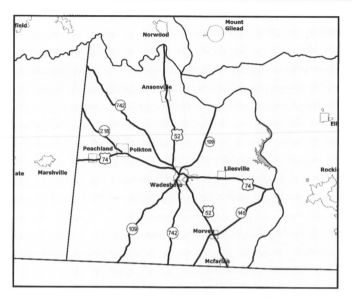

ANSON COUNTY

K-6   JOHN J. McRAE
1815-1868
Governor of Mississippi, 1854-1857. Member, U.S. Senate and House; Confederate congressman. Born 5 miles southeast.

NC 52 in Morven / 1938

K-7   SNEEDSBOROUGH
Laid out 1795. Promoted as inland port town on Pee Dee River by Archibald D. Murphey. Only graveyard remains, five miles southeast.

NC 52 in Morven / 1938

K-11   LEONIDAS L. POLK
President Nat'l Farmers' Alliance 1889-92; founder Progressive Farmer; a founder of N.C. State and Meredith Colleges. Birthplace stands here.

Old US 74 in Polkton / 1940

K-14   SHERMAN'S MARCH
Kilpatrick's Cavalry, a part of Sherman's army marching from Savannah to Goldsboro, passed through Wadesboro, March 3-5, 1865.

US 52/74 in Wadesboro / 1940

K-17   SAMUEL SPENCER
Jurist & Antifederalist leader. Member of court which in 1787 issued the first reported precedent for judicial review. His home stood 3 miles N.E.

SR 1730 (Old US 74) at SR 1744 (Clark Mountain Road) east of Lilesville / 1941

Leonidas L. Polk (K 11)

K-22 NORTH CAROLINA- SOUTH CAROLINA

NORTH CAROLINA

Colonized, 1585-87, by first English settlers in America; permanently settled c. 1650; first to vote readiness for independence, Apr. 12, 1776.

(Reverse) SOUTH CAROLINA

Formed in 1712 from part of Carolina, which was chartered in 1663, it was first settled by the English in 1670. One of the 13 original states.

US 52 in McFarlan at NC/SC boundary / 1941

K-29 CAROLINA FEMALE COLLEGE, 1850-67

Established by local planters, later operated by Methodist Church. Building was 150 yds. W.

US 52 (Main Street) in Ansonville / 1949

K-40 THOMAS SAMUEL ASHE

Associate Justice, State Supreme Court, 1878-1887; Member of Congress, 1873-1877; Member of Confederate Congress; legislator. Home is one mile west.

US 52/74 (Salisbury Street) in Wadesboro / 1966

K-41 BOGGAN-HAMMOND HOUSE

Eighteenth-century house built by Patrick Boggan, Revolutionary soldier & a founder of Wadesboro. Now historical museum. Located 2 blocks south.

US 52/74 (Salisbury Street) at Washington Street in Wadesboro / 1968

K-51 ROCKY RIVER CHURCH

Missionary Baptist. Began before 1772 as a branch of Little River Church; was independent by 1790. Present bldg. 3 mi. N.E.

NC 742 at SR 1610 (Wightmans Church Road) at Burnsville / 1976

K-55 HUGH HAMMOND BENNETT 1881-1960

"Father of soil conservation." First chief of the Soil Conservation Service, U.S. Dept. of Agriculture, 1935-1952. Born 4 miles southwest.

US 74 at SR 1259 (Anson High School Road) west of Wadesboro / 1995

K-57 RALF FREEMAN

Free black served as a Baptist pastor at Rocky River Church until law in 1831 barred blacks from public preaching. Buried 500 yards west.

US 52 at Cemetery Road in Ansonville / 1998

KK-1 THE BROWN CREEK SOIL CONSERVATION DISTRICT FIRST IN AMERICA

Here was established the first district in America for a systematic program of land erosion control. Known as the Brown Creek District because it embraced the area of the Brown Creek Watershed, it heralded the beginning of a national program of soil conservation districts.

The Brown Creek District included the plantation birthplace of Hugh H. Bennett, "father of soil conservation." Bennett, born in 1881, graduated from the University of North Carolina in 1903, and became a soil surveyor in the Bureau of Soils, Department of Agriculture. Observing that soil erosion ruined much good land throughout the United States, Bennett slowly initiated a program to prevent this waste. On April 27, 1935, Bennett became director of the Soil Conservation Service, a position he held until his retirement in 1952. By this time soil conservation was a national concern, largely because of the work of Hugh Bennett and his associates.

The success of the soil conservation district program was due to local participation by farmers and landowners. Conservation districts were created throughout the United States. Bennett and his specialists worked with the farmers in the districts for an effective program.

The Brown Creek District was established in 1937. In May thirty local property-owners petitioned the State Soil Conservation Committee "That there is need, in the interest of the public health, safety, and welfare, for a soil conservation district to function in the territory hereinafter described." The district would embrace 120,000 acres, much of it badly eroded. The petition was approved on May 31. A public hearing, held on July 3 at Wadesboro and followed by the mailing of ballots to the local farmers, resulted in an overwhelmingly favorable vote for creating the district. The North Carolina Secretary of State issued a certificate setting up the district on August 4. The Brown Creek District became the example for districts of the future.

US 74 east of Polkton / 1962

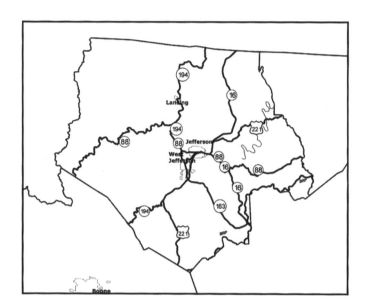

ASHE COUNTY

M-15   NORTH CAROLINA-
VIRGINIA
NORTH CAROLINA
Colonized, 1585-87, by first English settlers in America; permanently settled c. 1650; first to vote readiness for independence, Apr. 12, 1776.

(Reverse)   VIRGINIA
First permanent English colony in America, 1607, one of thirteen original states. Richmond, the capital, was seat of Confederate government.

NC 194 north of Helton at NC/VA boundary / 1942

M-16   NORTH CAROLINA-
VIRGINIA
NORTH CAROLINA
Colonized, 1585-87, by first English settlers in America; permanently settled c. 1650; first to vote readiness for independence, Apr. 12, 1776.

(Reverse)   VIRGINIA
First permanent English colony in America, 1607, one of thirteen original states. Richmond, the capital, was seat of Confederate government.

SR 1573 (Healing Springs Road) at NC/VA boundary / 1942

M-20   ASA GRAY
American botanist and Harvard professor. In July, 1841, investigated flora of this region. Headquarters were in house standing 50 yds. N.

NC 16/US 221 east of Jefferson / 1949

M-28   ORE KNOB MINE
Copper mine operated one mile north in the 1870s & 1880s. Site of Ore Knob, boom mining town, chartered 1875.

NC 88 at SR 1595 (Little Peak Road) east of Jefferson / 1954

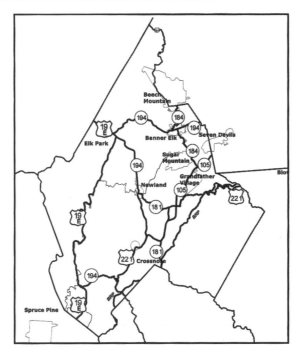

AVERY COUNTY

N-5 YELLOW MOUNTAIN ROAD
Along a route nearby the "Over-Mountain Men" marched to victory at King's Mountain, 1780.

US 19 East at Roaring Creek bridge
southwest of Frank / 1938

N-6 CRANBERRY MINES
Iron ore deposits near here were mined from ca. 1826 until 1930. Supplied iron to the Confederacy.

US 19 East at NC 194 north
of Cranberry / 1939

N-15 NORTH CAROLINA-
TENNESSEE
NORTH CAROLINA
Colonized, 1585-87, by first English settlers in America; permanently settled c. 1650; first to vote readiness for independence, Apr. 12, 1776.

(Reverse) TENNESSEE
Settled before 1770 by North Carolina-Virginia pioneers, ceded by North Carolina to the United States, 1789, admitted to the Union, 1796.

US 19 East northwest of Elk Park at NC/TN
boundary / 1941

N-18 ASA GRAY
American botanist and Harvard professor. In July, 1841, investigated flora of this region. He visited Grandfather Mountain.

US 221 northeast of Linville at Grandfather
Mountain / 1949

N-22 ANDRÉ MICHAUX
French botanist, pioneer in studying flora of western North Carolina, visited Grandfather Mountain, August, 1794.

US 221 northeast of Linville at Grandfather
Mountain / 1949

N-36 SHEPHERD M. DUGGER
Author of *The Balsam Groves of the Grandfather Mountain, 1892*; educator and humorist. Grave one block South.

NC 184/194 in Banner Elk / 1971

N-43 LEES-McRAE COLLEGE
Presbyterian. Founded in 1900 by Edgar Tufts. Named for teacher Elizabeth McRae & benefactor Mrs. S. P. Lees. Senior college since 1988.

NC 184/194 in Banner Elk / 1993

N-44   CROSSNORE SCHOOL
Founded by Mary Martin Sloop, physician, 1913, to serve region's youth. Weaving

Room, est. 1920, boosted revival of handicrafts. Campus 1/2 mi. W.

US 221/NC 194 at Crossnore / 1997

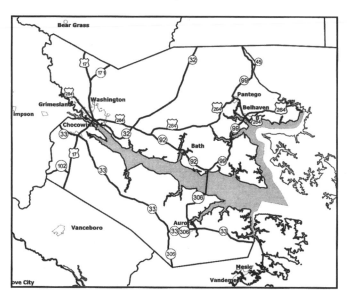

BEAUFORT COUNTY

B-3   ST. THOMAS CHURCH
Episcopal, oldest church building in the State of North Carolina, was constructed in 1734.

Craven Street in Bath / 1936

B-5   CHRISTOPHER GALE
First Chief Justice of North Carolina, appointed 1712, lived here at "Kirby Grange," his plantation.

NC 92 southeast of Back Creek bridge in Bath / 1937

B-6   FIRST PUBLIC LIBRARY
In North Carolina was set up near this spot about 1700. Books sent from England by Rev. Thos. Bray.

Main Street in Bath / 1938

B-8   GRANVILLE GRANT
Formed northern half of colony of North Carolina. Its southern boundary was surveyed in 1743 to a point near here.

US 264 west of Bunyan / 1938

B-14   DR. SUSAN DIMOCK
Native of Washington, Zurich graduate, head of a Boston hospital, 1st woman member N.C. Medical Society, 1872. Her girlhood home was here.

East Main Street in Washington / 1939

**B-15   ATTACK ON
            WASHINGTON**
Town taken by Federals, March, 1862. Confederate efforts to recapture it failed, 1862 and 1863.

*US 17 at Tar River bridge south
of Washington* / 1939

**B-16   BURNING OF
            WASHINGTON**
The town was burned and shelled by evacuating United States troops in April, 1864.

*US 17 (Bridge Street) at West Second Street
in Washington* / 1939

B-17 FORT HILL
Site of Confederate batteries on Pamlico River which enabled Gen. D. H. Hill's forces to besiege Washington in spring of 1863. 5 mi. E.
NC 33 southeast of Chocowinity / 1939

B-21 FIRST POST ROAD
The road from New England to Charleston, over which mail was first carried regularly in North Carolina, 1738-39, passed near this spot.
Main Street in Bath / 1942

B-24 JOSEPHUS DANIELS
Secretary of the Navy, 1913-21; Ambassador to Mexico; editor; author. Birthplace stood here.
East Main Street in Washington / 1948

B-25 JOHN F. TOMPKINS
Agricultural reformer, a founder of the State Fair, published and edited the "Farmer's Journal," 1852-53, in Bath. This was his home.
Main Street in Bath / 1949

B-27 MATTHEW ROWAN
Acting governor, 1753-54. Councilor, assemblyman, and Surveyor-General. Merchant in the Irish trade. His home was here.
Main Street in Bath / 1951

B-28 DeMILLE FAMILY
Home of motion picture producer Cecil B. DeMille & his father, playwright Henry C. DeMille, stood five blocks west.
Market Street in Washington / 1951

B-33 DANIEL G. FOWLE
Governor, 1889-91, state Adjutant General, 1863, Confederate officer, superior court judge, state legislator. His home stood here.
West Main Street in Washington / 1953

B-36 C. C. CAMBRELENG
Congressman from New York, 1821-39; House leader for Jackson & Van Buren; minister to Russia; merchant. Was born in this town, 1786.
US 17 (Bridge Street) in Washington / 1955

B-39 SIEGE OF WASHINGTON
Confederates failed to recapture town, March-April, 1863, but held it March-Nov., 1864.
US 17 at Tar River bridge south of Washington / 1959

B-46 TRINITY CHURCH
Episcopal. Originally Blount's Chapel. Built ca. 1774 by Rev. Nathaniel Blount. Moved in 1939 from original site nearby.
NC 33 in Chocowinity / 1968

B-47 EDWARD TEACH
Notorious pirate called "Blackbeard." Lived in Bath while Charles Eden was governor. Killed at Ocracoke, 1718.
Main Street in Bath / 1967

B-48 ALEXANDER STEWART
Anglican minister to N.C., 1753-71. Served parish of St. Thomas & as chaplain to Gov. Arthur Dobbs. Erected first glebe house on record in the colony.
Craven Street in Bath / 1968

**B-51 JOHN GRAY BLOUNT
1752-1833**
Merchant & land speculator. Shipping interests across eastern N.C.; also invested in western N.C. land. Home stood here.
Main Street at Market Street in Washington / 1987

**B-56 JAMES ADAMS
FLOATING THEATRE**
Toured coastal towns, 1913-1941. Edna Ferber's 1925 visit to ship, then docked nearby, was basis for her novel *Show Boat*.
Main Street in Bath / 1989

**B-59 ST. JOHN
THE EVANGELIST CHURCH**
The first Roman Catholic church in North Carolina. Consecrated, 1829. Burned by Federal troops, 1864. Stood one block east.
US 17 (Bridge Street) at Third Street in Washington / 1996

The James Adams Floating Theater (B 56), a popular attraction in eastern North Carolina coastal towns from 1913 to 1941

BB-1   COLONIAL BATH

Bath, oldest town in North Carolina, was established in 1705. The first settlers were French Huguenots from Virginia. Among the early English inhabitants were John Lawson, author of the first history of Carolina (1709) and Christopher Gale, Chief Justice of the colony (1712-17, 1722-24, 1725-31). Thomas Cary, Governor 1708-11, was a principal figure in the uprising known as Cary's Rebellion.

By 1708 Bath consisted of 12 houses and a population of 50 people. Trade in naval stores, furs, and tobacco was the foremost occupation. In 1707 a grist mill was established by a group of the leading citizens. A library, given to St. Thomas Parish in 1701 by the Reverend Thomas Bray, was the first public library in North Carolina.

Bath's early history was disturbed by political rivalries, fever epidemics, Indian wars, and piracy. Cary's Rebellion (1711) was a struggle between former Governor Thomas Cary and Governor Edward Hyde (1711-12) over the role of the Quaker Party in the politics of the colony. It was settled when troops from Virginia arrived in the Bath area in July, 1711. Hyde remained in power, Cary being sent to England for trial.

In the summer of 1711 occurred a severe epidemic of yellow fever from which many inhabitants died. Immediately began the Tuscarora War, 1711-15, fought between the settlers and the powerful Tuscarora Indian nation occupying the region between the Neuse River and Virginia. On September 22, 1711, the Indians attacked without warning the plantations around Bath, and many persons fled to the town for refuge. Troops under Colonel James Moore were sent from South Carolina to assist the North Carolinians. On March 23, 1713, Moore took Fort Nooherooka, principal Tuscarora stronghold, freeing the Bath area from the threat of further Indian attack.

Bath was also a haunt of the pirate Edward Teach, better known as "Blackbeard." Teach, a friend of Governor Charles Eden and Tobias Knight his secretary, was privately encouraged by them in his piratical activities. He was killed by Lieutenant Robert Maynard of the British Navy in the fall of 1718.

After this period of turbulence ended, Bath became a center of more peaceful, settled life. St. Thomas Church (Episcopal), the oldest standing church building in North Carolina, dates from 1734. Reverend George Whitefield, pioneer evangelist, visited Bath on several occasions between 1739 and 1765.

The Palmer-Marsh House, Bath's oldest and in the colonial period its largest residence, was erected about 1744.

The General Assembly met in Bath in 1744 and 1752. In 1746 the town was considered for capital of the colony. Governors Thomas Cary and Charles Eden (1714-22) made Bath their home for a time, as did Edward Moseley, long-time Speaker of the General Assembly.

In the late Colonial period Bath lost much of its importance to the new town of Washington, located 12 miles up the Pamlico River. With the removal of the Beaufort County seat of government to Washington in 1785, Bath lost much of its trade and importance. It has since remained the small country town it is today.

Three early buildings are now available for public inspection: St. Thomas Church, built in 1734, the Palmer-Marsh House, dating from about 1744, and the Bonner House, a 19th Century residence built on the site of John Lawson's 18th Century home. Other sites and buildings are marked.

State Historic Site Visitor Center in Bath / 1962

BB-2   HISTORIC BATH

Bath, the oldest incorporated town in North Carolina, was established in 1705. By 1708 the town consisted of twelve houses and a population of fifty people. Among the early inhabitants were John Lawson, Surveyor General of the colony and author of *A New Voyage to Carolina*, the first history of North Carolina; Christopher Gale, the first Chief Justice of the colony (1712-17, 1722-24, 1725-31); Governors Thomas Cary (1705-06, 1708-11) and Charles Eden (1714-1722); and the pirate Edward Teach, known as "Blackbeard."

The early history of Bath was disturbed by political rivalry, yellow fever epidemics, Indian wars, and piracy. After this period of turbulence ended, the town entered an era of peaceful development. It was a trade center, exporting naval stores, furs, tobacco; seat of government for Beaufort County; and in 1744 and 1752 the meeting place of the General Assembly. The political and economic importance of Bath declined after the Beaufort County seat was moved to the town of Washington in 1785.

State Historic Site Visitor Center in Bath / 1970

BB-3   PALMER-MARSH HOUSE

Colonial home of Colonel Robert Palmer, Surveyor-General of North Carolina 1753-1771 and Collector of Customs for the Port of Bath. Built c. 1744, probably by Michael Coutanche, it is one of the oldest surviving dwelling-houses in the State. Governor William Tryon described Palmer's home as "a very excellent house . . . at Bath which I often resided in with my family, being Hospitably entertained." After Colonel Palmer left for England in 1771 his son lived in the house until the mid 1780's. In the 19th Century it was the home of the Jonathan Marsh family, shipowners and merchants, originally from Rhode Island.

Main Street in Bath / 1962

C-36   TRINITY SCHOOL

Episcopal boys school founded in 1851 by The Rev. N. C. Hughes. Open off and on until 1908. Many students entered ministry. Stood here.

US 17 at NC 33 in Chocowinity / 1959
[Numbered C-36 in error; should be in the B district.]

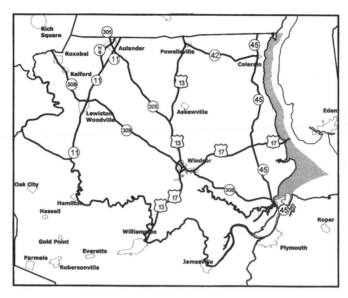

BERTIE COUNTY

A-2   INDIAN WOODS
Reservation established in 1717 for Tuscaroras remaining in N.C. after war of 1711-1713. Sold, 1828. Five miles N.W.

US 17/13 south of Windsor / 1936

A-7   DAVID STONE
Governor, 1808-10; U.S. Senator; Congressman. "Hope," his home, stands 4 miles northwest.

NC 308 (Sterlingworth Street) at US 13 Bypass in Windsor / 1936

**A-10   SALMON CREEK
AND EDEN HOUSE:
SEEDBED OF THE COLONY**
Along the banks of the Chowan River and Salmon Creek, the seeds were planted for the colony and state of North Carolina. From these roots in the 1600s emerged the refined plantation life of the ruling colonial gentry in the 1700s, made possible by the displacement of Indians and with slave labor. The earliest settlers in this region, largely natives of the British Isles, transplanted their folkways, building techniques, agricultural methods, and adventurous spirit to these shores.

Explorers venturing south from Virginia included John Pory who in 1622 visited the Chowan River area, reporting the natives friendly and prospects for settlement good. Among the first permanent European settlers was Nathaniel Batts, a trader in animal pelts.

In 1655 he hired a carpenter to build a house about three miles south near the mouth of Salmon Creek. By the time Charles II of England granted a charter to the Lords Proprietors in 1663, a small but growing community was in place along this river. The area was designated one of three official ports of entry in 1676.

While the proprietors legally headed the government, power rested in the hands of the governor and the council. Six colonial governors lived nearby during the proprietary (1663-1729) and royal (1729-1776) periods:
* Samuel Stephens, the first of the leaders to settle on Salmon Creek, encountered dissension and despair among the colonists during his term, 1667-1670.
* Seth Sothel in 1678 acquired 4,000 acres where Batts and Stephens had lived. As governor beginning in 1682, Sothel incurred charges of oppression, tyranny, extortion, and bribery, leading to his conviction and banishment in 1689.
* Edward Hyde also served a stormy tenure as governor, 1711-1712, witnessing the outbreak of the Tuscarora War that devastated the colony. Hyde, who took up residence on Salmon Creek in 1710, was the first governor of the separate colony of North Carolina, the division of Carolina taking place in 1712.
* Thomas Pollock, who had been jailed by Sothel, served as acting governor, 1712-1714 and again in 1722. His plantation

house, "Balgra," was two miles south on the north side of Salmon Creek. There he and Hyde withstood a small naval attack in 1711 during Cary's Rebellion.

* Charles Eden, governor from 1714 to 1722, purchased the property in this immediate vicinity in 1719 and constructed "Eden House" a few yards north. His home in time became an elegant center of social life for the Albemarle aristocracy. Following his death in 1722, the "Town on Queen Anne's Creek" was renamed Edenton and soon supplanted this area as the social and political center.

* Gabriel Johnston, who served as royal governor from 1734 to 1752, married Eden's stepdaughter Penelope Golland around 1740 and lived at Eden House. By the close of his term North Carolina was undergoing tremendous growth and settlement had extended to the foothills of the Appalachian mountains.

Over time the colonial estates along the Chowan River and Salmon Creek have been lost to shoreline erosion, fire, or decay. The area south of Salmon Creek, owned through most of the 1700s by three generations of the Duckenfield family, was acquired by the Capeheart family in 1829 and afterwards known as "Avoca." Pollock's grave at "Balgra" and those at Eden House were moved to Edenton around 1890. In 1996, prior to construction of the improved US 17 bridge, archaeologists excavated an area a short distance southeast uncovering remnants of two houses constructed in the late 1600s and later owned by the Eden family.

US 17 at Chowan River bridge east of Windsor / 1936 (revised 2000)

A-36   LOCKE CRAIG
1860-1925
Governor, 1913-1917; teacher, lawyer, state legislator. His birthplace is one mile N.E.

NC 308 at SR 1225 (Republican Road) northwest of Windsor / 1949

A-41   WILLIAM BLOUNT
Member of Continental Congress, signer of the Federal Constitution, governor S.W. Territory, Senator from Tennessee. Birthplace 1/5 mi. S.W.

US 17 (King Street) at Gray Street in Windsor / 1951

A-48   ROANOKE RIVER
Early channel of trade, its valley long an area of plantations. Frequent floods until 1952; since controlled by Kerr Dam. Old name was "Moratuck."

US 17/13 at Roanoke River bridge southwest of Windsor / 1954

A-49   "SCOTCH HALL"
Plantation setting for the novel "Bertie" by George R. Throop (1851), tutor in the family of Geo. W. Capehart. House built 1838 is 8 mi. S.E.

US 17 at NC 45 south of Taylors Store / 1959

A-57   NAVAL BATTLE, 1864
The Confederate ironclad ram *Albemarle,* led by Capt. J. W. Cooke, crossed Batchelor's Bay, May 5, 1864, and fought seven Union warships 15 mi. E.

NC 45 at Batchelor's Bay Drive southeast of Windsor / 1962

A-74   "WINDSOR CASTLE"
Built 1858 by Patrick H. Winston, Jr. Birthplace of sons George T., educator; Francis D., lt. gov., 1905-1909; & Robert W., writer. 100 yards east.

NC 308 (Sterlingworth Street) at Watson Street in Windsor / 1989

William Blount (A 41)

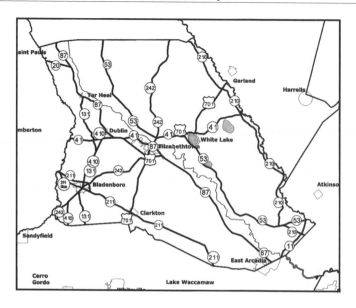

BLADEN COUNTY

I-7   JOHN OWEN
1787-1841

Governor, 1828-1830; state legislator; and Whig party leader. His home stood 4 miles NW.

NC 41/87 west of Battle of Elizabethtown /
1938

I-11   BATTLE
OF ELIZABETHTOWN

Whigs broke Tory power in Bladen Co., August, 1781, driving them into Tory Hole, 50 yards N.

NC 41/87 (Broad Street) in Elizabethtown /
1939

I-37   THOMAS ROBESON

Colonel in Revolution, member of provincial congresses and state senator. Robeson County is named for him. His home stood 1/2 mile N.E.

NC 87 in Tar Heel / 1953

I-66   THE BARTRAMS

Naturalists John and William Bartram, in 1765 and later, used their kinsman's house, Ashwood, as operating base. Stood 2 mi. E.

NC 87 at SR 1725 (Brady Road) north of
Westbrook / 1986

I-76   FUTURE FARMERS
OF AMERICA

Began in N.C. as Young Tar Heel Farmers, 1928, to promote vocational agriculture in schools. Camp here since 1928.

NC 53 in White Lake / 1989

I-78   WHITE LAKE CCC CAMP

An installation of the Civilian Conservation Corps. Initiated modern park improvements. Est. here 1935; closed 1942.

US 701 in White Lake / 1992

John Owen (I 7)

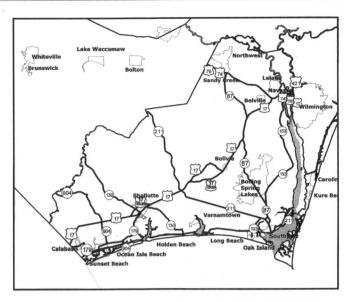

BRUNSWICK COUNTY

D-3   **ORTON**

Fine colonial home, built about 1725 by Roger Moore. Later Gov. Benjamin Smith's home. Stands 16fl mi. south.

NC 133 in Belville / 1936

D-4   **STAMP ACT**

Resisted by armed band, Feb., 1766, at Brunswick, where Royal Governor Tryon lived. Site 18fl mi. south.

NC 133 in Belville / 1936

D-8   **FORT CASWELL**

Named for Gov. Caswell. Begun by U.S. in 1826; seized by N.C. troops, 1861; abandoned by Confederates, 1865. Stands five miles southeast.

NC 133 north of Southport / 1936

D-11   **FORT JOHNSTON**

Built, 1748-64; burned by Whigs, 1775; rebuilt by U.S. government, 1794-1809. Only the officers quarters remain.

Bay Street in Southport / 1938

D-14   **ARTHUR DOBBS**

Royal Governor 1754-65, author, member Irish Parliament, promoter of search for Northwest Passage, is buried at Saint Philips Church.

NC 133 in Belville / 1939

D-16   **SPANISH ATTACK**

A Spanish expedition captured the town of Brunswick, 1748, during King George's War, but was soon driven away by the colonial militia.

NC 133 in Belville / 1939

D-24   **ROBERT HOWE**

Major general in the Revolution, commander of the American Army in the South, 1776-78. His home stood 17 miles S.

NC 133 in Belville / 1940

D-25   **ALFRED MOORE**

Associate Justice United States Supreme Court, 1799-1804, officer in the Revolution, state attorney general, judge. Home was 18fl mi. S.

NC 133 in Belville / 1940

Rice farming at Orton Plantation (D 53)

D-29   NORTH CAROLINA-
            SOUTH CAROLINA
         NORTH CAROLINA

Colonized, 1585-87, by first English settlers in America; permanently settled c. 1650; first to vote readiness for independence, Apr. 12, 1776.

(Reverse) SOUTH CAROLINA

Formed in 1712 from part of Carolina, which was chartered in 1663, it was first settled by the English in 1670. One of the 13 original states.

US 17 at NC/SC boundary / 1940

D-30   FIRST POST ROAD

The road from New England to Charleston, over which mail was first carried regularly in North Carolina, 1738-39, passed near this spot.

US 17 at NC/SC boundary / 1941

D-48   CHARLES TOWN

Center of a colony from Barbados led by John Vassall, 1664. Abandoned by 1667. Was located 2 mi. E. on Town Creek.

NC 133 at Town Creek bridge north of
Pinelevel / 1951

D-53   ORTON PLANTATION

House built c. 1725, subsequent additions. Home first of Roger Moore, later of Gov. Benjamin Smith, still later of James Sprunt. 3/4 mi. E.

NC 133 at Orton / 1954

D-54   BRUNSWICK

Founded c. 1725, long a principal port of N.C., site of Spanish attack, 1748, and of Stamp Act resistance, 1766. Later abandoned. Was 2 mi. S.E.

NC 133 at Orton / 1954

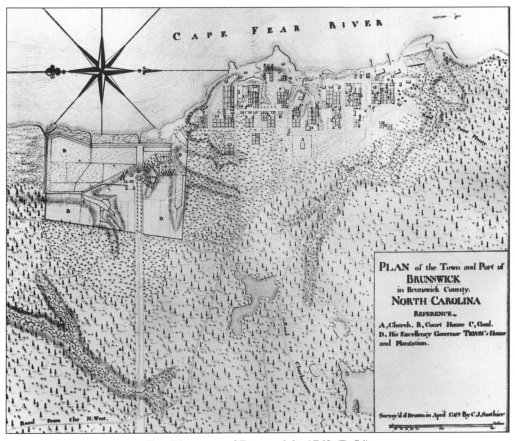

Sauthier map of Brunswick, 1769 (D 54)

D-55 ST. PHILIPS CHURCH

Anglican, built under act of 1751. Graves of Governors Arthur Dobbs and Benjamin Smith and U.S. Justice Alfred Moore. Ruins 2 mi. S.E.

NC 133 at Orton / 1954

D-62 FORT CASWELL

Seized by N.C. Militia three months before firing on Fort Sumter, Governor Ellis ordered its return to Federal authority; three mi. E.

NC 133 in Yaupon Beach / 1960

D-66 BALD HEAD LIGHTHOUSE

First lighthouse erected 1796. Present octagonal tower, built 1817, is 109 ft. tall. Used until 1935.

Bay Street in Southport / 1962

A dedication program held at Brunswick in 1968

**D-70   WASHINGTON'S
                SOUTHERN TOUR**
President Washington, on April 27, 1791, was a guest at the home of William Gause, Jr., which stood four miles south.

*US 17 at SR 1184 (Ocean Isle Beach Road)
southwest of Shallotte* / 1965

D-73   JOHN LaPIERRE
Ordained 1707; came to America 1708. Served in many churches in area as missionary of Society for the Propagation of the Gospel, 1732-1755.

*SR 1553 (Saint Philips Church Road) at
Brunswick Town State Historic
Site* / 1968

D-79   BOUNDARY HOUSE
Commissioners met here to run boundary in 1764. Popular stop for colonial travelers. Ruins used to est. present state line in 1928. Located 2fl mi. S.E.

*US 17 at SR 1168 (Country Club Road) in
Calabash* / 1976

D-82   RUSSELLBOROUGH
Home of royal governors Dobbs and Tryon. Site of Stamp Act resistance in 1765. Burned in American Revolution.

*SR 1533 (Saint Philips Church Road) at
Brunswk Town State Historic
Site* / 1982

**D-85   BENJAMIN SMITH
                1756-1826**
Governor, 1810-1811, legislator, soldier, benefactor of UNC. His plantation, "Belvedere," was 6 miles northeast.

*US 17/NC 87 at Jackeys Creek bridge
southwest of Belville* / 1987

D-89   JOSIAH MARTIN
Last royal governor of North Carolina, 1771-75. Fearing capture, in June 1775 he sought refuge here. Fled offshore to HMS *Cruizer* in July.

Bay Street in Southport / 1988

**D-92   DANIEL L. RUSSELL
                1845-1908**
Governor, 1897-1901; Superior Court judge, 1868-1874; member of Congress, 1879-1881. Born two miles N.W.

*US 17/NC 87 at SR 1521 (Funston Road)
east of Winnabow* / 1990

**D-93   ROBERT RUARK
                1915-1965**
Columnist and author. His 1957 novel *The Old Man and the Boy* based on childhood visits with grandparents 1 block W.

*NC 211 (Howe Street) at Nash Street in
Southport* / 1991

DDD-1   FORT ANDERSON
Large Confederate fort stands 2 mi. E. After a strong Union attack it was evacuated Feb. 18, 1865, resulting in the fall of Wilmington.

*NC 133 at Brunswick Town State Historic
Site* / 1961

DDD-2   FORT ANDERSON
Large Confederate fort stands 13 mi. S. After a strong Union attack it was evacuated Feb. 18, 1865, resulting in the fall of Wilmington.

NC 133 in Belville / 1961

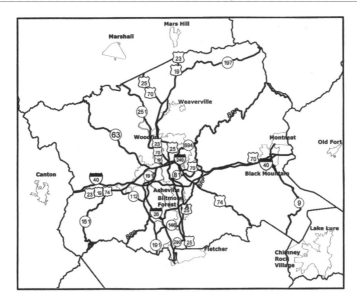

BUNCOMBE COUNTY

P-2 ZEBULON B. VANCE
Governor, 1862-5, 1877-9; U.S. Senator, 1879-94. Birthplace 6 miles northeast.

US 19/23 Business at SR 1003 (Reems Creek Road) south of Weaverville / 1935

P-3 RIVERSIDE CEMETERY
Graves of Thomas Wolfe and "O.Henry," authors; Zebulon B. Vance, governor; Thomas L. Clingman and Robert R. Reynolds, U.S. senators. One mile N.W.

Patton Avenue at North French Broad Avenue in Asheville / 1935

P-5 DAVID L. SWAIN
Governor and political leader. President of the University of North Carolina, 1835-1868. Was born three miles E.

US 25 (Merrimon Avenue) at Beaverdam Road in Asheville / 1938

P-9 STONEMAN'S RAID
On a raid through western North Carolina Gen. Stoneman's U.S. Cavalry occupied Asheville on April 26, 1865.

US 25 (Hendersonville Road) south of I-40 in Asheville / 1940

P-16 BINGHAM SCHOOL
A boys' military school, operated by Robert Bingham, 1891-1928. Moved from Mebane. Plant is 1 mile S.W.

NC 251 north of Asheville / 1948

P-17 THOMAS WOLFE
Author of "Look Homeward Angel" (1929), "Of Time and the River," and other works. Home stands 200 yards N., birthplace 500 yds. N.E.

College Street at Spruce Street in Asheville / 1948

P-18 NEWTON ACADEMY
Established before 1793 as Union Hill Academy. Named for Rev. George Newton. Present Newton Academy School is 4th building on this site.

Biltmore Avenue at Unadilla Avenue in Asheville / 1949

P-21 ANDRÉ MICHAUX
French botanist, pioneer in studying flora of western North Carolina, visited Black Mountains, August, 1794.

US 70 (State Street) in Black Mountain / 1949

P-22   LOCKE CRAIG
Governor, 1913-1917; teacher, lawyer, state legislator. His home stands here.

US 74 Alternate/NC 81 (Swannanoa River Road) in Asheville / 1949

**P-29   LEE'S SCHOOL
1846-1879**
A school for boys, conducted by Stephen Lee, West Point graduate, Confederate colonel, stood 1/2 mile north.

US 70/74 Alternate (Tunnel Road) at Chunn's Cove Road in Asheville / 1951

**P-30   FORSTER A. SONDLEY
1857-1931**
Historian, lawyer, and bibliophile. Gave to Asheville the Sondley Reference Library. His home is 2.7 mi. north.

US 70 at Beverly Road in Asheville / 1951

P-32   JETER C. PRITCHARD
United States Senator, 1895-1903, Republican leader, newspaperman, federal judge. His home is 3/10 mile east; grave is 1.3 mi. west.

US 25 (Merrimon Avenue) at Chestnut Street in Asheville / 1951

P-33   FRANCIS ASBURY
Bishop of the Methodist Episcopal Church, 1784-1816, often visited and preached at the home of Daniel Killian which was one mile east.

US 25 (Merrimon Avenue) at Beaverdam Road in Asheville / 1951

P-35   DR. L. B. McBRAYER
Leader in fight against tuberculosis in North Carolina, Superintendent of State Sanatorium in Hoke County, 1914-24. His birthplace is 400 ft. W.

NC 191 southwest of Asheville / 1952

P-36   RICHMOND PEARSON
Congressman, 1895-1901, U.S. Minister to Persia, 1902-07, and to Greece and Montenegro, 1907-09. His home, "Richmond Hill," is 2 miles north.

US 240 (Patton Avenue) at French Broad River bridge in Asheville / 1952

P-37   RUTHERFORD TRACE
The expedition led by Gen. Griffith Rutherford against the Cherokee, September, 1776, passed nearby on the banks of the Swannanoa River.

US 25 north of I-40 in Asheville / 1953

P-38   RUTHERFORD TRACE
The expedition led by Gen. Griffith Rutherford against the Cherokee, Sept., 1776, passed nearby.

NC 191 southwest of Asheville / 1954

P-39   RUTHERFORD TRACE
The expedition led by Gen. Griffith Rutherford against the Cherokee, Sept., 1776, camped nearby along Hominy Creek.

US 19/23/74 at Enka / 1954

P-44   KIFFIN Y. ROCKWELL
World War I soldier, aviator. First pilot of Escadrille Lafayette to shoot down enemy plane. Killed in action, Sept. 23, 1916. Home 200 yds. W.

US 25 (Merrimon Avenue) at Hillside Street in Asheville / 1954

Kiffin Y. Rockwell (P 44), seated, and his brother Paul

P-46   SWANNANOA TUNNEL
Longest (1,800 ft.) of 7 on railroad between Old Fort and Asheville. Constructed by convict labor, 1877-79. West entrance 300 yds. S.E.

I-40/US 70 access road east of Ridgecrest / 1955

P-49   JOSEPH LANE
Territorial Governor of Oregon, 1848-50, Vice-Presidential candidate, 1860, U.S. Senator, major general in Mexican War. Born 3 miles east.

US 25 (Merrimon Avenue) at Beaverdam Road in Asheville / 1959

P-53   SULPHUR SPRINGS
Health & social resort during the nineteenth century; patronized by low-country planters. Springs are 600 yds. S.

US 19/23 Business (Haywood Road) in Asheville / 1959

P-54   WILLIAM MOORE
Captain of militia force which marched against the Cherokee in Nov., 1776. A fort which he built stood near here. His home was 200 yds. E.

SR 3412 (Sand Hill Road) east of Enka / 1960

P-55   STONEMAN'S RAID
Southern troops turned back Stoneman's U.S. cavalry, raiding through western North Carolina, at Swannanoa Gap, near here, April 20, 1865.

I-40/US 70 access road east of Ridgecrest / 1960

P-56   UNIVERSITY OF N.C. AT ASHEVILLE
Established 1927; became Asheville-Biltmore College 1936. Moved here in 1961. A campus of The University of North Carolina, 1969.

Broadway Street at Weaver Boulevard in Asheville / 1976

P-57   CONFEDERATE ARMORY
Manufactured Enfield-type rifles. In 1863 plant moved to Columbia, S.C. Building was located 1/4 mi. SE. Burned in 1865.

College Street in Asheville / 1965

P-60   SHERRILL'S INN
Established in 1834 to serve travelers crossing Hickory Nut Gap. In continuous service until 1909. House stands 300 yards south.

US 74 Alternate at Hickory Nut Gap southeast of Fairview / 1970

P-61   ASHEVILLE NORMAL SCHOOL
Presbyterian. Opened 1887 as Home Industrial School. Teacher's College 1892-1944. Stood nearby.

US 25 (McDowell Street) in Asheville / 1972

P-63   ALEXANDER INN
Built around 1820 to serve travelers crossing Swannanoa Gap. One-time stage stop and tavern, later a boarding house. Stands 75 yds. N.

SR 2435 (Old US 70) at Swannanoa / 1985

P-64   BLACK MOUNTAIN COLLEGE
Est. in 1933; closed 1956. Experimental school with emphasis on fine arts & progressive education. Campus was 3 mi. NW.

US 70 (State Street) at SR 2435 (Old US 70) in Black Mountain / 1986

P-68   BILTMORE HOUSE
Designed for George W. Vanderbilt by Richard M. Hunt. Constructed, 1890-1895. Opened to public, 1930. Three miles west.

US 25 (McDowell Street) in Asheville / 1986

P-69   WARREN WILSON COLLEGE
Founded in 1894 by the Presbyterian Church as Asheville Farm School. A four-year college since 1966. 1fi mi. E.

US 70 at SR 2412 (New Salem Road) west of Swannanoa / 1987

P-72   MOUNT MITCHELL RAILROAD
Opened Black Mountains to logging and tourism. Built, 1911-1914. Ran from point nearby to Camp Alice, 21 mi. NE.

Old US 70 at Old Toll Road east of Black Mountain / 1989

P-74   WEAVER COLLEGE
Founded as Weaverville College, 1873; Methodist, coeducational. In 1934 merged with Rutherford to form Brevard College. Campus was one block W.

US 19/23 Business (Main Street) at Brown Street in Weaverville / 1990

P-77   BUNCOMBE TURNPIKE
Opened up western N.C. Built, 1824-28; the 75-mi. long route from S.C. line to Tenn. line, used by settlers & livestock drovers, passed nearby.

Broadway Street at Weaver Boulevard in Asheville / 1993

**P-78   OLIVE TILFORD DARGAN
1869-1968**
Writer of fiction and poetry. "Fielding Burke," her pen name. Author of Call Home the Heart and Highland Annals. Home, 1925-68, was 1/4 mile N.

US 19/23 Business (Haywood Road) at Balsam Avenue in Asheville / 1994

**P-79   LILLIAN EXUM
CLEMENT STAFFORD
1894-1925**
First female legislator in the South. Elected to N.C. House, 1920. Her law office was 400 yds. west; home 1/2 mi. NE.

Charlotte Street at College Street in Asheville / 1998

**PPP-1   BATTLE OF
ASHEVILLE**
On April 3, 1865, Union Col. Isaac M. Kirby left East Tenn. with 1100 men on a raid against Asheville. On April 6, Kirby's force was defeated by local militia under Col. G. W. Clayton. Earthworks remain 100 yds. N.

Broadway Street in Asheville / 1963
[Marker numbered P-56 in error.]

N-32   SWANNANOA GAP
Used by Indians and pioneers in crossing Blue Ridge. General Rutherford's expedition against Cherokee passed here, September 1776.

I-40/US 70 access road east of Ridgecrest / 1956
[Numbered N-32 in error; should be in the P district.]

Lillian Exum Clement Stafford (P 79)

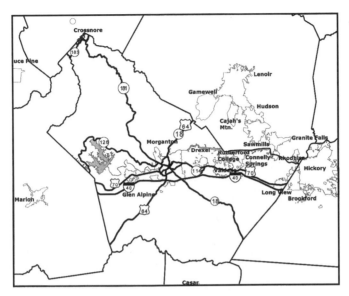

BURKE COUNTY

N-2 WALDENSES
A religious body dating from the Middle Ages. The town of Valdese was founded by members of this group in 1893.
US 64/70 (Main Street) in Valdese / 1937

N-3 QUAKER MEADOWS
Rendezvous for "Over-Mountain Men" prior to Battle of Kings Mountain, 1780. Home to Joseph & Charles McDowell, military & political leaders.
*NC 181 at NC 126 (Green Street)
in Morganton / 1937*

N-8 TOD R. CALDWELL
Governor, 1870-1874, during Reconstruction, member State Convention of 1865. His home stood here.
*US 64/70 Business (Meeting Street)
in Morganton / 1939*

N-13 STONEMAN'S RAID
On a raid through western North Carolina Gen. Stoneman's U.S. cavalry fought a skirmish with southern troops near here, April 17, 1865.
*NC 18/US 64 at Catawba River bridge in
Morganton / 1940*

N-17 CAMP VANCE
Training Camp for State Troops, 1861-64, named for Col. Zeb. B. Vance, War Governor, was here. The Camp was raided by Federal Troops in 1864.
US 64/70 southwest of Drexel / 1942

N-21 ANDRÉ MICHAUX
French botanist, pioneer in studying flora of western North Carolina. Spent nights of Sept. 8, 1794, and May 2, 1795, at "Swan Ponds," 3 mi. S.W.
*NC 181 at NC 126 (Green Street)
in Morganton / 1949*

N-28 WAIGHTSTILL AVERY
First attorney general of North Carolina, 1777-79, member provincial congresses, colonel in Revolution. "Swan Ponds," his home, was 3 mi. S.W.
*NC 181 at NC 126 (Green Street)
in Morganton / 1953*

N-29 RUTHERFORD COLLEGE
Evolved from private school opened c. 1853 by R. L. Abernethy. Operated 1900-1933 by Methodist Church. Closed 1935. The original site 1.3 mi. N.
*Malcolm Boulevard in Rutherford College /
1954*

North Carolina School for the Deaf (N 40)

N-34   BURKE COURTHOUSE

Built of local cut stone, ca. 1835, by James Binnie. August terms of State Supreme Court held here, 1847-61. Raided by Union force 1865. Remodeled 1901.

NC 18 South (South Sterling Street)
in Morganton / 1963

N-39   BROUGHTON HOSPITAL

State hospital for care of mentally ill; opened 1883. Named in 1959 for J. Melville Broughton, governor, 1941-1945.

NC 18 in Morganton / 1989

N-40   N.C. SCHOOL FOR THE DEAF

Opened 1894 under superintendent Edward McKee Goodwin. Main building designed by A. G. Bauer.

US 64 at Fleming Drive
in Morganton / 1989

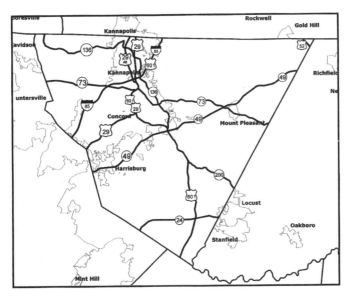

CABARRUS COUNTY

L-4 JEFFERSON DAVIS
President, Confederate States of America, spent the night of April 18, 1865, in house which stood here.

North Union Street in Concord / 1936

L-7 REED GOLD MINE
Gold discovered there 1799. Many gold mines were later operated in this area. N.C. was the chief gold-mining state to 1849. N. 4 mi.

NC 24/27 at SR 1100 (Reed Mine Road) near Cabarrus/Stanly County line / 1936

L-8 NATHANIEL ALEXANDER
Surgeon in Revolution; Congressman; Governor, 1805-07. Birthplace stands 3 miles north.

NC 49 at SR 1300 (Morehead Road) in Harrisburg / 1936

L-13 GRANVILLE GRANT
Formed northern half of colony of North Carolina. Southern boundary surveyed to a point near here in the fall of 1746.

US 29/601 at Cabarrus/Rowan County line north of Kannapolis / 1938

Reed Gold Mine (L 7)

L-33 TRADING PATH
Colonial trading route started in 17th century; extended from southern Va. to land of Catawba & Waxhaw Indians in N.C. Passed near this spot.

US 601 Business (Union Street) at Wilshire Avenue in Concord / 1941

**L-49   STONEWALL JACKSON
                TRAINING SCHOOL**
State home and school for boys, opened
1909. Manual industrial, and agricultural
training.
*SR 1157 (Old Charlotte Road) south
of Concord / 1952*

L-50   W. R. ODELL
Textile manufacturer, State Senator, 1905-07.
Friend of education. His home is 1 block W.
*NC 73/US 601 Business (Church Street) at
Buffalo Street in Concord / 1952*

L-52   JAMES P. COOK
Leader in founding of the Stonewall Jackson
Training School, state senator, editor Con-
cord "Standard" (1888-96) and "Uplift."
Home 1/2 block W.
*US 601 Business (Union Street) at Corban
Street in Concord / 1954*

**L-55   JAMES W. CANNON
                1852-1921**
Textile pioneer; founder of Cannon Mills,
1887, and Kannapolis, 1906; leading manufacturer of towels. Grave 2 mi. S.
*US 29/601 (Cannon Boulevard)
in Kannapolis / 1955*

**L-65   MOUNT PLEASANT
                COLLEGIATE INSTITUTE**
Lutheran junior college for men, 1903-33, on
site of North Carolina College, 1853-1902.
Two blocks north.
*NC 73 (Franklin Street) at Main Street in
Mount Pleasant / 1962*

**L-66   MONT AMOENA
                SEMINARY**
Lutheran school for girls, 1859-1927. The
name is Latin for "Mt. Pleasant." Site is one
block south.
*NC 73 (Franklin Street) at Main Street in
Mount Pleasant / 1962*

L-72   ST. JOHN'S CHURCH
Lutheran. Began ca. 1745 as Dutch Buffalo
Creek Church. Adolph Nussman was first
regular pastor, 1773. Building erected 1845.
300 yards north.
*NC 73 at SR 2414 (Saint John's Road)
northwest of Mount Pleasant / 1968*

L-74   "MILL HILL"
Early example of Greek Revival architecture
in South. Built, circa 1821, by Jacob Stire-
walt. House stands one mile southeast.
*SR 1616 (Stirewalt Road) at SR 1609
(Mooresville Road) west of
Kannapolis / 1970*

L-76   SAMUEL SUTHER
Early minister of German Reformed Church
in N.C., 1768-1782. Preached at Coldwater
Union Church which stood 500 yards N.
*NC 73 at SR 2408 (Gold Hill Road)
east of Concord / 1970*

L-77   ROCKY RIVER CHURCH
Presbyterian. Founded in early 1750s. Hugh
McAden preached here 1755. First regular
pastor, Alexander Craighead, 1758. Present
church constructed 1860.
*SR 1139 (Rocky River Road) and SR 1136
(Lower Rocky River Road)
at Rocky River / 1971*

**L-82   BETHEL UNITED CHURCH
                OF CHRIST**
Began 1745 as Dutch Buffalo Creek Church.
German Reformed & Lutheran, 1806-1875.
Present structure, 1929, is 2 miles East.
*NC 49 at SR 2453 (Lentz Road) northeast
of Mount Pleasant / 1974*

Warren Coleman (L 91)

L-84   RED HILL
Home and tavern of John & Martin Pheifer. Gov. Wm. Tryon and President George Washington among guests. Stood 1fi mi. W.

US 29/601 Bypass at SR 1394 (Poplar Tent Road) west of Concord / 1975

L-91   WARREN COLEMAN
1849-1904
Founder of the nation's first textile factory owned and operated by blacks, 1897-1904. Mill building is 350 yds. N.

US 601 Bypass at Main Street in Concord / 1987

L-93   ISRAEL PICKENS
1780-1827
Congressman from N.C., 1811-1817. Moved to Alabama where he was governor, 1821-1825, & U.S. Senator. Born 2 mi. SW.

NC 73 at SR 1442 (Odell School Road) west of Concord / 1991

L-96   CHARLES A CANNON
1892-1971
Cannon Mills president, 1921-1962; advanced the marketing of textiles. Civic leader and health care benefactor. Grave is one mile south.

US 29/601 in Concord / 1995

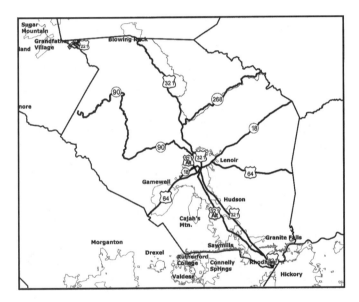

CALDWELL COUNTY

N-1   FORT DEFIANCE
Home of Wm. Lenoir, leader in Revolution and public affairs, built 1788-92 on site of frontier Fort Defiance, is 3 mi. E.

NC 268 at Yadkin River bridge south of Patterson / 1937

N-11   STONEMAN'S RAID
On a raid through western North Carolina Gen. Stoneman's U.S. cavalry passed through Lenoir Mar. 28, and were there again Apr. 15-17, 1865.

NC 18 Bypass (Morganton Boulevard) in Lenoir / 1940

N-24   COLLETT LEVENTHORPE
Confederate general, physician, author. Born in England, settled in North Carolina about 1847. Grave is 150 yds. north.

NC 268 northeast of Patterson / 1950

N-30   DAVENPORT COLLEGE
For women; chartered 1859 by Methodist Episcopal Church, South; merged with Greensboro College, 1933. Two bldgs. stand 100 ft. S.W.

US 321 Alternate (South Main Street) at College Avenue in Lenoir / 1956

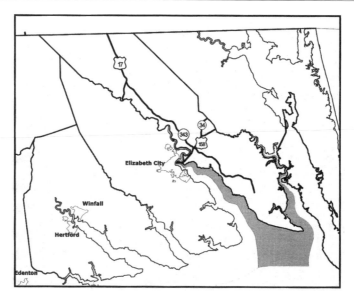

CAMDEN COUNTY

A-8   BATTLE OF SOUTH MILLS
Confederates, on Apr. 19, 1862, repelled Union army here, prevented demolition of Dismal Swamp Canal locks three miles N.W.

NC 343 southeast of South Mills / 1936

A-12   DISMAL SWAMP CANAL
Connects Albemarle Sound with Chesapeake Bay. Begun 1790; in use by War of 1812.

SR 1243 (Old NC 343) at South Mills / 1936

A-29   DEMPSEY BURGESS
Member of provincial congresses, 1775-1776; lieutenant colonel of militia in Revolution; Congressman, 1795-99. Grave is 7 miles S. E.

US 158/NC 34 at Camden / 1948

A-30   ISAAC GREGORY
Member provincial congress, 1775; brigadier general of militia in Revolution; member N.C. conventions, 1788-1789. Home is 4 miles S.E.

US 158/NC 34 at Camden / 1948

A-38   LEMUEL SAWYER
Author of "Blackbeard, a Comedy," 1824, an early drama on North Carolina, & other works. Member of Congress. Grave 160 yds. N.W.

US 158/NC 34 southwest of Camden / 1951

A-42   WILLIAM REED
Acting governor, 1722-1724; president of the Provincial Council. His home stood 3/4 mile east.

NC 343 southeast of Camden / 1953

A-63   McBRIDE CHURCH
Methodist since 1792. Begun as Anglican c. 1733. Visited by bishops Francis Asbury and Thomas Coke. Building erected 1837; remodeled 1882. 2fi mi. E.

US 17 Business at South Mills / 1968

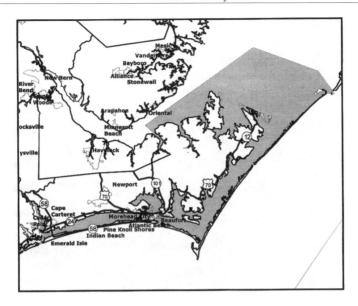

CARTERET COUNTY

C-4   OCRACOKE INLET
Once chief trade inlet of N.C. Pirate "Black-beard" killed near there, 1718, seventeen miles northeast across sound.
NC 12 at Cedar Island ferry landing / 1936

C-8   SPANISH ATTACK
Spanish force landed and captured Beaufort, 1747. Driven away a few days later by local troops.
Turner Street in Beaufort / 1936

C-9   FORT MACON
Built 1826-34 to protect Beaufort Inlet. Replaced Fort Hampton. State park. 5fi miles southeast.
US 70 (Arendell Street) in Morehead City / 1936

C-13   SALT WORKS
Established by order of the Provincial Congress, April 24, 1776, for Revolutionary War use. They were located 1fi miles east.
Turner Street in Beaufort / 1939

C-21   WHALE FISHERY
At Shackleford Banks, six miles southeast by boat, was located a whale fishery of the 18th and 19th centuries.
Turner Street in Beaufort / 1941

**C-24   CAPE LOOKOUT
LIGHTHOUSE**
Constructed, 1857-1859, to replace original 1812 tower. Present lighthouse, 150 feet tall, is four miles south.
*SR 1335 (Harkers Island Road)
at Shell Point* / 1989

C-35   CORE SOUND MEETING
Quaker center for more than 100 yrs. after 1733. Migration west was one cause of decline. Meeting house was 50 yards W.
NC 101 southeast of Harlowe / 1959

**C-40   TEACHER'S ASSEMBLY
(NORTH CAROLINA
EDUCATION ASSN.)**
Headquarters and annual meeting-place, 1888-1900; razed 1934. The building stood here.
Arendell Street in Morehead City / 1962

C-43   OLD BURYING GROUND
Deeded to town, 1731, by Nathanael Taylor. Capt. Otway Burns of the War of 1812, Revolutionary and Civil War soldiers are buried here.
Ann Street in Beaufort / 1965

**C-48   NORTH CAROLINA
          BANKERS ASSOCIATION**
Organized at Teacher's Assembly Hall, July 24, 1897. Thomas H. Battle elected first president.

Arendell Street in Morehead City / 1970

**C-49   CONFEDERATE
          SALT WORKS**
The largest Confederate salt works in Carteret County was 50 yards S. It was burned by Union forces in April, 1862.

Arendell Street in Morehead City / 1962

C-55   FORT HANCOCK
Erected in 1778 by Le Chevalier de Cambray & Capt. de Cottineau to protect Cape Lookout Bay. Dismantled, 1780. Site 8 miles south.

*SR 1355 (Harriss Road)
at Marshallberg / 1977*

C-56   ATLANTIC HOTEL
A prominent resort hotel opened June 21, 1880, and visited by citizens from N.Y. to Ga. Burned April 15, 1933. Stood here.

Arendell Street in Morehead City / 1978

C-57   NEWPORT BARRACKS
Command post for Union defense system from New Bern to Morehead City, 1862-1865. Was 1/3 mi. E.

*SR 1247 (Old US 70) at SR 1140 (Roberts
Road) south of Newport / 1962*

C-58   UNION ARTILLERY
Union artillery was placed in this area during the siege of Fort Macon, March 23-April 26, 1862.

*SR 1190 (Fort Macon Road) at Fort Macon
State Park / 1962*

C-59   VERRAZZANO
Florentine sailing under French flag. His voyage along the coast in 1524 marked the first recorded European contact with North Carolina.

NC 58 in Pine Knoll Shores / 1986

C-62   HOOPHOLE CREEK
Union forces led by General John G. Parke landed here March 29, 1862, during the Fort Macon campaign.

*NC 58 (Fort Macon Boulevard) in Atlantic
Beach / 1962*

**In 1988 the United States Coast Guard Auxiliary sponsored a dedication ceremony for the
Camp Glenn marker (C 63) in Morehead City.**

C-63   CAMP GLENN

National Guard camp, 1911-1918; later site of U.S. Navy base, and first U.S. Coast Guard air station, 1920-1921.

US 70 (Arendell Street) in
Morehead City / 1987

C-69   MARINE RESEARCH

The area around Beaufort and Morehead City long has been valued by marine biologists for its research potential. Army surgeons at Fort Macon in the 1870s published articles about marine life. In the 1880s The Johns Hopkins University for six summers used the Gibbs House on Front Street in Beaufort as a seaside laboratory. In 1899 the federal government chose Beaufort as the site for a fisheries laboratory, the nation's second after Woods Hole, Mass. That lab moved 1fi miles west to Pivers Island in 1902. Duke University founded its marine laboratory on the island in 1938. The University of North Carolina since 1947 has operated a marine studies facility at Camp Glenn in Morehead City. Rachel Carson (1907-1964), pioneer environmentalist and author of *Silent Spring* and *The Edge of the Sea*, conducted research in Beaufort in her later years. The estuarine sanctuary across from the Beaufort waterfront is named in her memory.

Front Street at Live Oak Street
in Beaufort / 1992

CC-3   SIEGE OF FORT MACON

PRELUDE: On February 8, 1862, Union General Ambrose E. Burnside captured Roanoke Island, key to the important Sound Region of Northeastern North Carolina. On February 10, Elizabeth City fell followed by strategic New Bern on March 14. Washington was taken on March 20. The Union forces were now ready to attack Fort Macon, the strategic fort some 5 miles southeast of this point, which protected the deepwater harbor of Beaufort.

UNION ADVANCE: General John G. Parke's 3rd Division advanced against the fort by way of the Atlantic and North Carolina Railroad from New Bern. After some difficulty experienced in moving their artillery, the Union force arrived at Carolina City, a former Confederate camp, on March 21. Morehead City was occupied on March 22; Beaufort on March 26. A request for surrender was sent to Colonel Moses J. White, Fort Macon's commander, on March 23. This request was quickly refused. On March 29 Union forces landed unopposed on Bogue Banks at the mouth of Hoophole Creek. Siege mortars and other artillery were soon brought over the Sound from Carolina City.

The Confederates in Fort Macon soon exchanged cannon fire with the Union Fleet, commanded by Captain Samuel Lockwood. A company of infantry was sent to contest the Union advance.

CONTACT: On April 8 contact was established between the opposing forces. The Confederates were driven into the fort after several days of heavy skirmishing. Fort Macon was now completely invested by the Union forces.

Union artillery was placed into position in 3 batteries, between 1680 and 1280 yards from the fort. Two of these batteries contained mortars; the third was composed of Parrott guns. These positions were protected by sand dune gun emplacements. The Confederates, having no mortars, attempted to substitute 6 old carronades, placed at 40 degree elevations. This effort failed due to a lack of sufficient ammunition for the guns.

On April 25 the Union guns began to bombard the fort. This attack was aided by the Union Fleet. The fleet was soon forced to withdraw, however, due to heavy seas and to the accuracy of Confederate fire.

At 4:30 P.M. on April 25, after a heavy Union cannonade, the Confederates displayed a flag of truce. A cease-fire was arranged, which was followed by the surrender of the fort on April 26 at 9:30 A.M.

The capture of Fort Macon is important because the Union forces now held control over the entire Northeastern North Carolina coastal area. The Union Navy had obtained an excellent deepwater supply base (Beaufort Harbor) on the coast of North Carolina.

TROOPS ENGAGED: Union: 4th and 5th R.I. Inf.; 9th N.J. Inf.; 8th Conn. Inf.; 1st U.S. Art. (1 co.); 3rd N.Y. Art. (1 co.). General John G. Parke commanding. Confederate: 10th N.C. Regt. (Art.—4 cos.); 20th N.C. Regt. (Art.—1 co.). Colonel Moses J. White commanding.

US 70 (Arendell Street) in
Morehead City / 1962

CCC-1   FORT MACON
Built by U.S. Corps of Engineers, 1826-34. Good example of brick fort. Seized by Confederates, April 14, 1861. Scene of battle, April 25, 1862.

SR 1190 (Fort Macon Road) at Fort Macon State Park / 1962

CCC-2   CAROLINA CITY
A large Confederate camp which extended over an area of 1 sq. mi. stood here; taken by Union Army Mar. 23, 1862, in the Fort Macon Campaign.

US 70 (Arendell Street) in Morehead City / 1962

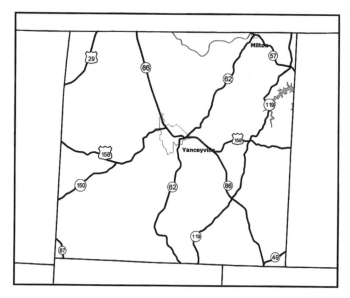

CASWELL COUNTY

G-5   BRIGHT LEAF TOBACCO
In 1850s on a farm in this area Abisha Slade perfected a process for curing yellow tobacco. His slave Stephen discovered process in 1839.

SR 1511 (Blanch Road) west of Blanch / 1936

G-6   CASWELL COURTHOUSE
Erected about 1861. Murder of Sen. J. W. Stephens here in 1870 led to martial law and Kirk-Holden "War."

US 158 in Yanceyville / 1936

G-8   BEDFORD BROWN
U.S. Senator, 1829-40; state legislator, opponent of secession, 1860. This is "Rose Hill," his home.

US 158 north of Locust Hill / 1936

G-12   ROMULUS M. SAUNDERS
Was Minister to Spain, 1845-49; congressman, judge, legislator, and political leader. This was his home.

NC 62 southwest of Milton / 1938

G-18   BARTLETT YANCEY
Congressman. A State legislator and political leader. Died in 1828 at the age of 42. His home and grave are here.

US 158 west of Yanceyville / 1938

G-25   RED HOUSE CHURCH
Presbyterian. Founded about middle of 18th century. Hugh McAden, its noted pastor, was buried in the churchyard, 1781. One mi. S.

NC 57 at Semora / 1939

G-43   CALVIN GRAVES
Speaker N.C. House of Commons and Senate. He cast deciding vote for the North Carolina Railroad, 1849. This was his home.

NC 150 and SR 1128 (Wagonwheel Road) at Locust Hill / 1948

G-61   SOLOMON LEA
First president Greensboro College, 1846-47. Founder and master of the Somerville Female Institute, 1848-1892. Home stands 100 yds. N.

US 158 at Leasburg / 1954

G-67 BETHESDA CHURCH

Presbyterian, began as "Hart's Chapel," about 1765. Mother of many churches. The present building erected 1944, stands 3/4 mile south.

US 158 at SR 1153 (Bethesda Church Road) west of Yanceyville / 1956

G-71 JACOB THOMPSON

Secretary of Interior, 1857-1861, Confederate secret agent in Canada, U.S. Representative from Mississippi. Birthplace stands 100 yds. southeast.

US 158 at Leasburg / 1959

G-75 WILLIAM L. POTEAT

Wake Forest College president, 1905-1927. Champion of freedom of scientific thought. Birthplace and family home stands here.

NC 62 northeast of Yanceyville / 1959

G-77 GRIERS PRESBYTERIAN CHURCH

Organized in 1753. Rev. Hugh McAden served as its first minister. Present building dates from 1856. Stands 1 mi. E.

NC 119 northeast of Hightowers / 1960

G-93 THOMAS DAY
ca. 1801-1861

Free black cabinetmaker in Milton, 1824-1861. Home and shop located here in the old Union Tavern, 1848-1858.

NC 62/57 (Broad Street) in Milton / 1976

G-104 ARCHIBALD DEBOW MURPHEY

Advocate of improved schools, roads, canals. Jurist, teacher, legislator. Born 7/10 mi. S.

NC 57 and NC 119 at Semora / 1988

North Carolinians have long prized items, such as this wardrobe, crafted by Thomas Day (G 93).

G-110 WASHINGTON'S SOUTHERN TOUR

George Washington's last overnight stop in N.C., June 3, 1791, was at the home of Dudley Gatewood, which stood 1 mi. N.E.

NC 86 and SR 1503 (Walters Mill Road) at Gatewood / 1992

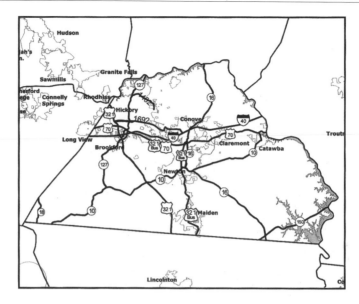

CATAWBA COUNTY

O-23   HOKE SMITH
Secretary of Interior, 1893-1896, Governor
of Georgia, United States Senator, was born,
1855 at Catawba College, then located at this
point.

South College Avenue in Newton / 1942

O-32 "MIRACLE OF HICKORY"
Outbreak of polio in June 1944 led to the
founding of an emergency hospital 1/2 mile
N.E. Closed, 1945.

*US 321 at SR 1314 (Old Lenoir Road)
in Hickory* / 2000

O-46   LENOIR RHYNE
Coeducational, Lutheran college, named for
W. W. Lenoir and D. E. Rhyne. Opened as
Lenoir College in academic year, 1891-92.

*Eighth Street NE at Eighth Avenue NE
in Hickory* / 1954

O-51   CATAWBA COLLEGE
Coeducational, liberal arts. Affiliated with
Evangelical & Reformed Church. Opened
1/2 mi. N., 1851. Moved to Salisbury, 1925,
& enlarged.

*US 321 (Westside Boulevard)
in Newton* / 1956

O-53   CLAREMONT COLLEGE
Founded in 1880 by the Evangelical &
Reformed Church as a school for women.
Closed in 1916. Stood 300 yards east.

*NC 127 (Second Street NE)
in Hickory* / 1959

**O-55   GRAVE EVANGELICAL
        LUTHERAN CHURCH**
Organized before 1797 by German settlers
from Pennsylvania. Present building, erected
1950, stands 2fi miles south.

*NC 10 at SR 2019 (Rocky Ford Road)
southwest of Startown* / 1960

O-62   CHARLES H. MEBANE
Superintendent of Public Instruction, 1897-
1901; president of Catawba College, 1901-
04; newspaper editor. Home 3 blocks E.

*US 321 (Westside Boulevard) at West Ninth
Street in Newton* / 1971

**O-63   OLD ST. PAUL'S
        LUTHERAN CHURCH**
Organized before 1771 as a union church by
German settlers. Present building erected ca.
1820.

US 70/321 west of Conover / 1971

O-64　ST. JOHN'S CHURCH

Lutheran. Organized prior to 1798. J. G. Arends was first pastor. Building is fourth on site 1/4 mile East.

NC 16 at SR 1712 (St. John's Church Road)
north of Conover / 1973

O-68　M. L. McCORKLE
1817-1899

Superior Court judge; a founder of Catawba College; state senator & Confederate colonel. His home stood here.

NC 16 South (South Main Street)
in Newton / 1975

O-70　CONCORDIA COLLEGE
1881-1935

Lutheran. A precursor of Lenoir-Rhyne College; burned, 1935. Church now on site 1 block south.

East Main Street in Conover / 1979

O-74　POTTERY INDUSTRY

Begun in 18th century by Hartsoe, Hilton, Johnson, Propst, Ritchie, Seagle, and Reinhardt families living in 4 mi. radius.

NC 10 east of Corinth / 1987

OO-2　BUNKER HILL
COVERED BRIDGE

One of the last surviving covered bridges in North Carolina, built in 1894, stands 500 yards north on Lyles Creek.

US 70 at Lyle Creek east
of Claremont / 1958

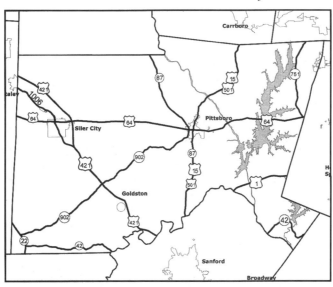

CHATHAM COUNTY

H-10　CAPTAIN JOHNSTON
BLAKELEY

After many victories, War of 1812, was lost at sea with his sloop Wasp. Lived at "Rockrest," 3 miles east.

NC 87 northwest of Pittsboro / 1937

H-12　JOHN OWEN
1787-1841

Governor, 1828-1830; state legislator; and Whig party leader. His grave is 400 yards W.

US 15/501 (Hillsborough Street) at
Salisbury Street in Pittsboro / 1938

H-14　GRANVILLE GRANT

Formed northern half of colony of North Carolina. Southern boundary was surveyed to a point just south of here in 1746.

US 1 at Haw River bridge northeast
of Moncure / 1938

H-15　TORY RAID

David Fanning and his Tories captured many Whig leaders here at old Chatham Courthouse, July, 1781.

US 15/501 (Sanford Road)
in Pittsboro / 1939

H-16   CHARLES MANLY
Governor, 1849-51. Whig Party leader. His law office, relocated & restored, stands 70 yds. N.

US 64 (East Street) at Masonic Street in Pittsboro / 1938

H-17   JAMES I. WADDELL
Commander of the famous Confederate cruiser, "Shenandoah," lived in a house which stands 3 blocks west.

US 15/501 (Hillsborough Street) in Pittsboro / 1939

H-18   RAMSEY'S MILL
Cornwallis, following the battle of Guilford Courthouse, spent several days building a bridge over Deep River, at point 300 yards N.W.

SR 1011 (Old US 1) at SR 1012 (Moncure Road) at Moncure / 1939

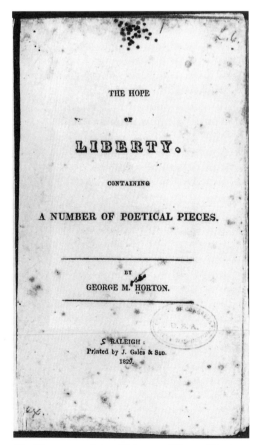

THE HOPE
OF
LIBERTY.
CONTAINING
A NUMBER OF POETICAL PIECES.
BY
GEORGE M. HORTON.
RALEIGH:
Printed by J. Gales & Son.
1829.

No likeness exists of George Moses Horton (H 108). This is the title page of his 1829 book, *The Hope of Liberty*.

H-24   WILCOX IRON WORKS
Important source of munitions during the American Revolution, operated occasionally since. Furnace was 100 yards southwest.

SR 1176 (Old US 421) at Mount Vernon Springs / 1939

H-61   HERMAN HUSBAND
1724-1795
Leader during War of the Regulation, 1768-1771; a reformer and pamphleteer. Later in Whiskey Rebellion in Pa. Lived nearby.

Chatham Avenue at Loves Creek in Siler City / 1951

H-72   ABRAHAM RENCHER
Congressman; Minister to Portugal; Governor of the Territory of New Mexico, 1857-1861; poet and essayist. Buried two blocks West.

US 15/501 (Hillsborough Street) at Salisbury Street in Pittsboro / 1965

H-73   ROCKY RIVER CHURCH
Baptist, organized about 1757. Used by Regulators for meetings after 1768. Stands 200 yards east.

SR 1004 (Snow Camp Road) northeast of Siler City / 1960

H-78   O'KELLY CHAPEL
CHRISTIAN CHURCH
Organized, 1794, by Jas. O'Kelly, founder of the denomination. Present building fourth on site.

NC 751 south of Chatham/Durham County line / 1968

H-84   ROCKY RIVER
FRIENDS MEETING
Established under care of Cane Creek Meeting, 1753; a Monthly Meeting since 1908. Fourth building was constructed in 1926.

SR 1300 (Foust Road) north of Siler City / 1973

H-88   HENRY A. LONDON
1846-1918
Lawyer, state senator. Author of 1901 "London Libel Law." Editor of *Chatham Record*, 1878-1918. Home was here.

US 15/501 (Hillsborough Street) in Pittsboro / 1977

H-108   **GEORGE MOSES HORTON**
ca. 1798-1883
Slave poet. His *The Hope of Liberty* (1829)

was first book by a black author in South. Lived on farm 2 mi. SE.

US 15/501 at SR 1700 (Mount Gilead Church Road) north of Pittsboro / 1999

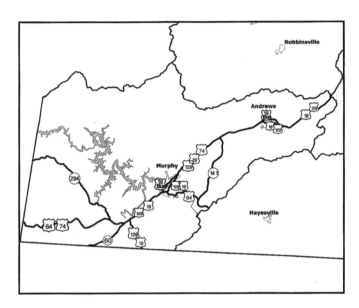

CHEROKEE COUNTY

Q-10   **CHEROKEE WAR**
Major George Chicken of South Carolina led first English military expedition against the Cherokee in this area, 1715.

Peachtree Street in Murphy / 1939

Q-11   **FORT BUTLER**
One of forts in which Gen. Winfield Scott gathered the Cherokee before moving them west in 1838. Stood 1/4 mile southwest.

Lakeside Avenue in Murphy / 1939

Q-21   **DE SOTO**
In 1540 an expedition of Spaniards led by De Soto, first Europeans to explore this area, passed near here.

US 64 at Peachtree Creek east of Murphy / 1940

Q-22   **DE SOTO**
In 1540 an expedition of Spaniards led by De Soto, first Europeans to explore this area, passed near here.

US 19 Business (Valley River Avenue) in Murphy / 1940

Q-23   **DE SOTO**
In 1540 an expedition of Spaniards led by De Soto, first Europeans to explore this area, marched out of North Carolina near here.

US 294 west of Liberty at NC/TN boundary / 1940

Q-27   **JUAN PARDO**
In 1567 an expedition of Spaniards, sent out from Florida by Pedro Menendez de Aviles and led by Juan Pardo, passed near here.

Peachtree Street in Murphy / 1941

Hernando De Soto (Q 21, Q 22, and Q 23)

**Q-29   NORTH CAROLINA-
GEORGIA**

NORTH CAROLINA

Colonized, 1585-87, by first English settlers in America; permanently settled c. 1650; first to vote readiness for independence, Apr. 12, 1776.

(Reverse)   GEORGIA

The colony of Georgia was chartered in 1732, named for King George II of England, and settled in 1733. It was one of the 13 original states.

*US 19/129 southwest of Bell View at NC/GA
boundary* / 1941

**Q-31   NORTH CAROLINA-
TENNESSEE**

NORTH CAROLINA

Colonized, 1585-87, by first English settlers in America; permanently settled c. 1650; first to vote readiness for independence, Apr. 12, 1776.

(Reverse)   TENNESSEE

Settled before 1770 by North Carolina-Virginia pioneers, ceded by North Carolina to the United States, 1789, admitted to the Union, 1796.

*US 64/74 west of Ranger at NC/TN
boundary* / 1941

**Q-33   NORTH CAROLINA-
GEORGIA**

NORTH CAROLINA

Colonized, 1585-87, by first English settlers in America; permanently settled c. 1650; first to vote readiness for independence, Apr. 12, 1776.

(Reverse)   GEORGIA

The colony of Georgia was chartered in 1732, named for King George II of England, and settled in 1733. It was one of the 13 original states.

*NC 60 southwest of Culberson at NC/GA
boundary* / 1942

Q-40   BAPTIST MISSION

For Cherokee Indians, established in 1817, consisting of a chapel, school, farm, and mills. Was 3fi miles north.

US 64 southeast of Murphy / 1951

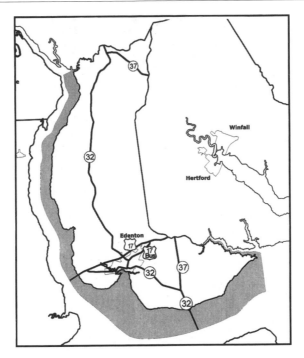

CHOWAN COUNTY

A-1 ST. PAUL'S EPISCOPAL CHURCH

Parish formed in 1701, present structure begun in 1736, succeeding two earlier wooden buildings.

US 17 Business (North Broad Street) in Edenton / 1936

A-4 JOSEPH HEWES

Signer of Declaration of Independence, leader in Continental Congress, merchant. His store was three blocks S.

US 17 Business (North Broad Street) in Edenton / 1936

A-5 JAMES IREDELL 1751-1799

Justice of U.S. Supreme Court, 1790-99. Attorney General of N.C. during Revolution. Home stands 200 ft. east.

US 17 Business (North Broad Street) at NC 32 (Church Street) in Edenton / 1936

A-9 SAMUEL JOHNSTON

Revolutionary leader, Governor, U.S. Senator. His home, "Hayes," and grave are one mile S.E.

US 17 Business (North Broad Street) in Edenton / 1936

A-11 CHOWAN COUNTY COURTHOUSE

Oldest courthouse in use in North Carolina. Built about 1767. Whig centre in Revolution. Stands 3 blocks S.E.

US 17 Business (Broad Street) in Edenton / 1936

A-22 EDENTON TEA PARTY

Fifty-one women met at Mrs. Elizabeth King's home, which stood 1100 ft. S.E., and resolved, Oct. 25, 1774, to support the American cause.

US 17 Business (West Queen Street) in Edenton / 1940

A-25 FIRST POST ROAD

The road from New England to Charleston, over which mail was first carried regularly in North Carolina, 1738-39, passed near this spot.

US 17 Business (North Broad Street) in Edenton / 1942

"Hayes," the Edenton home of Samuel Johnston (A 9)

A-27   MACKEYS FERRY
Established 1735 over Albemarle Sound, succeeding Bells Ferry. Discontinued in 1938. Northern terminus was four blocks south.

US 17 Business (West Queen Street)
in Edenton / 1942

A-34   DR. HUGH WILLIAMSON
Signer of the Federal Constitution, member of Congress, historian. Home was 4 blocks S.E.

US 17 Business (North Broad Street)
in Edenton / 1949

A-46   WEAPEMEOC
The principal town of the Weapemeoc Indians, visited by Ralph Lane and his colonists in 1585-1586, stood near present-day Edenton.

US 17 Business (West Queen Street)
in Edenton / 1954

A-50   JAMES IREDELL, JR.
1788-1853
Governor, 1827-28; U.S. Senator; and legislator. Compiler of revisal of N.C. laws. His home two blocks south; grave at Hayes one mile S.E.

US 17 Business (West Queen Street)
in Edenton / 1959

A-53   THOMAS CHILD
Attorney-General of Colony, 1745-1761. Leader of faction which opposed Governor Dobbs. Secretary to Lord Granville. Home was 2 blocks S.

US 17 Business (West Queen Street)
in Edenton / 1959

A-55   BARKER HOUSE
Home of Thomas Barker, N.C. agent to England, and his wife Penelope, reputed leader of the Edenton "Tea Party," 1774. Stands 3 blocks south.

US 17 Business (North Broad Street)
in Edenton / 1959

A-67   THOMAS C. MANNING
1825-1887
U.S. Minister to Mexico; Chief justice, La. Supreme Court, 3 yrs., assoc. for 7 yrs.; adjutant gen. of La., 1863-65; taught at Edenton Academy. Lived here.

NC 32 (East Church Street)
in Edenton / 1973

A-69   FRANCIS CORBIN
(d) 1767

Granville agent, jurist, legislator. Provoked "Enfield Riot." Home, "the Cupola House," 2 blks. S.

US 17 Business (North Broad Street) at
Queen Street in Edenton / 1982

A-72   HARRIET JACOBS
c. 1813-1897

Fugitive slave, writer, & abolitionist. *Incidents in the Life of a Slave Girl* (1861) depicts her early life. Lived in Edenton.

US 17 Business (North Broad Street)
in Edenton / 1996

A-73   HENDERSON WALKER
c. 1660-1704

Acting governor, 1699-1703; attorney general, judge, and vestryman. Grave is 75 feet west.

US 17 Business (North Broad Street)
in Edenton / 1988

A-78   INGLIS FLETCHER
1879-1969

Novelist. Wrote *Raleigh's Eden* (1940), first of 12-volume "Carolina Series," based on early N.C. history. Her home, "Bandon," stood 1/2 mile northwest.

SR 1222 (Rocky Hock Road)
at Arrowhead Beach / 1993

Chowan County Courthouse, as it appeared in 1971 (A 11)

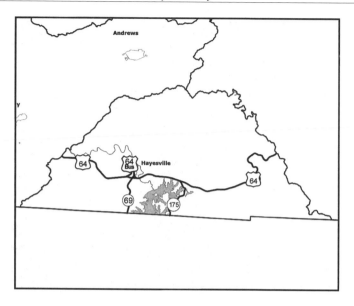

CLAY COUNTY

Q-15   FORT HEMBREE
One of the forts where General Winfield Scott's United States forces gathered the Cherokee before moving them west, stood 3/4 mi. N.W.

US 64 Business (Main Street)
in Hayesville / 1939

Q-19   DE SOTO
In 1540 an expedition of Spaniards led by De Soto, first Europeans to explore this area, passed near here.

SR 1353 (Old US 64) at
Shooting Creek / 1941

Q-20   DE SOTO
In 1540 an expedition of Spaniards led by De Soto, first Europeans to explore this area, passed near here.

US 64 Business (Main Street)
in Hayesville / 1940

Q-26   JUAN PARDO
In 1567 an expedition of Spaniards, sent out from Florida by Pedro Menendez de Aviles and led by Juan Pardo, passed near here.

US 64 northeast of Brasstown / 1941

**Q-35   NORTH CAROLINA-
                GEORGIA**
NORTH CAROLINA
Colonized, 1585-87, by first English settlers in America; permanently settled c. 1650; first to vote readiness for independence, Apr. 12, 1776.

(Reverse)   GEORGIA
The colony of Georgia was chartered in 1732, named for King George II of England, and settled in 1733. It was one of the 13 original states.

NC 69 south of Hayesville at NC/GA
boundary / 1949

Q-37   GEORGE W. TRUETT
Pastor First Baptist Church, Dallas, Texas, 1897-1944, president of Baptist World Alliance. His birthplace stands one mile northwest.

US 64 southwest of Hayesville / 1950

**Q-49   JOHN C. CAMPBELL
                FOLK SCHOOL**
Est. in 1925 by Olive D. Campbell and Marguerite Butler, who adapted the Danish folk school model to study of the region.

SR 1100 (Phillips Road)
at Brasstown / 1986

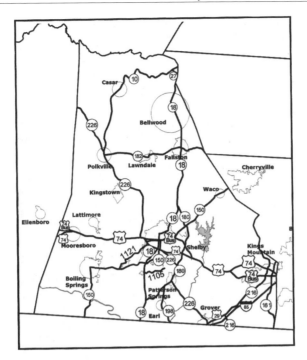

CLEVELAND COUNTY

**O-1 KINGS MOUNTAIN
BATTLEGROUND**
Scene of decisive British defeat, Oct. 7, 1780.
Seven miles south in S.C. National Park.

*US 74 Business (King Street) at NC 216
(Battleground Avenue) in
Kings Mountain / 1936*

**O-5 KINGS MOUNTAIN
BATTLEGROUND**
Site of decisive British defeat on Oct. 7,
1780. National Military Park located 5 mi.
southeast in South Carolina.

US 29 at NC 216 northeast of Grover / 1938

O-6 CORNWALLIS
Entered North Carolina near here, January,
1781, on his second invasion of the state,
pursuing Morgan and Greene.

US 29 in Grover at NC/SC boundary / 1938

O-13 PATRICK FERGUSON
Tory force led by Col. Ferguson camped
nearby Oct. 4-5, 1780. Two days later Ferguson died in major British defeat at Kings
Mountain, 5 mi. SE.

*US 29 at NC 226 in Grover at NC/SC
boundary / 1940*

**O-22 NORTH CAROLINA-
SOUTH CAROLINA
NORTH CAROLINA**
Colonized, 1585-87, by first English settlers
in America; permanently settled c. 1650; first
to vote readiness for independence, Apr. 12,
1776.
(Reverse) SOUTH CAROLINA
Formed in 1712 from part of Carolina, which
was chartered in 1663, it was first settled by
the English in 1670. One of the 13 original
states.

US 29 in Grover at NC/SC boundary / 1941

O-24 PLATO DURHAM
Confederate captain; legislator; member of
conventions of 1868, '75; conservative leader
in Reconstruction period. His home was 100
ft. S.

*US 74 Business/NC 150 (East Marion
Street) at Washington Street
in Shelby / 1948*

Clyde R. Hoey (O 48), Governor (1937-41) and U.S. Senator (1945-54)

O-27   O. MAX GARDNER
Governor, 1929-33; Under Secretary of U.S. Treasury; appointed Ambassador to Great Britain, 1946. Birthplace stands here, grave 300 yds. N.

US 74 Business (Marion Street) at Martin Street in Shelby / 1949

O-43   GARDNER-WEBB UNIVERSITY
Baptist. Founded 1905 as Boiling Springs High School; junior college, 1928-1971. University since 1993.

NC 150 (Main Street) in Boiling Springs / 1952

O-48   CLYDE R. HOEY
United States Senator, 1945-54, congressman, governor, N.C. legislator, lawyer, editor. Home is 1 mi., grave 1.2 mi., N.E.

US 74 Bypass (Dixon Boulevard) at Gold Street in Shelby / 1955

O-59   GRAHAM'S FORT
Home of Col. William Graham. Site of Tory raid, 1780. Served as Revolutionary War fort. Site is 300 yds. N.E.

NC 226 at Buffalo Creek bridge northwest of Grover / 1967

**O-71   W. J. CASH
1900-1941**
Author of *The Mind of The South*. Editor & journalist. His grave is located 1600 ft. N.

US 74 Business (Marion Street) at Martin Street in Shelby / 1982

**O-72   THOMAS DIXON, JR.
1864-1946**
Minister, politician, & author. Film "Birth of a Nation" was based on his novel *The Clansman*. Grave is 1500 ft. N.

US 74 Business (Marion Street) at Martin Street in Shelby / 1982

O-75   MOUNT HARMONY UNITED METHODIST CHURCH
Congregation organized by 1791. Cemetery and present building, the church's fourth, are one mile west.

NC 226 at SR 1379 (Mount Harmony Church Road) northwest of Polkville / 1988

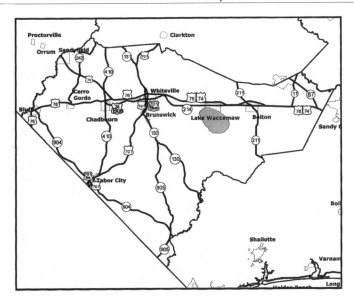

COLUMBUS COUNTY

D-21   CORNWALLIS
Marching to Wilmington after the Battle of Guilford Courthouse, passed with his army near here, April, 1781.

NC 87 west of Acme / 1940

D-27   NORTH CAROLINA-
SOUTH CAROLINA
NORTH CAROLINA
Colonized, 1585-87, by first English settlers in America; permanently settled c.1650; first to vote readiness for independence, Apr. 12, 1776.
(Reverse) SOUTH CAROLINA
Formed in 1712 from part of Carolina, which was chartered in 1663, it was first settled by the English in 1670. One of the 13 original states.

US 76 at NC/SC boundary / 1941

D-28   NORTH CAROLINA-
SOUTH CAROLINA
NORTH CAROLINA
Colonized, 1585-87, by first English settlers in America; permanently settled c.1650; first to vote readiness for independence, Apr. 12, 1776.
(Reverse) SOUTH CAROLINA
Formed in 1712 from part of Carolina, which was chartered in 1663, it was first settled by the English in 1670. One of the 13 original states.

US 701 Business in Tabor City at NC/SC boundary / 1940

D-74   MILLIE-CHRISTINE
McKOY
Black Siamese twins born near here, 1851. Exhibited in U.S. and Europe. Died in 1912. Grave is five miles N.

US 74/76 Business at SR 1700 (Red Hill Road) northeast of Whiteville / 1969

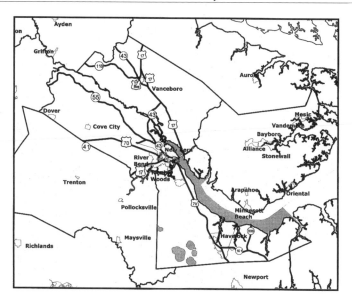

CRAVEN COUNTY

C-1 JOHN WRIGHT STANLY HOUSE
Home of Revolutionary War leader; and his son John, Congressman & state legislator. House moved and restored 1966-70 by the Tryon Palace Commission.

George Street in New Bern / 1935

C-2 TRYON PALACE
Historic Capitol and Governor's residence of N.C., 1770-1794. Burned 1798, and restored in 1952-1959. Open to the public. One block south.

US 70 Business (Broad Street) at George Street in New Bern / 1935

C-3 FIRST PRINTING PRESS IN N.C.
Set up near this spot 1749, by James Davis, who published first book and newspaper in the colony.

US 70 Business (Broad Street) at Middle Street in New Bern / 1935

C-5 ABNER NASH
Governor during British invasion, 1780-81. Member of Provincial and Continental Congresses. Grave 3$^1/_3$ miles S.W.

US 70 Business at SR 1004 (Brice's Creek Road) south of Trent River bridge and New Bern / 1936

C-6 WILLIAM GASTON
N.C. Supreme Court justice, 1833-44, congressman, champion religious liberty, author State song. Home one block north.

US 70 Business (Broad Street) at Craven Street in New Bern / 1936

C-7 RICHARD DOBBS SPAIGHT
A signer of the U.S. Constitution; governor, 1792-95. R. D. Spaight, Jr., governor, 1835-36. Graves two miles S.W.

US 70 Business at SR 1004 (Brice's Creek Road) south of Trent River bridge and New Bern / 1936

C-10 BARON DE GRAFFENRIED
Citizen of Bern, Switzerland, landing here with Swiss and Palatines, founded New Bern, 1710.

US 17 at Neuse River bridge in New Bern / 1938

C-11 BATTLE OF NEW BERN
The victory of Union General Ambrose Burnside here on March 14, 1862, caused the fall of New Bern.

US 70 Business at SR 1004 (Brice's Creek Road) south of Trent River bridge and New Bern / 1938

C-12 FORT TOTTEN

Here stood one of the forts built around New Bern by Union forces after they took the town in March, 1862.

Trent Boulevard at Second Street in New Bern / 1938

C-14 GEORGE E. BADGER

Secretary of the Navy, 1841; United States Senator, 1846-55; judge of the superior court; staunch nationalist. Birthplace was 80 yds. S.

US 70 Business (Broad Street) at Middle Street in New Bern / 1939

C-17 WASHINGTON'S SOUTHERN TOUR

President Washington, on April 20, 1791, was a guest at the home of Col. John Allen, which was 5 mi. E.

NC 55 at Fort Barnwell / 1939

C-19 WASHINGTON'S SOUTHERN TOUR

President Washington visited in the Stanly home two nights, April 20-21, 1791.

Pollock Street in New Bern / 1940

C-20 BAYARD vs SINGLETON

Early American precedent for judicial review of legislation, was decided nearby, 1787, by Judges Samuel Ashe, Samuel Spencer, John Williams.

US 70 Business (Broad Street) at Middle Street in New Bern / 1940

C-22 FIRST POST ROAD

The road from New England to Charleston, over which mail was first carried regularly in North Carolina, 1738-39, passed near this spot.

East Front Street in New Bern / 1942

C-23 STREETS FERRY

Established near here by Richard Graves before 1730. Named for later owner Samuel Street. Replaced by bridge, 1961.

NC 43 at Neuse River bridge north of Lima / 1942

C-25 FORT POINT

Site of Fort Caswell, built by N.C., 1775-76, to protect New Bern, renamed Fort Lane by Confederacy. Taken by U.S., Mar., 1862. 1/2 mi. E.

Junction of SR 1113 (Old Cherry Point Road) and SR 1129 (Green Springs Road) near James City / 1948

C-27 DE BRETIGNY

French marquis, State purchasing agent in Martinique, 1781-82, fought at Guilford Courthouse, Councillor of State. Home was nearby.

Pollock Street at Jones Street in New Bern / 1949

C-30 F. M. SIMMONS 1854-1940

U.S. Senator, 1901-1931. Chaired Senate Finance Committee during World War I. U.S. House, 1887-1889. Lived here.

East Front Street in New Bern / 1950

C-32 FORT BARNWELL

Constructed by Colonel John Barnwell of South Carolina in campaign against the Tuscarora Indians in April 1712. Remains are 2 mi. N.E.

NC 55 at Fort Barnwell / 1954

C-33 JAMES WALKER HOOD

Asst. Superintendent Public Instruction, 1868-70; a founder Livingstone College, 1885; Bishop A.M.E. Zion Church; founded St. Peters, 1864. One blk. N.

US 70 Business (Broad Street) at George Street in New Bern / 1972

C-39 POLITICAL DUEL

John Stanly killed Richard Dobbs Spaight, former governor of North Carolina, in a duel near this spot, September 5, 1802.

US 70 Business (Broad Street) at Hancock Street in New Bern / 1962

C-42 CHRIST CHURCH

Episcopal. Craven Parish created 1715. First Church erected 1750, this one in 1875. Communion service, given by George II, 1752, still in use. One block S.

US 70 Business (Broad Street) at Craven Street in New Bern / 1965

**C-50   FIRST PROVINCIAL
                CONGRESS**
In America to be called and held in defiance
of British orders met in this town, Aug. 25-
27, 1774, with 71 delegates present.
*US 70 Business (Broad Street) at Craven
Street in New Bern* / 1973

C-51   BATCHELDER'S CREEK
Site of Union outpost captured by Confederate Generals Hoke & Pickett on February 1,
1864. The earthworks are 300 yards North.
NC 55 west of New Bern / 1974

**C-53   GEORGE H. WHITE
                1852-1918**
Lawyer; member of N.C. legislature, 1881 &
1885. U.S. Congressman, 1897-1901. Born
into slavery. Home stands 2 blocks N.
*US 70 Business (Broad Street) at Metcalf
Street in New Bern* / 1976

**C-60   CALEB BRADHAM
                1867-1934**
"Brad's Drink," which he created in pharma-
cy here, was marketed as Pepsi-Cola after
1898.
*Pollock Street at Middle Street
in New Bern* / 1986

C-61   NEW BERN ACADEMY
First school chartered in N.C. Assembly
levied a tax for its support in 1766. Present
building was completed in 1810.
*Hancock Street at New Street
in New Bern* / 1986

C-64   JAMES CITY
Community founded here in 1863 as resettle-
ment camp for freed slaves. Named for
Horace James, Union Army chaplain.
US 70 at James City / 1989

C-66   RAINS BROTHERS
Brig. Gen. Gabriel Rains and Col. George
Rains, graduates of West Point, inventors of
explosives for Confederacy. This was their
boyhood home.
East Front Street in New Bern / 1989

C-67   USRC DILIGENCE
U.S. Revenue Cutter built in N.C., 1791. Ship
was commissioned in 1792 by Revenue
Marine (now U.S. Coast Guard). 1/4 mi. W.
*East Front Street at South Front Street in
New Bern* / 1989

C-68   CHERRY POINT
U.S. Marine Corps Air Station activated 1941
as Cunningham Field for first USMC aviator
A. A. Cunningham. MCAS Cherry Point
since May 1942.
*NC 101 at Cunningham Boulevard
in Havelock* / 1992

**C-70   BAYARD WOOTTEN
                1875-1959**
Pioneer photographer of N.C. and the South.
An advocate of equal rights for women.
Began career ca. 1904 in this house where
she was born.
East Front Street in New Bern / 1992

Bayard Wootten (C 70)

CC-1   BATTLE OF NEW BERN

PRELUDE: Union General Ambrose E. Burnside's Division captured Roanoke Island on February 8, 1862. This success provided the Union forces with an excellent base for their next operation—the capture of New Bern.

ACTION: On March 12, 1862 Union land and naval forces under joint command of General Burnside and Commodore S. C. Rowan, arrived at the mouth of Slocum's Creek. Early on March 13 gunboats shelled the nearby woods. Soon Union infantry landed unopposed and began marching in the direction of New Bern, 16 miles northwest.

The Union Fleet moved up the Neuse River to Fisher's Landing where a Confederate force, under Colonel James Sinclair, awaited the Union advance. However, the Confederates were soon driven away by heavy naval gunfire.

The Union Army advanced rapidly past the undefended Croatan Earthwork, the first line of Confederate defenses. By nightfall Union troops were only 1fi miles from the main Confederate line, the Fort Thompson Earthwork.

At 7:30 A.M. on March 14 the battle began with an attack on the Confederate left flank by General John G. Foster's Brigade. The Confederates, ably led by General Lawrence O'B. Branch and protected by the heavy guns of Fort Thompson, were able to hold their position.

Soon, General Jesse L. Reno's Brigade attacked the Confederate right flank. Here the Confederate defense line ended at the railroad. About 150 yards to the rear, Colonel Zebulon B. Vance's 26th North Carolina Regiment occupied a line of rifle pits, which extended 1/2 mile west toward Brice's Creek. The weak spot in the Confederate line was the 150 yards of railroad track, guarded by some North Carolina Militia under Colonel H. J. B. Clark. This militia retreated immediately after being exposed to Union gunfire. The 35th North Carolina Regiment, sent to help the militia, soon followed their example. Unsuccessful in their efforts to turn the Confederate flanks, the Union forces were able to exploit this weak spot. After an initial failure, Foster's and Reno's troops, assisted by General John G. Parke's Brigade, managed to occupy the Fort Thompson Line from the river to the railroad. Vance, whose men continued to resist, soon learned that the other Confederate forces were retreating toward New Bern. After some delay Vance managed to withdraw his men across Brice's Creek in the direction of Kinston.

By nightfall New Bern had been occupied by Burnside's Army. The Confederates were in full retreat toward Kinston, 35 miles inland.

The victory at New Bern provided the Union Army with an excellent base strategically located on the mainland of North Carolina. The town would remain under Union control for the rest of the war. The stage was now set for the Fort Macon Campaign, March 23-April 26, 1862.

East Front Street in New Bern / 1962

CC-2   BATTLE OF NEW BERN

For a detailed account of the battle please read the large map-marker "Battle of New Bern" on US Highway 17 at New Bern, 5/ miles northwest of this road. The Croatan Earthwork, an extensive fortification not used during the battle, can be seen $6^3/_{10}$ miles southeast of this highway. Here, extensive earthworks can be seen on both sides of the highway in a direct line with this marker.

Troops engaged in the Battle of New Bern:

Union:

Major General Ambrose E. Burnside, commanding Division; Brigadier General John G. Parke's Brigade; 4th and 5th R.I. Inf.; 8th and 11th Conn. Inf.; Brigadier General Jesse L. Reno's Brigade; 21st Mass., 51st N.Y., 9th N.J., and 51st Pa. Inf.; Brigadier General John G. Foster's Brigade; 23rd, 24th, 25th, and 27th Mass. and 10th Conn. Inf.

Confederate:

Brigadier General Lawrence O'B. Branch, commanding Brigade; 7th, 26th, 27th, 28th, 33rd, 35th, and 37th N.C. Inf.; 19th N.C. Regt. (1st Cavalry); Captain Thomas H. Brem's and Captain A. C. Latham's artillery batteries. Confederates in Fort Thompson: Captain John N. Whitford's and Captain W. A. Herring's artillery companies. (The men in the other Confederate forts did not directly participate in the battle.)

US 70 Business southeast
of New Bern / 1962

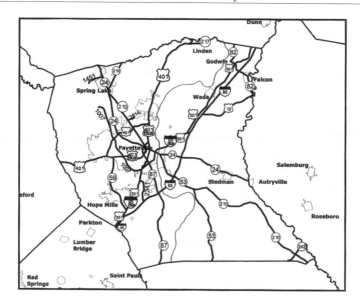

CUMBERLAND COUNTY

I-1   OLD BLUFF CHURCH
Presbyterian. Organized in 1758 by Rev. James Campbell. Present building erected about 1858. N.W. 1 mi.

US 301 at SR 1802 (McLellon Road)
northeast of Wade / 1935

I-2   U.S. ARSENAL
Authorized by Congress, 1836. Taken over by Confederacy, 1861. Destroyed March 1865, by Sherman. Ruins stand 2 blocks S. W.

Hay Street at Bradford Avenue
in Fayetteville / 1935

I-4   JAMES C. DOBBIN
Secretary of United States Navy, 1853-57. Helped found State Hospital for Insane. Home one block north.

Raeford Road in Fayetteville / 1936

I-8   ROBERT ROWAN
Officer in the French and Indian wars and in the Revolution, member Provincial Congresses, state legislator. His grave is 1/2 mile N.E.

Green Street at Old Street
in Fayetteville / 1938

I-9   CORNWALLIS
Marching to Wilmington after the Battle of Guilford Courthouse, stopped with his army in this town in April, 1781.

Green Street in Fayetteville / 1938

I-10   CROSS CREEK
Colonial village and trading center, merged in 1778 with town of Campbelton and in 1783 renamed Fayetteville.

Bow Street at Person Street
in Fayetteville / 1939

I-12   LAFAYETTE
On March 4-5, 1825, was guest of Fayetteville (named for him 1783), staying at home of Duncan McRae, on site of present courthouse.

Gillespie Street in Fayetteville / 1939

I-13   MacPHERSON CHURCH
Presbyterian. Founded by early Scottish settlers. Graves of Alexander MacPherson and T. H. Holmes, a Confederate general, 1fi miles N.

Raeford Road at MacPherson Church Road
in Fayetteville / 1939

I-14   OLD TOWN HALL
Built on site of the "State House," burned 1831, where the North Carolina Convention of 1789 ratified the Federal Constitution.

*Green Street at Market Square
in Fayetteville* / 1939

I-17   FORT BRAGG
Established 1918 as U.S. field artillery training center. Named for N.C. native Braxton Bragg, Lt. Col., USA; Gen., CSA.

*NC 24 (Bragg Boulevard) and Randolph
Street at Fort Bragg* / 1940

I-18   SHERMAN'S ARMY
Invading North Carolina, Sherman's army occupied Fayetteville, Mar. 11-14, 1865, destroying the Confederate Arsenal, which stood 1 mile W.

Hay Street in Fayetteville / 1940

I-21   PLANK ROADS
Fayetteville was the focal point for five plank roads, chartered 1849-52. The longest was built to Bethania, 129 miles northwest.

*Green Street at Market Square
in Fayetteville* / 1940

Excavation by archaeologists in Fayetteville in 1985 uncovered the remains of one of the five plank roads (I 21) that converged in the town.

I-26   ROBERT STRANGE
U.S. Senator, 1836-40; author of "Eoneguski, or Cherokee Chief," first novel about North Carolina (1839). Home and grave are 350 yds. east.

*Ramsey Street at Kirkland Street
in Fayetteville* / 1948

**I-28   FIRST PRESBYTERIAN
CHURCH**
Organized in 1800. The original building, begun in 1816, rebuilt on same walls after fire of 1831, stands one block east.

*Green Street at Bow Street
in Fayetteville* / 1950

**I-29   CONFEDERATE
BREASTWORKS**
Thrown up early in 1865 to defend Fayetteville from Sherman's army. Remains are here.

US 401 in Fayetteville / 1950

**I-31   FAYETTEVILLE STATE
UNIVERSITY**
Est. 1867 as Howard School. State-supported since 1877. A part of The University of North Carolina since 1972.

*NC 87/210 (Murchison Road)
in Fayetteville* / 1950

**Charles W.
Chesnutt
(I 32)**

**I-32   CHAS. W. CHESNUTT
1858-1932**
Negro novelist and short story writer, teacher and lawyer. Taught in a school which stood here.

Gillespie Street in Fayetteville / 1950

I-33   BABE RUTH
Hit his first home run in professional baseball, March, 1914. 135 yds. N.W. In this town George Herman Ruth acquired the nickname "Babe."
Gillespie Street in Fayetteville / 1951

I-42   MOORE'S CAMP
Prior to the Battle of Moores Creek Bridge, forces of Gen. James Moore, Whig commander, camped, Feb. 15-21, 1776, 1fi miles northeast.
NC 87 south of Fayetteville / 1954

I-52   REV. JAMES CAMPBELL
One of early Presbyterian ministers in N.C., 1757-1780. Organized Bluff, Barbecue, and Longstreet churches. Grave is 8 mi. east.
US 401 at SR 1609 (Elliott Bridge Road)
southwest of Linden / 1959

I-54   CAMPBELTON
Colonial river port, incorporated in 1762. Later merged with Cross Creek to form the town of Fayetteville.
Person Street at Broad Street
in Fayetteville / 1960

I-55   METHODIST COLLEGE
Co-educational. Four year liberal arts college. Chartered in 1956. Opened September, 1960.
US 401 Business (Ramsey Street)
in Fayetteville / 1966

I-59   DUNN'S CREEK
QUAKER MEETING
Started about 1746; joined yearly meeting, 1760; discontinued about 1781. Site and cemetery are 2.5 miles S.E.
NC 87 south of Fayetteville / 1972

I-60   FRANK P. GRAHAM
1886-1972
First president of Consolidated U.N.C., 1932-1949. U.S. senator; U.N. mediator, India & Pakistan. Birthplace was 50 yds. W.
US 401 Business (Ramsey Street) at Quincey
Street in Fayetteville / 1973

I-61   THE FAYETTEVILLE
OBSERVER
Oldest N.C. newspaper still being published. Begun 1816 as weekly; daily since 1896. E. J. Hale, editor, 1824-1865.
Whitfield Street in Fayetteville / 1973

I-62   HENRY EVANS
Free black cobbler & minister. Built first Methodist church in Fayetteville. Died 1810. Buried 2 blocks north.
Person Street at Cool Spring Street
in Fayetteville / 1977

I-63   C. M. STEDMAN
1841-1930
Last Confederate officer in Congress, 1911-1930; lawyer & lt.-governor. Grave is 2 blks. east.
US 401 Business (Ramsey Street)
in Fayetteville / 1979

I-64   CONFEDERATE
WOMEN'S HOME
Built in 1915 for the widows and daughters of state's Confederate veterans. Closed, 1981. Cemetery 300 yds. W.
Fort Bragg Road at Glenville Avenue
in Fayetteville / 1986

I-65   WARREN WINSLOW
1810-1862
Acting Governor, 1854; Congressman, 1855-1861. Negotiated surrender of local U.S. arsenal in 1861. Grave 40 yds. SE.
Grove Street at Cool Spring Street
in Fayetteville / 1986

I-70   CHARTER OF THE
UNIVERSITY OF N.C.
William R. Davie's bill to charter the University was adopted by the General Assembly meeting nearby, Dec. 11, 1789.
Gillespie Street at Market Square
in Fayetteville / 1989

I-71   RHETT'S BRIGADE
The brigade of Colonel A. M. Rhett was repulsed 300 yds. W. on March 16, 1865, by Union troops under Col. Henry Case.
NC 82 north of Godwin / 1961

I-72 CONFEDERATE FIRST LINE

Gen. W. B. Taliaferro's division occupied trenches crossing the road at this point, March 15-16, 1865.

NC 82 north of Godwin / 1961

I-73 "OAK GROVE"

Plantation home of John Smith, used as a Confederate hospital during the Battle of Averasboro, March 16, 1865.

NC 82 north of Godwin / 1961

I-74 FEDERAL ARTILLERY

From a point 50 yards west three batteries of artillery under Major J. A. Reynolds shelled the Confederate first line of earthworks.

NC 82 north of Godwin / 1961

I-75 FEDERAL HOSPITAL

The 1865 home of Wm. Smith, 100 yds. E., was used as a hospital for Union troops in the Battle of Averasboro, March 15-16, 1865.

NC 82 north of Godwin / 1961

I-77 CAPE FEAR BAPTIST CHURCH

Constituted in 1756 as Particular Baptist. Stephen Hollingsworth, first minister. Present (1859) building 2 mi. E.

NC 87 at SR 2234 (Blossom Road) south of Fayetteville / 1991

I-79 JOHN ENGLAND 1786-1842

Bishop of Charleston. He organized Roman Catholics in N.C. at Fayetteville convention, & consecrated St. Patrick Church, 1829. Present church 4/10 mi. E.

Owen Drive at Village Drive in Fayetteville / 1996

I-80 BANK OF THE UNITED STATES

Second national bank opened branch in 1818 in Fayetteville. Bank operated, 1820-1835, in house one block east.

Gillespie Street at Holliday Street in Fayetteville / 2000

I-81 DAVID M. WILLIAMS 1900-1975

"Carbine" Williams, designer of short stroke piston, which made possible M-1 carbine rifle, widely used in WWII. Lived nearby.

US 301 in Godwin / 2000

II-1 BATTLE OF BENTONVILLE March 19, 20, and 21, 1865

At Bentonville, General William T. Sherman's Union Army, advancing from Fayetteville toward Goldsboro, met and battled the Confederate Army of General Joseph E. Johnston. General Robert E. Lee had directed the Confederates to make a stand in North Carolina to prevent Sherman from joining General U. S. Grant in front of Lee's Army at Petersburg, Virginia.

Johnston had been able to raise nearly 30,000 men from South Carolina, Alabama, Mississippi, Tennessee, and eastern North Carolina. His army included a galaxy of generals: two full generals besides Joseph E. Johnston; four lieutenant generals; fourteen major generals; and many brigadier generals. Ahead of Sherman with his force, he looked for an opportunity to strike.

Sherman's Army of 60,000 men was divided into two wings: 30,000 men in the Left Wing marching via Averasboro and Bentonville, and 30,000 men in the Right Wing marching on a parallel route to the southeast. Sherman's North Carolina objective was Goldsboro, where 40,000 additional troops and fresh supplies would reinforce and nourish his weary army.

The three-day battle ended in a stalemate. After an initial success on the first day, the Confederates were unable to destroy the united Federal Left and Right Wings (60,000 men) and on the night of March 21-22 they withdrew. The Union Army, anxious to reach Goldsboro, did not pursue.

Troops involved: 85,000 to 90,000

Casualties:	*Killed*	*Wounded*	*Missing*
Confederate	239	1,694	673
Union	304	1,112	221
Total	543	2,806	894

Total killed, wounded, and missing: 4,243

The Battle of Bentonville was important because it was :

1. The only major Confederate attempt to stop Sherman after the Battle of Atlanta,

August, 1864.

2. The last major Confederate offensive in which the Confederates chose the ground and made the initial attack.

3. The largest battle ever fought on North Carolina soil.

The Harper House, residence in which John and Amy Harper raised their 8 children, has been restored on the battleground. This home was used during the battle as a Union hospital and after the battle as a Confederate hospital.

In the Confederate Cemetery are buried 360 soldiers.

The museum and 6,000-acre battleground are open for tours on a regular schedule. To reach the Battleground, proceed on I-95 thirty miles to intersection of US 701. Turn right and follow signs eleven miles.

I-95 (northbound) at rest area
near Fayetteville / 1962

II-2 PRELUDE TO AVERASBORO

Late in 1864, two large Union armies, one in Virginia and the other in Georgia, were beginning to squeeze the Confederacy to defeat. Grant held Lee's Army of Northern Virginia immobile at Petersburg, while Sherman, with 60,000 men, captured Atlanta and began the famous March to the Sea. Savannah fell by Christmas, 1864, and mid-January, 1865, Sherman's invasion of the Carolinas was begun. Columbia was captured on February 17th and Fayetteville on March 11th.

After leaving Fayetteville, Sherman sought to confuse General Joseph E. Johnston's Confederate forces by making a pretended advance against Raleigh with the left wing of his army. This wing, commanded by General H. W. Slocum, began its march from Fayetteville along Old Stage Road (present U.S. 401) which connected with Raleigh. Some 25 miles above Fayetteville the road branched near the village of Averasboro: one branch continued north to Raleigh, the other ran to the east toward Smithfield and Goldsboro. While Sherman's left wing moved in the direction of Averasboro, his right wing advanced toward Goldsboro on a parallel road about 20 miles to the east.

The Confederates faced a difficult military situation in North Carolina by mid-March, 1865. General Johnston, ordered to stop Sherman, found his small army scattered over a wide area. It would take time to organize the various units into an effective fighting force. The only corps in position to hinder the Union advance was the 6,500 man force under General W. J. Hardee. This corps was ordered to resist Slocum's advance, thus began the Battle of Averasboro.

NC 82 north of Godwin / 1961

II-3 BATTLE OF AVERASBORO
Phase One—March 15, 16, 1865

You are standing near the center of the first phase of fighting in the Battle of Averasboro, March 15-16, 1865.

On March 15th the left wing of General Sherman's Union army, commanded by General H. W. Slocum, was advancing along this road from Fayetteville to Averasboro. General H. J. Kilpatrick's cavalry division was in the lead, skirmishing with General Joseph Wheeler's Confederate cavalry which contested the Union advance.

At 3:00 P.M. the Union forces struck a heavy Confederate skirmish line. General Smith Atkins' 9th Michigan cavalry drove the skirmishers back into the first of three lines of breastworks erected across the road. The Union cavalry then constructed heavy barricades in front of the Confederate works.

At 6:00 P.M. Confederate General W. B. Taliaferro, whose division was holding position, ordered an attack along his line. The Union forces, though hard-pressed, were able to hold their position due to the arrival of reinforcements from the 14th Corps. Nightfall found the two armies in nearly the same positions they had held throughout the afternoon. General W. T. Sherman, Union commander, arrived on the field during the night.

At 6:00 A.M. on March 16th, the Union forces attacked Taliaferro's line, driving the Confederates before them. Then the Southerners launched a desperate counter-attack. A disaster for the Union forces was averted when portions of the 20th Corps arrived upon the field. Three batteries of artillery were placed in the position near the John Smith house. These began firing upon the Confederates, driving them back into their breastworks.

At 11:00 A.M. two newly-arrived Union brigades engaged the Confederates in front, while the brigade of Colonel Henry Case assaulted the Confederate right flank. This attack forced the Confederates to withdraw into their second line of works.

NOTE: For the remainder of the battle, drive two miles north on this road and read the map-marker on phase two of the battle.

NC 82 north of Godwin / 1961

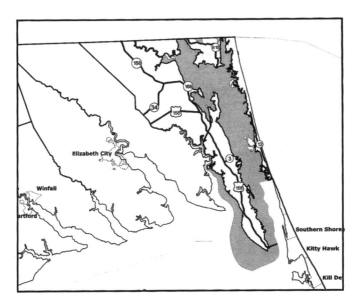

CURRITUCK COUNTY

A-6   THOMAS J. JARVIS
Governor, 1879-1885; Minister to Brazil; U.S. Senator; was born in a house which stood here.

US 158 at Jarvisburg / 1936

A-15   DIVIDING LINE
Commissioners drove the first stake for the Virginia-Carolina boundary, Mar. 18, 1728, three miles N.E., across Currituck Sound.

NC 615 on Knotts Island / 1938

A-16   DIVIDING LINE
In 1728 the Virginia-Carolina boundary was first surveyed from the Atlantic coast to a spot two hundred twenty miles west of here.

NC 168 at NC/VA boundary / 1938

A-47   YEOPIM
Reservation established for Yeopim Indians in 1704; sold after 1739. Northern boundary nearby; village was 2 miles S.E.

US 158 at SR 1149 (Indian Town Road) south of Shawboro / 1998

A-59   JOSEPH PILMOOR
Preached first Methodist sermon in colony, 1772, at Currituck Courthouse. Pilmoor Memorial Methodist Church is near the site. About 300 ft. north.

NC 168 at Currituck / 1966

A-62   HENRY M. SHAW
Member of N.C. Assembly and U.S. Congress. Confederate colonel. Killed in attack on New Bern, Feb. 1, 1864. Home & grave about 150 feet West.

NC 34 at Shawboro / 1967

A-66   McKNIGHT'S SHIPYARD
Thomas McKnight, colonial merchant and legislator; Loyalist during Revolution. Operated large shipyard which stood near here.

US 158 at SR 1149 (Indian Town Road) south of Shawboro / 1971

A-76   ALBEMARLE AND CHESAPEAKE CANAL
Constructed 1855-59 by steam dredges to assist commerce. Now part of Intracoastal Waterway. N.C. Cut 5 miles long.

US 158 at Coinjock / 1991

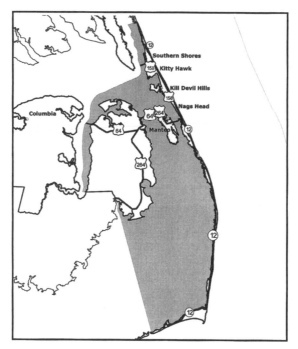

DARE COUNTY

B-1   FIRST ENGLISH COLONIES

Explored in 1584. Site of first English settlements in new world, 1585-1587. Birthplace of Virignia Dare, first child born of English parents in America.

US 64/264 rest area northwest of Manteo / 1935

B-2   FORT HUGER

Principal Confederate fort on Roanoke Island. Mounted twelve guns. Surrendered Feb. 8, 1862. Earthworks are 100 yards south.

US 64/264 boat access ramp at Croatan Sound bridge northwest of Manteo / 1961

This marker in Dare County dedicated to the Roanoke colonies (B 1), shown here in a postcard view, was among the first five signs approved by the Marker Advisory Committee in 1935.

B-4   WRIGHT BROTHERS
On December 17, 1903, from site near foot of Kill Devil Hill, Orville and Wilbur Wright made first successful powered flight 1/5 mile west.

US 158 in Kill Devil Hills / 1936

B-26   R. A. FESSENDEN
Inventor, Pioneer in radio communication, conducted wireless experiments, 1901-02, from a station, 600 yds. S.W.

*US 64/264 rest area northwest
of Manteo / 1949*

B-30   "MIRLO" RESCUE
A German submarine sank the British tanker "Mirlo" off coast nearby, Aug. 16, 1918. Coast Guard, led by J. A. Midgett, saved most of the crew.

NC 12 at Salvo / 1953

**B-31   THE WRECK OF THE
"HURON"**
Near this spot, Nov. 24, 1877, the U.S.S. "Huron" ran ashore with loss of ninety-eight lives.

*NC 12 (Virginia Dare Boulevard) at Bladen
Street in Nags Head / 1953*

**B-32   BILLY MITCHELL
1879-1936**
Brigadier general of the Army Air Service, demonstrated air power by bombing battleships off coast, Sept. 5, 1923. Landing field was here.

NC 12 north of Buxton / 1953

B-37   COLINGTON ISLAND
Granted to Sir John Colleton, Sept. 8, 1663. Colonized in 1665 by a company under Peter Carteret. Two miles W.

NC 12 in Kill Devil Hills / 1959

B-38   CONFEDERATE FORTS
Fort Hatteras and Fort Clark, 2 miles s. west, fell to Union troops on Aug. 29, 1861, after two days of heavy naval bombardment.

NC 12 at Hatteras ferry landing / 1959

B-41   DIAMOND SHOALS
"Graveyard of Atlantic." German submarines sank over 100 ships here, 1941-42, in the "Battle of Torpedo Junction." Shoals are 3 mi. south.

NC 12 at Buxton / 1954

**The Wreck of the "Huron" (B 31), as depicted in
Frank Leslie's Illustrated Newspaper in 1877**

B-44   ANDREW CARTWRIGHT

Agent of the American Colonization Society in Liberia, founded the A.M.E. Zion churches in Albemarle area. His first church, 1865, near here.

NC 345 at US 64/264 southeast
of Manteo / 1965

B-50   U.S.S. MONITOR

Fought C.S.S. "Virginia" ("Merrimac") in first battle of ironclad ships. Lost Dec. 31, 1862, in gale 17 miles southeast. First marine sanctuary.

NC 12 north of Buxton / 1976

B-52   FORT FORREST

Confederate, mounting seven guns. Protected west side of Croatan Sound. Destroyed on Feb. 8, 1862. Earthworks stood 1 mile N.

US 64/264 at Manns Harbor / 1961

B-53   RADIO MILESTONE

From near here in 1902 R. A. Fessenden sent the first musical notes ever relayed by radio waves. Received 48 miles north.

NC 12 north of Buxton / 1988

B-54   CAPE HATTERAS
LIGHTHOUSE

Tallest brick lighthouse in nation at 208 feet. Constructed, 1869-1870, to mark Diamond Shoals. Replaced 1802 structure.

NC 12 at Buxton / 1989

B-60   PORT FERDINANDO

Roanoke voyages, 1585-1590, based operations at inlet near here. Long closed, it was named for pilot Simon Fernandes.

NC 12 south of Nags Head / 2000

BB-4   BATTLE OF
ROANOKE ISLAND

At 3 P.M. Feb. 7, 1862, Union forces under Gen. Ambrose Burnside landed at Ashby Harbor. By midnight 7,500 Federals were ashore. A Confederate force of 400 men and 3 field-pieces was sent to resist the Federal landing. The Confederates were driven away by gunfire from the Federal fleet in Croatan Sound.

The Confederates withdrew north along the only road on the island, situated a little to the west of the present State Highway 345, across which a line of breastworks had been constructed to delay the Federal advance. The Confederates relied on the swamps on each side of the road to protect their flanks. The Confederate right and left flanks were protected by skirmishers.

The Federal 1st Brigade assaulted the Confederates in front, supported by 6 cannon. Federal infantry attempted to advance, but were repulsed by heavy Confederate fire. Troops were ordered into the swamp to crush the Confederate left.

At this time Gen. J. L. Reno arrived with 4 regiments of the Federal 2nd Brigade, which he moved through the swamp against the Confederate right. By the time the Federals reached both flanks of the Confederate position, Gen. J. G. Parke, commanding the Federal 3rd Brigade, arrived and made an attack upon the Confederate front. Under pressure from three sides, the Confederates withdrew to the northern end of the island.

Additional Confederate forces arrived in time to become involved in the retreat. One hour later the Confederate commander surrendered his entire force, 2,488 men, to Gen. Burnside. Roanoke Island was lost—and with it Confederate control of the North Carolina Sound region.

Confederate Troops Engaged: Company B, 8th and Companies B, F, and E, 31st North Carolina Regiments; Companies E and K, 59th, two companies of the 46th, and one company of the 49th Virginia Regiments.

Federal Troops Engaged: 21st, 23rd, 25th, and 27th Massachusetts Regiments; 9th and 51st New York Regiments; 9th New Jersey Regiment; 10th Connecticut Regiment.

Total number of troops engaged: Federal: over 5,000; Confederate: 400.

NC 345 south of junction with US 64/264
in Manteo / 1961

BB-5   NAVAL BATTLE OF
ROANOKE ISLAND

During late January, 1862, a Federal land-sea expedition assembled at Hatteras Inlet to take Roanoke Island and capture control of the North Carolina Sound region. This force was under the joint command of General Ambrose Burnside and navy Flag-Officer Louis Goldsborough. After several delays due to bad weather, the Union fleet, consisting of numerous troop transports and more than 20 war vessels, arrived at the southern end of Roanoke Island. On February 7, 1862,

Federal ships bombarded Fort Bartow, southernmost of the Confederate defenses. The fort returned the fire but with little effect. The Confederate fleet, under Captain W. F. Lynch, waited to engage the Federals behind a line of obstructions placed in Croatan Sound to retard the Federal advance. However, the Confederates, after a sharp engagement which was ended only by darkness, were forced to retire due to lack of ammunition. On February 8, 1862, the Federal fleet bombarded various positions on Roanoke Island in support of General Burnside's land offensive. After the Union victory on the afternoon of February 8, a detachment of Federal ships under Commodore S. C. Rowan was sent into Albemarle Sound in pursuit of the Confederate fleet. The Union forces were now in control of most of the inland waters of northeastern North Carolina.

US 64/264 rest area northwest of Manteo / 1961

BBB-1   FORT BLANCHARD
Confederate earth fort mounting four guns. Smallest on Roanoke Island. Surrendered on Feb. 8, 1862. Earthworks are 300 yds. S.

US 64/264 boat access ramp at Croatan Sound bridge northwest of Manteo / 1961

BBB-2   FORT BARTOW
Confederate earth fort mounting nine guns. Bombarded by Federal fleet February 7, 1862. Earthworks 2fi mi. W.

US 64/264 in Manteo / 1961

BBB-3   CONFEDERATE CHANNEL OBSTRUCTIONS
Wood pilings placed to stop Federal fleet in Croatan Sound, still visible at low tide. Remains are 2 1/2 mi. W.

US 64/264 in Manteo / 1961

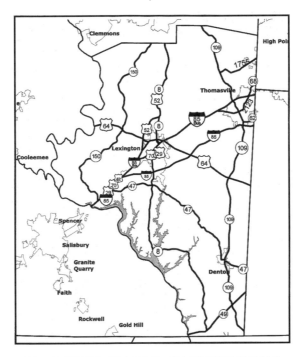

DAVIDSON COUNTY

K-15   STONEMAN'S RAID
Southern troops turned back Stoneman's U.S. cavalry, raiding through western North Carolina, at the Yadkin River bridge, April 12, 1865.

US 29/70/NC 150 at Yadkin River bridge southwest of Lexington / 1940

K-16   JEFFERSON DAVIS
President Davis, fleeing southward after Lee's surrender, with members of his cabinet spent the night Apr. 16, 1865, in a pine grove nearby.

I-85 Business/US 29/70 east of Lexington / 1941

K-20   TRADING PATH
Colonial trading route, dating from 17th century, from Petersburg, Virginia, to Catawba and Waxhaw Indians in Carolina, passed nearby.

*SR 2205 (Old US 64) at NC 109 north
of Denton* / 1941

K-21   TRADING PATH
Colonial trading route, dating from 17th century, from Petersburg, Virginia, to Catawba and Waxhaw Indians in Carolina, passed nearby.

NC 8 north of Southmont / 1941

K-24   YADKIN COLLEGE
A Methodist Protestant institution. Opened in 1856, made co-educational in 1878, closed in 1924. Building stands 1 mi. N.

*US 64 at SR 1186 (Koontz Road) east of
Yadkin River and northwest
of Lexington* / 1941

K-32   JOHN H. MILLS
First head of Oxford Orphanage (1873-1884) and Thomasville Baptist Orphanage (Mills Home), president Oxford Female College. Grave 100 yds. S.

*I-85 Business/US 29/52/70 west
of Thomasville* / 1950

**K-35   JOHN W. THOMAS
1800-1871**
Founder of Thomasville. As legislator led fight for N.C. Railroad; friend of education. His home, Cedar Lodge, was nearby.

*SR 2184 (Old NC 109) at SR 2168 (Cedar
Drive) south of Thomasville* / 1952

**K-44   OLD DAVIDSON COUNTY
COURTHOUSE**
Completed 1858. Interior was burned, 1865, rebuilt ca. 1867. Fine example of Classical Revival style.

*NC 8 (Main Street) at Center Street
in Lexington* / 1972

K-49   PILGRIM CHURCH
Established ca. 1757 as German Reformed. Known early as Leonard's Church. Fourth building to occupy site stands 3/8 mi. NW.

*SR 1844 (Atlantic Street) at SR 1813 (Ridge
Road) northeast of Lexington* / 1978

**K-56   WM. RAINEY HOLT
1798-1868**
Physician. Advocate of scientific agriculture. His plantation "Linwood" was 6 miles southwest. Built home here, 1834.

*US 29/70 Business (South Main Street)
in Lexington* / 1995

John H. Mills (K 32)

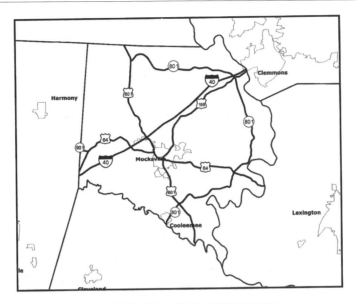

DAVIE COUNTY

M-3 DANIEL BOONE'S PARENTS
Squire and Sarah Boone are buried here. Daniel Boone, 1734-1820, lived many years in this region.

US 601 northwest of Mocksville / 1938

M-27 JOHN STOKES
First U.S. Judge for District of N.C., 1790, captain in Revolution, state legislator, member of convention of 1789. His plantation was nearby.

US 601 at SR 1103 (Pineridge Road) east of Cooleemee / 1952

M-33 HINTON R. HELPER
Author of *The Impending Crisis*, a bitterly controversial book which denounced slavery; U.S. Consul at Buenos Aires, 1861-66. Born 150 yds. N.

US 64 west of Mocksville / 1959

M-41 "COOLEEMEE"
Fine example of "Anglo-Grecian Villa." Built on 4,000 acre plantation by Peter W. Hairston in 1855. House stands 1 mi. south.

US 64 at SR 1812 (Peter Hairston Road) west of Yadkin River bridge east of Mocksville / 1970

M-44 COKESBURY SCHOOL
Short lived. The first Methodist school in North Carolina. Began about 1790. Was two miles east.

NC 801 at SR 1657 (Underpass Road) northwest of Advance / 1977

M-47 BOONE TRACT
In 1753 Lord Granville granted 640 acres on Bear Creek to Squire Boone who sold it in 1759 to his son Daniel. This was a part of the original Boone tract.

US 64 at Bear Creek west of Mocksville / 1979

The tombstone of Squire and Sarah Boone, parents of Daniel Boone (M 3), near Mocksville

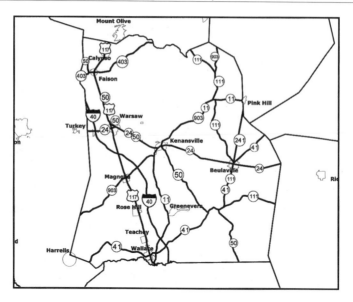

DUPLIN COUNTY

F-4   GROVE CHURCH
Presbyterian. First church founded by Scotch-Irish who settled here about 1736.

NC 11/24/50/903 (South Main Street) in Kenansville / 1936

F-6   HUGH McADEN
Presbyterian clergyman, lived nearby. Served Duplin and New Hanover congregations, 1759-1769. Moved to Caswell County where he died in 1781.

NC 24 east of Kenansville / 1939

F-7   BATTLE OF ROCKFISH
The British under Major Craig defeated the North Carolina Militia, Aug. 2, 1781, 300 yards S.E.

NC 11 southeast of Wallace / 1939

F-8   E. E. SMITH
1852-1933
President for over 40 years of State Colored Normal School (Fayetteville State University). U.S. minister to Liberia, 1888-90. Born 2fi mi. SE.

NC 403 at SR 1306 (Beautancus Road) northeast of Faison / 1993

F-14   WILLIAM HOUSTON
Stamp master of North Carolina, 1765, resigned during demonstration in Wilmington against the Stamp Act; a physician at Sarecta, four mi. E.

NC 11/903 at SR 1700 (Sarecta Road) northeast of Kenansville / 1940

F-22   THOS. O. LARKIN
Was U.S. Consul at Monterey, Cal., 1844-1848. Played part in winning California for the United States. Home, 1825-29, was nearby.

NC 41 in Wallace / 1949

F-26   JAMES KENAN
Revolutionary leader, member Provincial Congresses, conventions 1788, '89; militia brigadier general; trustee of University. Grave 2 mi. N.

NC 24 west of Warsaw / 1949

F-27   CONFEDERATE ARMS
FACTORY
Stood here. Made bowie knives, saber-bayonets, and other small arms. Destroyed by Federal cavalry, July 4, 1863.

NC 11/24/50/903 (South Main Street) in Kenansville / 1949

F-29   SAMSON L. FAISON
Brigadier General, U.S. Army, in World War I. Decorated for helping break the Hindenburg Line. His birthplace is 350 yards northwest.

US 117 (East Center Street)
in Faison / 1950

F-47   LIBERTY HALL
Plantation of Thomas S. Kenan, legislator & U.S. Congressman, whose son, Owen Rand, legislator, Confederate Congressman, and major, was born here.

NC 11/24/50/903 (South Main Street)
in Kenansville / 1972

F-48   ROCKFISH CHURCH
Presbyterian. Organized about 1756. Served by Hugh McAden, Robert Tate, & others. Third building on site 10 yds. north.

NC 41 west of Wallace / 1972

F-50   JAMES M. SPRUNT
1818-1884
Educator, botanist, C.S.A. chaplain, county official, & Presbyterian minister. His grave is 4 mi. West.

NC 24 (Main Street) in Beulaville / 1972

F-63   HENRY L. STEVENS, JR.
1896-1971
Veterans leader. National Commander of American Legion, 1931-32; Superior Court judge, 1939-62. He lived 2 blocks N.

US 117 at NC 24 in Warsaw / 1998

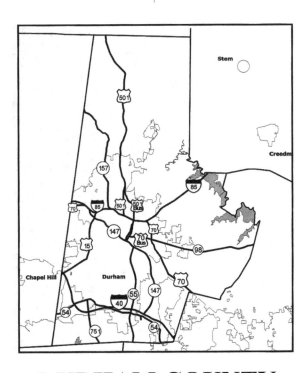

DURHAM COUNTY

G-28   WILLIE P. MANGUM
Member of United States Senate for 18 years and president pro tempore, 1842-45; Congressman; Whig party leader. Home site, grave, 10 mi. N.E.

US 501 at SR 1793 (Bahama Road) southwest of Bahama / 1940

G-29   STAGVILLE
Plantation established by Richard Bennehan in 1776. Later a part of vast holdings of the Cameron family. House is 7 miles northeast.

US 501 Business (Roxboro Street)
at Braggtown in Durham / 1941

G-32   TRADING PATH

Colonial trading route, dating from 17th century, from Petersburg, Virginia, to Catawba and Waxhaw Indians in Carolina passed nearby.

US 501 north of Durham / 1941

G-41   JAMES O'KELLY
ca. 1735-1826

Founded the Christian Church, after dissenting from Methodist-Episcopal Church, 1792. His grave is 4 miles south.

NC 54 at NC 751 (Hope Valley Road)
in Durham / 1948

G-50   STEPHEN B. WEEKS

Historian, bibliographer, collector of North Carolina books and manuscripts, professor at Trinity College, 1891-93. Grave 6 mi. N.E.

US 501 at SR 1793 (Bahama Road)
southwest of Bahama / 1949

G-53   NORTH CAROLINA
CENTRAL UNIVERSITY

Founded 1910 by James E. Shepard for Negroes. State liberal arts college, 1925-1969. Now a regional university.

NC 55 (South Alston Avenue) at Lawson
Street in Durham / 1950

G-57   JAMES E. SHEPARD

Negro educational and religious leader. Founder of a college (1910), now N.C. Central University, its president to 1947. Grave is 1fi miles S.E.

NC 751 (Hope Valley Road) at University
Drive in Durham / 1951

G-63   DUKE HOMESTEAD

Birthplace of J. B. and B. N. Duke, tobacco and hydroelectric magnates, philanthropists (Duke University, the Duke Endowment), is 1 mi. S.W.

US 15/501 North (Roxboro Road)
in Durham / 1954

G-65   MOUNT BETHEL
METHODIST CHURCH

Non-denominational meeting house built about 1750 by Nathaniel Harris. Was attended by Washington Duke. Methodist since 1808.

SR 1793 (Bahama Road) at Bahama / 1966

G-68   WILLIAM B. UMSTEAD

Governor, 1953-54; U.S. Senator, congressman; Democratic leader; and lawyer. Birthplace is 6 1/2 mi., grave 5fi mi., N.E.

US 501 at SR 1793 (Bahama Road) south-
west of Bahama / 1956

G-80   BENNETT PLACE

Farm home of James Bennett, where Confederate Gen. Joseph E. Johnston surrendered his army to Union Gen. William T. Sherman, Apr. 26, 1865. Johnston's surrender followed Lee's at Appomattox by 17 days and ended the Civil War in the Carolinas, Georgia, and Florida.

Bennett Memorial Road at Neal Road
in Durham / 1962

Industrialist and philanthropist James Buchanan (Buck) Duke (G 63), photographed in 1919 with his daughter Doris

G-85   BULL CITY BLUES

During the 1920s-1940s, Durham was home to African American musicians whose work defined a distincitve regional style. Blues artists often played in the surrounding Hayti community and downtown tobacco warehouse district. Prominent among these were Blind Boy Fuller (Fulton Allen) (1907-1941) and Blind Gary Davis (1896-1972), whose recordings influenced generations of players.

Fayetteville Street at Simmons Street in Durham / 2000

G-97   DUKE UNIVERSITY

Formerly Trinity College. Name was changed in 1924 to honor Washington Duke whose son James B. Duke endowed the institution.

US 70 Business (Main Street) in Durham / 1979

G-98   N.C. SOCIETY OF ENGINEERS

Organized in 1918 in the Malbourne Hotel, which stood here. J. N. Ambler elected first president.

US 15/501 North (Roxboro Street) in Durham / 1986

**G-101   JULIAN S. CARR
1845-1924**

Industrialist & civic leader. Benefactor of Trinity College. Headed United Confederate Veterans. Grave 1/4 mi. S.

Chapel Hill Street in Durham / 1987

**G-102   JOHN SPRUNT HILL
1869-1961**

Banker and attorney. Leader in credit union movement. Benefactor, UNC Library. Lived here.

Duke Street in Durham / 1987

**G-109   JOHN MERRICK
1859-1919**

Black business leader. In 1898 he founded what is now N.C. Mutual Life Insurance Company. His grave is 85 yds. N.W.

Fayetteville Road at Cornwallis Road in Durham / 1992

G-112   N.C. SCHOOL OF SCIENCE AND MATHEMATICS

Opened in 1980 as state-supported, residential high school. Campus was site of Watts Hospital (1909-1976), built by Geo. Washington Watts.

Broad Street in Durham / 1994

G-113   DURHAM COUNTY PUBLIC LIBRARY

Oldest public library in North Carolina supported by local taxpayers. In 1898 opened its doors at site 1/2 mile west.

US 15/501 North (Roxboro Street) in Durham / 1995

G-114   RURAL CREDIT UNION

Lowes Grove credit union, first in South, formed to serve local farmers. Est. Dec. 9, 1915, on initiative of John Sprunt Hill.

NC 54 at Alston Avenue in Durham / 1999

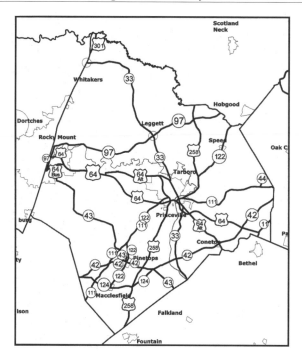

EDGECOMBE COUNTY

E-18   TOWN COMMON
Established in 1760 by the Legislative Act which created the colonial town of Tarboro.

NC 33 (Main Street) in Tarboro / 1939

E-20   ELIAS CARR
Governor, 1893-1897, president of the North Carolina Farmers' Alliance. "Bracebridge Hall," his home, stands one mile north.

NC 42/43 southeast of Pinetops / 1939

**E-24   WASHINGTON'S
               SOUTHERN TOUR**
President Washington spent the night, April 18, 1791, in the town of Tarboro.

NC 33 (Main Street) in Tarboro / 1939

E-40   W. L. SAUNDERS
Editor "Colonial Records of North Carolina," Confederate colonel, N.C. Secretary of State, 1879-91. His grave is four blocks east.

NC 33 (Main Street) in Tarboro / 1949

E-41   W. D. PENDER
Confederate major general; graduate of U.S. Military Academy, 1854. Mortally wounded at Gettysburg, age 29. Grave is 4 blocks east.

NC 33 (Main Street) in Tarboro / 1949

E-65   HENRY T. CLARK
Governor of North Carolina, 1861-1862. Speaker of the State Senate. Helped organize the State for war. Grave is 3 blocks E.

NC 33 (Main Street) in Tarboro / 1959

**Confederate Major General William
Dorsey Pender (E 41)**

John C. Dancy (E 85)

E-70   WILLIAM R. COX
Confederate general. His brigade fought in last infantry action at Appomattox. Later Congressman; Secretary U.S. Senate. Home here.
US 64 Alternate at SR 1225 (Kingsboro Road) east of Rocky Mount / 1965

E-74   DRED WIMBERLY
Former slave. Voted for better roads, schools, and colleges as State representative, 1879, 1887; and State senator, 1889. His home stands here.
US 64 Business (Raleigh Street) in Rocky Mount / 1966

E-85   JOHN C. DANCY
1857-1920
Editor of A.M.E. Zion Church papers; orator; a delegate to Methodist world conference; customs collector of Wilmington. Home stood 3 blks. E.
NC 33 (Main Street) at St. James Street in Tarboro / 1974

E-90   BRICK SCHOOL
Est. for blacks in 1895 through philanthropy of Mrs. Joseph K. Brick; became junior college in 1926. Closed, 1933. Buildings stood here.
US 301 at Bricks / 1979

E-95   JOHN SPENCER BASSETT
1867-1928
Historian. Professor at Trinity College, 1894-1906. Secretary, Amer. Historical Association, 1919-1928. Born here.
Wilson Street at Albemarle Avenue in Tarboro / 1987

E-96   JOSEPH BLOUNT
CHESHIRE, JR.
1850-1932
Bishop of the Episcopal Diocese of N.C., 1893-1932; lawyer & writer. Birthplace is one block W.; grave 100 yards S.
Church Street at Saint David Street in Tarboro / 1987

E-97   FREEDOM HILL
Community established here by freed blacks in 1865. Incorporated as Princeville in 1885.
US 258 at NC 33 in Princeville /1988

E-107   WESTRAY BATTLE
BOYCE LONG
1901-1972
Director of the Women's Army Corps, 1945-1947. First woman honored with Legion of Merit, 1944. Grave 175 yds. S.
NC 97 east of Rocky Mount / 1998

Joseph Blount Cheshire Jr. (E 96)

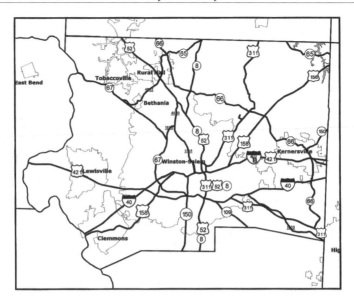

FORSYTH COUNTY

J-9   SHALLOW FORD
Colonial route across Yakdin River. Scene of Tory defeat by Whigs, 1780. Crossing used in 1781 by army of Lord Cornwallis. 600 yds. S.

SR 1001 (Shallowford Road) at Yadkin River bridge west of Lewisville / 1938

J-20   STONEMAN'S RAID
On a raid through western North Carolina Gen. Stoneman's U.S. cavalry fought a skirmish with southern troops at Shallow Ford, April 11, 1865.

SR 1001 (Shallowford Road) at Yadkin River bridge west of Lewisville / 1940

Plank Road marker (J 23) at Bethania

J-23 PLANK ROAD
The western terminus of the Fayetteville and Western Plank Road, 129 miles in length, longest in North Carolina, built 1849-1854, was here.
NC 65 at Bethania / 1941

J-31 WINSTON-SALEM STATE UNIVERSITY
Established for Negroes as Slater Industrial Academy, 1892. State supported since 1895; University since 1969.
US 311 (Martin Luther King Jr. Drive) at Cromartie Street in Winston-Salem / 1950

J-38 ROBERT B. GLENN 1854-1920
Governor, 1905-1909; legislator. Champion of Prohibition and of railroad regulation. Home stood 1 block W.
West Fourth Street at North Broad Street in Winston-Salem / 1952

J-40 GUERNSEY CATTLE
The first registered Guernsey cattle in N.C. were brought from Pa. by Dr. H. T. Bahnson, 1882, to his farm that lay south of this road.
NC 150 at Nelson Street in Winston-Salem / 1954

J-41 BETHABARA
First settlement by Moravians in North Carolina, 1753; known also as Old Town. Church erected 1788. Town is 1 mile N.E.
NC 67 (Reynolda Road) at Fairlawn Drive in Winston-Salem / 1955

J-50 WAKE FOREST UNIVERSITY
Founded 1834 in Wake County by N.C. Baptist Convention. Moved to Winston-Salem in 1956.
NC 67 (Reynolda Road) at Silas Creek Parkway in Winston-Salem / 1959

J-51 NAZARETH CHURCH
Lutheran. Begun about 1778 by German settlers. Formerly called "Old Dutch Meeting House." Present building, 1878.
NC 65 in Rural Hall / 1959

J-52 WM. CYRUS BRIGGS
Invented in 1898 one of the first successful automatic cigarette machines. Workshop was 3 blocks east, home 614 W. Fifth St.
South Main Street at West First Street in Winston-Salem / 1959

J-54 REYNOLDA HOUSE
Built in 1917 by founder of R. J. Reynolds Tobacco Co. Dedicated 1965 as center for advancement of arts and higher education.
NC 67 (Reynolda Road) at Coliseum Drive in Winston-Salem / 1970

J-63 FRIEDBERG CHURCH
Moravian. Begun in 1759, organized in 1773; first church and school built in 1769. Third structure, 1825; located 1.6 mi. W.
NC 150 at SR 3021 (Friedberg Road) south of Winston-Salem / 1974

J-65 FRATERNITY CHURCH OF THE BRETHREN
Oldest German Baptist (Dunker) congregation in North Carolina. Est. ca. 1775 near Muddy Creek, one mile south.
US 158 at SR 2991 (Fraternity Church Road) east of Clemmons / 1976

J-66 McKNIGHT'S MEETING HOUSE
Est. by Methodists ca. 1782. Annual Conferences held here in 1789, 1790, & 1791 by Bishop Asbury. Site was 400 yards N.W.
US 158 at SR 1202 (Lassister Lake Road) west of Clemmons / 1976

J-69 GREAT WAGON ROAD
Frontier road from Pennsylvania to Georgia in 18th century. A major avenue for settlers of the N.C. backcountry. Passed near here.
NC 65 and SR 1611 (Bethania Road) at Bethania / 1976

J-70 FRIES MANUFACTURING AND POWER CO.
First producer of hydroelectric power in North Carolina, April 20, 1898. Located 3 mi. S.W. at early ferry crossing.
US 158 at Yadkin River bridge west of Clemmons / 1976

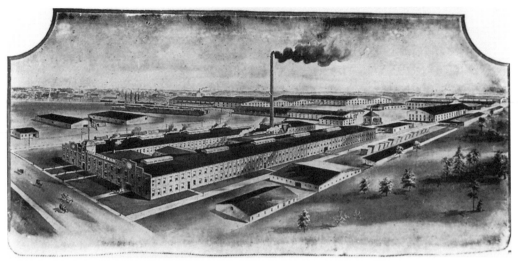

Nissen Wagon Works (J 71), circa 1918

J-71   NISSEN WAGON WORKS
Begun in 1834 by John Nissen. By 1919, fifty wagons a day were produced. Sold in 1925. Was located here.

Waughtown Street at Marble Street
in Winston-Salem / 1976

J-72   R. J. REYNOLDS
1850-1918
Founder of R. J. Reynolds Tobacco Company. In 1875 built his first factory in Winston. Grave 1 block E.

South Main Street at Cemetery Street
in Winston-Salem / 1976

J-83   NORTH CAROLINA
SCHOOL OF THE ARTS
Est. 1963; opened 1965. First state-supported school for performing arts in U.S. A campus of The University of North Carolina since 1971.

Waughtown Street in Winston-Salem / 1985

J-86   ROBERT M. HANES
1890-1959
Banker. Economic adviser to post-World War II Europe. A founder of the Research Triangle Park. Home was 50 yds. W.

Stratford Road at Warwick Road
in Winston-Salem / 1988

J-97   WASHINGTON'S
SOUTHERN TOUR
President Washington spent night of May 31, 1791, at the tavern in Salem. Two blocks east.

Old Salem Road at Walnut Street
in Winston-Salem / 1991

J-101   SIMON G. ATKINS
1863-1934
Founded Slater Academy, now Winston-Salem State Univ.; president, 1892-1904, 1913-34. Religious and community leader. Lived one block west.

US 311 (Martin Luther King Jr. Drive) at
Cromartie Street in Winston-Salem / 1995

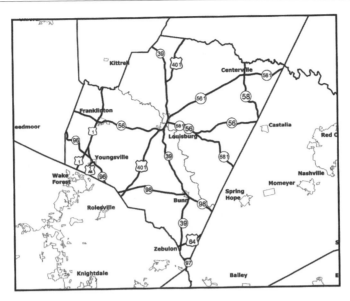

FRANKLIN COUNTY

E-1   GREEN HILL PLACE
Site of first annual conference of Methodist Episcopal Church, 1785. One mile south.

South Main Street at Bunn Road
in Louisburg / 1935

E-26   LOUISBURG COLLEGE
Opened in 1857 on the site of the Franklin Academy, chartered 1787. Now a Methodist junior college, coeducational.

North Main Street in Louisburg / 1940

E-27   GREEN HILL PLACE
Site of first annual conference of Methodist Episcopal Church, 1785. Stands 300 yards S.W.

Bunn Road in Louisburg / 1940

E-33   UNIQUE TOMB
200 yards west, cut in a large granite boulder and covered by a marble slab, is the tomb of William A. Jeffreys, state senator, 1844-45.

US 401 at SR 1101 (Evans Road) near
Franklin/Wake County line / 1942

E-52   THOMAS W. BICKETT
Governor, 1917-21, first in state nominated by a Democratic primary, N.C. Attorney General, member state house. Home stands 1/2 mi. S.W.

US 401/NC 39 (Bickett Boulevard) at NC
561 (Justice Street) in Louisburg / 1953

E-62   MOSES A. HOPKINS
1846-1886
U.S. minister to Liberia, 1885-1886; black clergyman. Founder & principal of Albion Academy which stood two blocks east.

US 1 Alternate (Main Street)
in Franklinton / 1959

E-77   EDWIN WILEY FULLER
Poet and novelist, 1847-1876, born in Louisburg. Wrote *The Angel in the Cloud* and *Sea Gift*. House is 4 blocks west.

US 401/NC 39 (Bickett Boulevard)
in Louisburg / 1968

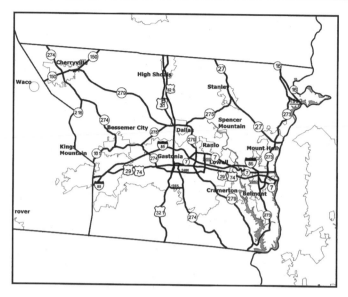

GASTON COUNTY

O-18   NORTH CAROLINA-
SOUTH CAROLINA

NORTH CAROLINA

Colonized, 1585-87, by first English settlers in America; permanently settled c.1650; first to vote readiness for independence, Apr. 12, 1776.

(Reverse) SOUTH CAROLINA

Formed in 1712 from part of Carolina, which was chartered in 1663, it was first settled by the English in 1670. One of the 13 original states.

US 321 south of Crowders at NC/SC boundary / 1941

O-29   TRYON COUNTY

Formed 1768, named for Governor William Tryon. Divided in 1779 into Lincoln and Rutherford Counties. Courthouse stood here.

NC 274 northwest of Bessemer City / 1948

O-39   OAK GROVE

Built 1782. Home of James Johnston, officer in Revolution, member Provincial Congress, legislature, convention of 1788. Is 2 mi. east.

NC 16 at Lucia / 1952

O-42   WILLIAM CHRONICLE

Major in Revolution, leader of Lincoln County forces at the battle of Kings Mountain, 1780, where he was killed. His home stood nearby.

NC 7 (Catawba Street) in Belmont / 1952

O-47   JOSEPH DICKSON
1745-1825

Colonel in Revolution, later brigadier general, member of legislatures of N.C. and Tenn., and of U.S. Congress. His home stands 1/4 mile W.

NC 27 northwest of Mount Holly / 1954

O-50   DALLAS

Named for G. M. Dallas. First seat of Gaston County, 1846-1911; site of Gaston College, now extinct. Courthouse built 1848 is here.

NC 275/279 (Trade Street) in Dallas / 1956

O-54   JOHN FULENWIDER

Founder of High Shoals Iron Works about 1795. One of first producers of pig iron by charcoal process. Revolutionary patriot. Buried 20 yards W.

NC 155 in High Shoals / 1959

Two remarkably similar views of the Tryon County marker (O 29) near Bessemer City, taken in 1949 and 1991

**R. Gregg Cherry (O 56),
Governor (1945-49)**

O-56   R. GREGG CHERRY
Governor of North Carolina, 1945-1949.
State legislator. Promoted good roads and
rural electrification. Grave is 3 miles S.E.

*US 29/74 (Franklin Avenue)
in Gastonia* / 1960

**O-57   BELMONT ABBEY
COLLEGE**
Roman Catholic. Liberal arts coeducational
college. Founded, 1876, by Order of St.
Benedict. One mile north.

US 29/74 in Belmont / 1965

**O-65   DANIEL E. RHYNE
1852-1931**
Textile, furniture, and wagon manufacturer
and banker. A benefactor of Lenoir Rhyne
College. His grave is 100 yards E.

*NC 279 (New Hope Road)
in Gastonia* / 1973

O-69   ST. JOSEPH'S
Built in 1843 for Irish immigrant gold min-
ers. Fourth Catholic church built in state.
This is the original building.

*NC 273 at SR 1918 (Sandy Ford Road)
north of Mount Holly* / 1979

**O-76   STUART W. CRAMER
1868-1940**
Engineer and inventor. Pioneered advances in
textile mill air conditioning. Home 3 mi. SW.

*US 29/74 at Lakewood Drive
in Cramerton* / 1989

**O-78   NORTH CAROLINA
ORTHOPEDIC HOSPITAL**
State institution for crippled children, 1921-
1979. R. B. Babington was its first president;
O. L. Miller, founding surgeon.

*NC 279 (New Hope Road)
in Gastonia* / 1992

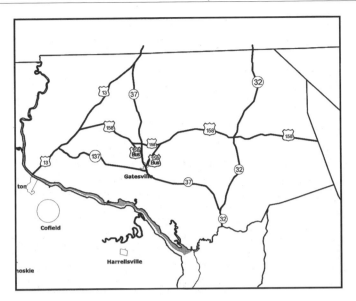

GATES COUNTY

A-17 GEORGE WASHINGTON
Owned a tract of land nearby. He surveyed and formed a company to drain a part of the Dismal Swamp, 1763.

NC 32 at SR 1325 (Savage Road) northeast of Sunbury / 1939

A-24   FIRST POST ROAD
The road from New England to Charleston, over which mail was first carried regularly in North Carolina, 1738-39, passed near this spot.

NC 32 at Corapeake / 1942

A-31   EARLY EXPLORATION
In 1622 an expedition from Jamestown, Va., led by John Pory, explored the Chowan River area.

US 13/158 Bypass at Chowan River bridge southwest of Eure / 1948

A-32   WILLIAM P. ROBERTS
A Confederate brigadier general at age 23, state auditor, a member of Convention of 1875. His grave is 700 yds. west.

NC 37 in Gatesville / 1949

A-35   NORTH CAROLINA-
VIRGINIA
NORTH CAROLINA
Colonized, 1585-87, by first English settlers in America; permanently settled c. 1650; first to vote readiness for independence, Apr. 12, 1776.

(Reverse)   VIRGINIA
First permanent English colony in America, 1607, one of thirteen original states. Richmond, the capital, was seat of Confederate government.

NC 32 at NC/VA boundary / 1949

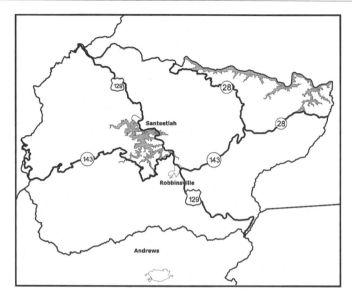

GRAHAM COUNTY

Q-2   JUNALUSKA
Cherokee Indian Chief, brave warrior under Andrew Jackson at Horse Shoe Bend, in Creek War, 1814. Grave one mile southwest.
Main Street in Robbinsville / 1937

Q-53   FONTANA DAM
Constructed, 1942-1944, by the Tennessee Valley Authority. At 480 feet tallest dam in eastern U.S. One mile north.
NC 28 and SR 1245 (Fontana Dam Road) at Fontana Village / 2000

Fontana Dam (Q 53)

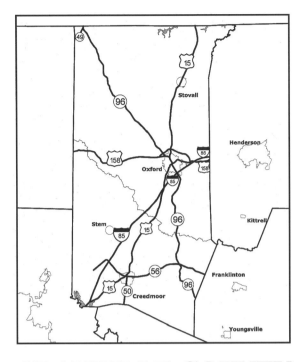

GRANVILLE COUNTY

G-1   JOHN PENN
1740-1788
One of North Carolina's three signers of the Declaration of Independence. His home stood three miles northeast.
US 15 in Stovall / 1936

G-7   OXFORD ORPHANAGE
Opened by Masons, 1873, with John H. Mills first head, in plant of St. Johns College, which they had operated, 1858-1861.
US 15 in Oxford / 1936

G-17   THOMAS PERSON
Leader of popular movements: Regulation, Revolution, and Antifederalism. His home in Goshen stood five miles north.
US 158 at Berea / 1938

G-27   HORNER MILITARY
SCHOOL
Established here by James H. Horner, 1851. Continued by his sons. Moved to Charlotte 1914.
US 158 (Williamsboro Street) at Military Street in Oxford / 1939

G-31   TRADING PATH
Colonial trading route, dating from 17th century, from Petersburg, Virginia, to Catawba and Waxhaw Indians in Carolina, passed nearby.
US 15 and SR 1445 (Buckhorn Road) at Bullock / 1941

John Penn (G 1)

The singing class (above) from the Oxford Orphanage (G 7), 1948, and (below) a class at the Central Orphanage of North Carolina (G 83), photographed several years after its founding in 1883

**G-45   OXFORD FEMALE
COLLEGE**

Opened 1851 by Baptists, operated by individuals after 1857. Franklin P. Hobgood, president, 1880-1924. School closed 1925. Campus was 2 blocks S.

*US 158 (Williamsboro Street) at Lanier
Street in Oxford* / 1948

**G-56   NATH'L ROCHESTER
1752-1831**

Officer in Revolution. Member, N.C. Provincial Congress & Legislature. Founded Rochester, N.Y., 1811. Home was nearby.

US 158 east of Oxford / 1951

**G-73   HARRIS MEETING
HOUSE**

Founded by Methodists prior to 1778. It was the mother church in this area. Disbanded in 1828. Stood 1 mi. N.

*US 158 at SR 1524 (Parham Road) east
of Oxford* / 1959

**G-83   CENTRAL ORPHANAGE
OF NORTH CAROLINA**

Founded 1883. Pioneer Negro child-caring institution, serving on state-wide basis.

NC 96 in Oxford / 1965

**G-86   HENRY PATILLO
1726-1801**

Presbyterian minister; legislator; author of textbooks. Served many churches in Virginia & North Carolina. Home & school 1/4 mile West.

US 15 north of Stovall / 1967

**G-94   HENRY P. CHEATHAM
1857-1935**

Born into slavery. U.S. Congressman, 1889-1893. Superintendent of Colored Orphanage of N.C., 1907-1935. Grave 8/10 mi. N.E.

*NC 96 (Linden Avenue) at Eighth Street
in Oxford* / 1976

G-105   CAMP BUTNER

World War II infantry training camp; housed Axis prisoners of war. Named for N.C. native, Gen. Henry W. Butner.

NC 56 at Butner / 1989

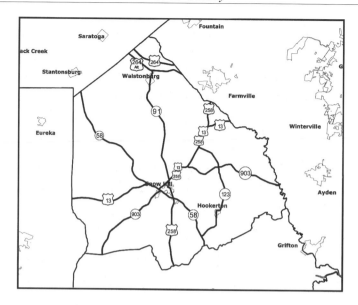

GREENE COUNTY

F-37   NOOHEROOKA
Tuscarora stronghold. Site of decisive battle of the Tuscarora War, March 20-23, 1713, when 950 Indians were killed or captured. Site 1 mi. N.

NC 58 at SR 1058 (Old SR 1201) northwest of Snow Hill / 1961

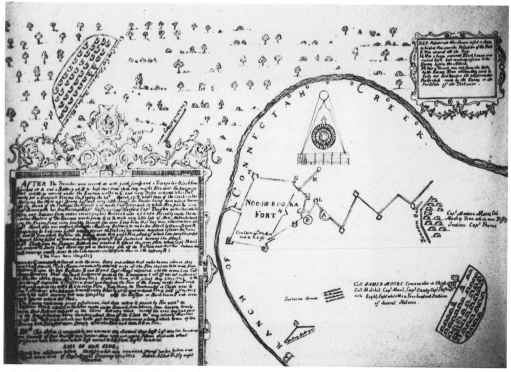

Archaeologists were aided in locating the site of Fort Nooherooka (F 37) by this undated, unsigned map, giving a plan of the vicinity with legends and a full account of the fight.

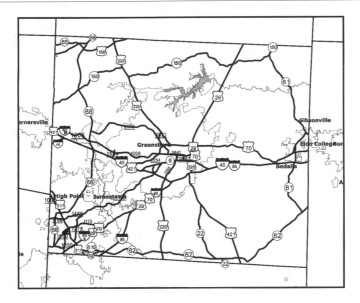

GUILFORD COUNTY

J-1 O. HENRY

William Sydney Porter, 1862-1910, short story writer, lived in a house which stood near here.

West Market Street in Greensboro / 1936

**J-2 DAVID CALDWELL
1725-1824**

Pioneer teacher, physician, and preacher. His famous academy stood 2fi miles northwest.

*South Aycock Street at Market Street
in Greensboro* / 1936

J-3 GUILFORD COURTHOUSE

Important battle of the Revolution between armies of Greene and Cornwallis. U.S. military park.

US 220 (Battleground Avenue) at New Garden Road in Greensboro / 1936

J-4 JOHN MOTLEY MOREHEAD

Governor, 1841-45. Pioneer in railroad and industrial development. "Blandwood," his home.

*West McGee Street at South Edgeworth
Street in Greensboro* / 1936

**J-5 CALVIN H. WILEY
1819-1887**

First Superintendent of N.C. Common Schools, 1853-1865. Author, editor. Born 1fi miles northeast.

*SR 3317 (Duluth Loop) south
of Greensboro* / 1936

**J-6 DOLLY MADISON
1768-1849**

Hostess and social leader. Wife of President Madison. Birthplace stood 1fi mi. northeast.

West Market Street in Greensboro / 1936

**J-10 UNIVERSITY OF N.C.
AT GREENSBORO**

Est. in 1891 as a normal school; became Woman's College of the University of North Carolina, 1932. Coeducational since 1963.

West Market Street in Greensboro / 1939

J-11 GREENSBORO COLLEGE

First college chartered for women in N.C., 1838. Founded by Methodist Church. Coeducational since 1954.

West Market Street in Greensboro / 1939

J-19   BEARD'S HAT SHOP
William Beard made & sold hats at his well-known shop, established before 1795 and later operated by his son David. Site $1^1/_3$ mi. N.

Greensboro Road at Penny Road
in High Point / 1940

J-21   JEFFERSON DAVIS
The President of the Confederacy held two meetings of his cabinet, April 12-13, 1865, at the home of J. T. Wood, which was a few yards N.

South Elm Street at McGee Street
in Greensboro / 1940

J-22   CONFEDERATE CABINET
Members of the cabinet, fleeing south, occupied a railroad car near this spot, Apr. 11-15, 1865.

South Elm Street at Asheboro Street
in Greensboro / 1940

J-24   PLANK ROAD
A section of the Fayetteville-Salem plank road, a toll road 129 miles long, built 1849-1854, followed this route.

US 311 (Main Street) at High Street
in High Point / 1948

J-27   JOSEPH G. CANNON
Member of Congress for 46 years from Illinois, Speaker of the House, 1903-11. His birthplace stood 1fi miles southwest.

US 220 (Battleground Avenue) at New Garden Road in Greensboro / 1949

J-29   N.C. A. & T. UNIVERSITY
Chartered in 1891 as a land grant college for blacks. Since 1972 a campus of The University of North Carolina.

East Market Street in Greensboro / 1949

J-30   CONFEDERATE HOSPITAL
Set up in the First Presbyterian Church to receive wounded from battle of Bentonville, 1865, was here.

Summit Avenue in Greensboro / 1950

J-32   ALAMANCE CHURCH
Presbyterian, organized about 1764. Synod of North Carolina formed here, 1813. The present building erected 1955.

SR 1005 (Alamance Church Road) southeast
of Greensboro / 1951

J-33   BUFFALO CHURCH
Presbyterian, organized about 1756. Present building, the third, was erected in 1827. Revolutionary soldiers buried here.

Church Street at Sixteenth Street
in Greensboro / 1951

J-34   EDGEWORTH FEMALE
SEMINARY
Established by John M. Morehead, operated, 1840-1862, 1868-1871. Building, burned in 1872, stood at this site.

West Market Street at Edgeworth Street
in Greensboro / 1951

J-35   GUILFORD COLLEGE
A coeducational college operated by the Society of Friends. Chartered as New Garden Boarding School in 1834. Opened in 1837.

Friendly Avenue at New Garden Road
in Greensboro / 1952

J-36   OAK RIDGE INSTITUTE
First building erected 1851-52. Opened during academic year 1852-53. Since 1929 Oak Ridge Military Institute.

NC 150 and NC 68 at Oak Ridge / 1952

J-37   WEITZEL'S MILL
Site of a skirmish between American forces under Col. O. H. Williams and British troops under Col. James Webster, Mar. 6, 1781, is 6 mi. E.

US 29 northeast of Greensboro / 1952

J-42   HIGH POINT UNIVERSITY
Founded by Methodist Church in 1924 with aid from City of High Point. University since 1991.

Montlieu Avenue at College Avenue
in High Point / 1955

J-46   LEVI COFFIN
1789-1877
Anti-slavery leader, reputed president of "Underground Railroad," was born about 4 miles north. Moved to Indiana in 1826.
Friendly Avenue in Greensboro / 1955

J-48   CENTRE FRIENDS
MEETING
Was begun in 1757 and organized as a Monthly Meeting in 1773. This is the fourth building on the original site.
NC 62 south of Greensboro / 1957

J-49   DEEP RIVER
FRIENDS MEETING
Was begun in 1753 and organized as a Monthly Meeting, 1778. Present building erected 1875.
Wendover Avenue and SR 1536 (Penny Road) at Deep River bridge north of High Point / 1957

J-55   BENNETT COLLEGE
Methodist. Begun 1874; reorganized as woman's college, 1926. Named for Lyman Bennett of Troy, N.Y. Campus 2 bl. S.
East Market Street at Dudley Street in Greensboro / 1962

J-57   OLD BRICK CHURCH
Originally German Reformed. Now United Church of Christ. Served in 1759 by James Martin. This church was begun in 1813 and was remodeled in 1840.
SR 3110 (Brick Church Road) at SR 3111 (May Road) south of Whitsett / 1966

J-58   HALEY HOUSE
Built 1786 by John Haley, blacksmith & sheriff, on the Petersburg-Salisbury Road. Later a tavern; now preserved as a museum.
Lexington Avenue at McGuinn Street in High Point / 1967

J-61   LOW'S LUTHERAN
CHURCH
Congregation organized ca. 1771; fourth church erected in 1971 on site of original log structure.
NC 61 north of Kimesville / 1972

J-62   CEDAR HILL FOUNDRY
AND MACHINE SHOP
Operated by Clapp, Gates and Company. Made rifles and military supplies for N.C. and the Confederacy, 1861-64. Site 1/4 mi. E.
SR 3056 (Rock Creek Dairy Road) southeast of Sedalia / 1974

J-64   T. GILBERT PEARSON
1873-1943
Ornithologist; teacher; internationally honored conservationist. Founded Audubon Society in N.C. Grave is 1/10 mi. N.E.
US 220 (Battleground Avenue) at Fisher Street in Greensboro / 1975

J-73   GREENSBORO O.R.D.
World War II training camp and overseas replacement depot, 1943-1946. Over 330,000 servicemen were processed here. This is center of 652 acre site.
US 70 (East Wendover Avenue) in Greensboro / 1977

J-74   IMMANUEL COLLEGE
Lutheran. Founded 1903, and moved here in 1905; prepared black students for work in theology & education. Closed 1961.
East Market Street at Benbow Road in Greensboro / 1979

J-75   NEW GARDEN
FRIENDS MEETING
Meeting for worship was begun in 1751; became a Monthly Meeting, 1754. Present bldg. is here.
New Garden Road at Friendly Avenue in Greensboro / 1979

J-77   LINDLEY FIELD
Est. in 1927. First air mail flight through N.C. landed here May 1, 1928. Now Regional Airport.
West Market Street in Greensboro / 1979

J-78   ALBION W. TOURGÉE
1838-1905
Union army officer, author, judge. Member of 1868 Convention. Home was 2 blocks S.
NC 6 (East Lee Street) at Martin Luther King Jr. Boulevard in Greensboro / 1979

J-79   SIT-INS
Launched the national drive for integrated
lunch counters, Feb. 1, 1960, in Woolworth
store 2 blocks south.

*Elm Street at Friendly Avenue
in Greensboro* / 1980

J-80   GEORGE PREDDY
1919-1944
World War II fighter pilot. N.C.'s leading ace.
Killed in action. Home 1 block east.

Summit Avenue in Greensboro / 1983

J-81   LINDSAY STREET
SCHOOL
The first permanent public graded school in
N.C. opened in 1875 in a building which
stood on this site.

*Lindsay Street at Church Street
in Greensboro* / 1962

**Charlotte Hawkins Brown leads group
singing at Canary Cottage, her home on
the campus of Palmer Memorial Institute
(J 87).**

J-84   MASONIC HOME
Established in 1912 by Grand Lodge of
Masons and Order of Eastern Star for their
aged.

Holden Road in Greensboro / 1986

J-85   PIEDMONT RAILROAD
Railroad line between Greensboro and
Danville. Constructed, 1862-1864, for the
Confederacy. Its terminus was nearby.

*Church Street at Washington Street
in Greensnboro* / 1988

J-87   PALMER MEMORIAL
INSTITUTE
Preparatory school for blacks founded 1902
by Charlotte Hawkins Brown. Named for
Alice Freeman Palmer. Closed in 1971. Now
state historic site.

US 70 at Sedalia / 1989

J-89   GUILFORD COUNTY
HEALTH DEPARTMENT
Established in 1911, it was the first county
health department in N.C. and second in U.S.
Now two blocks north.

*Market Street at Eugene Street
in Greensboro* / 1989

J-92   EDWARD R. MURROW
1908-1965
Radio correspondent in London during World
War Two. Television interviewer & commen-
tator. Born 75 yards northeast.

*NC 62 at SR 3433 (Davis Mill Road) south
of Greensboro* / 1990

J-95   SPRINGFIELD FRIENDS
MEETING
Established in 1773 and organized as a
Monthly Meeting, 1790. Building erected
1927 on original site is 1/2 mile east.

*US 311 (South Main Street) at NC 610
(Fairfield Road) in High Point* / 1990

J-96   CONE BROTHERS
Moses and Ceasar Cone pioneered marketing
of textiles; manufactured denim & flannel.
Their first mill, Proximity, 1895, was 1/4
mile N.E.

*Church Street at Wendover Avenue
in Greensboro* / 1991

Moses (left) and Ceasar Cone (J 96)

J-99   FRIEDENS CHURCH
Lutheran. Congregation organized before 1791; church shared with other denominations until the 1850s. This bldg., 1940.

NC 61 at SR 2746 (Friedens Church Road) north of Gibsonville / 1994

J-100   MODEL FARM
Established by Quakers 1867 to stem westward migration by promoting improved agricultural practices. Tract, sold in 1891, was 1/2 mi. E.

US 311 (South Main Street) at Model Farm Road in High Point / 1995

J-102   NORTH CAROLINA RAILROAD
Opened interior of N.C. The ground-breaking took place nearby, July 11, 1851. First president, John Motley Morehead.

South Elm Street in Greensboro / 1996

J-103   N.C. MANUMISSION SOCIETY
Antislavery organization formed by Quakers in central N.C. First met at Centre, July 1816. Disbanded in 1834.

NC 62 south of Greensboro / 1998

JJ-1   THE PRESBYTERIAN CHURCH IN NORTH CAROLINA
There were Presbyterians in North Carolina from the earliest days of the Colony. The most numerous groups, the Scotch-Irish and the Highland Scots, arrived in large numbers during the 18th century. The former settled largely in the Piedmont and the latter in the Cape Fear area.

The early Presbyterian settlers had no ministers. In response to many petitions the Synod of New York sent William Robinson to preach in the winter of 1742-43. The Synod of Philadelphia sent John Thompson in 1744. Hugh McAden arrived in 1755 and visited both the Piedmont and Cape Fear areas. James Campbell began ministering to the Highland Scots in 1757. In 1758 Alexander Craighead arrived in Mecklenburg

County. Among other Presbyterian ministers of the period were David Caldwell, who came as a missionary in 1764 and became a great teacher and statesman, and Henry Patillo, author of the first school textbook in the Colony, who arrived in 1765.

The first three Presbyteries were Orange (1770), Concord (1796), and Fayetteville (1813). The Synod of North Carolina was organized on October 6, 1813, at Alamance Church.

Presbyterians have always been strong supporters of education. In 1767 David Caldwell opened his "Log College" in Guilford County, forerunner of other academies conducted by such Presbyterian educators as Henry Patillo, Samuel E. McCorkle, James Hall, and William Bingham. At the request of Presbyterians, the Colonial Assembly chartered Queens College in 1771, but the act was disallowed by the King. Davidson College opened in 1837 with Robert H. Morrison as first president. Other Presbyterian colleges have included Flora Macdonald, Queens, and St. Andrews.

William R. Davie, a founder of the University of North Carolina, Archibald D. Murphey, early 19th century advocate of internal improvements, constitutional reform, and public education, and Calvin H. Wiley, first State Superintendent of Common Schools, were prominent Presbyterian laymen.

Early growth was slow but was accelerated by the Great Revival of the 18th century, which began with the preaching of James McGready, and by State-wide camp meetings. According to Synod records there were, in 1813, 3 presbyteries, 25 ministers, 102 churches, and 4,000 communicants. In 1963 there were 9 presbyteries, 623 ministers, 645 churches, and 147,262 communicants.

SR 1005 (Alamance Church Road) southeast of Greensboro / 1963

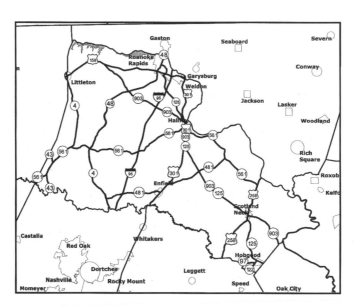

HALIFAX COUNTY

E-3   INDEPENDENCE
The "Halifax Resolves," first formal sanction of American Independence, adopted in this town, April 12, 1776.

US 301 north of US 301 Business (Main Street) in Halifax / 1935

E-4   WILLIAM R. DAVIE
Lived here. Revolutionary hero, member Federal Convention, governor, envoy to France, "Father of the University."

US 301 Business (Main Street) in Halifax / 1935

E-8   MASONIC LODGE
Chartered 1767. Building was erected in 1769. Joseph Montfort, "Grand Master of America," is buried there. 500 yds. E.

US 301 Bypass at US 301 Business (Main Street) north of Halifax / 1938

E-9   WILLIE JONES
Statesman of Revolutionary era, leading champion of democracy in N.C. His home, "The Grove," stood 400 yards west.

US 301 south of Halifax / 1938

E-11   RAM ALBEMARLE
Noted Confederate ironclad was built near this spot, 1863-64. Aided in recapture of Plymouth, April, 1864.

US 258/NC 561 at Roanoke River bridge north of Scotland Neck / 1938

E-12   CORNWALLIS
The British Army under Gen. Cornwallis marching to Virginia defeated the local Militia at the town of Halifax, in May, 1781.

US 301 north of US 301 Business (Main Street) in Halifax / 1939

E-16   JOHN BRANCH
Governor of N.C., 1817-20, and of the Florida Territory, Secretary of the Navy, U.S. Senator. Home was four blocks, grave is 1/2 mile, west.

US 301 (McDaniel Street) at East Franklin Street in Enfield / 1939

E-22   RALEIGH AND GASTON RAILROAD
Chartered 1835, completed 1840. Gaston, its terminal town, now extinct, was 3 mi. N.E.

US 158 northeast of Littleton / 1939

E-23   WILMINGTON AND WELDON RAILROAD
Longest railroad in the world when completed in 1840. Length 161fi mi. Terminus was nearby.

US 158 West (Second Street) in Weldon / 1939

The locomotive *Romulus Saunders* ran on the Raleigh and Gaston Railroad (E 22) in the 1850s.

E-25   WASHINGTON'S SOUTHERN TOUR

President Washington was a visitor in the town of Halifax, on April 16-17, 1791.

US 301 Business (Main Street) northeast of US 301 in Halifax /1939

E-28   LITTLETON COLLEGE

Chartered in 1883 as Central Institute and in 1887 as Littleton Female College. Burned 1919. Was located here.

US 158 in Littleton / 1940

E-34   ROANOKE CANAL

Canal and locks completed around river rapids, 1834. Highway crosses canal route here. A lock is 200 feet south.

NC 48 (Roanoke Avenue) in Roanoke Rapids / 1948

Claude Kitchin of Scotland Neck served in Congress from 1901 to 1923 (E 47 and E 49). His brother, William, was also a congressman and served as governor from 1909 to 1913 (E 46 and E 47).

E-35   ROANOKE CANAL

Canal and locks around river rapids completed 1834 by Roanoke Navigation Company. Highway crosses route of canal at this point.

Sycamore Street in Weldon / 1948

E-39   HUTCHINS G. BURTON ca. 1774-1836

Governor, 1824-1827; Attorney General of N.C.; Congressman. His home was 400 yds. W.

US 301 south of Halifax / 1948

E-43   WALTER CLARK 1846-1924

Champion of liberalism. Member, State Supreme Court, 1889-1924; Chief Justice, 1902-24. Editor, *State Records of N.C.* Home, "Airlie," was here.

NC 4 at Airlie / 1950

E-46   W. W. KITCHIN 1866-1924

Governor, 1909-1913; congressman, 1897-1908; & attorney. His grave is 240 yards south.

US 258 at SR 1117 (Mary Chapel Road) north of Scotland Neck / 1951

E-47   GALLBERRY

Built about 1885. Home of three congressmen, W. H. Kitchin and his sons Wm. W. (governor, 1909-1913) and Claude.

NC 125/903 northwest of Scotland Neck / 1951

E-48   WHITMEL HILL

Colonel in Revolution. Member of Continental Congress, 1778-1781; of Provincial Congresses; and of state legislature. Grave 125 yds. S.E.

US 258 north of Scotland Neck / 1951

E-49   CLAUDE KITCHIN

Congressman, 1901-23, Democratic majority leader, 1915-19. Opposed war declaration, later supported Wilson's war policies. Home is here.

US 258 (Main Street) in Scotland Neck / 1951

E-50   TRINITY CHURCH
Episcopal. Established about 1732. This building, the third, was erected in 1854, in part with brick from an older church.
US 258 north of Scotland Neck / 1951

E-51   "COLONIAL CHURCHYARD"
Graves of Confederate general Junius Daniel, editor Abraham Hodge, U.S. district Judge John Sitgreaves, are 1 bl. N.E.
US 301 Business (St. David Street) at King Street in Halifax / 1953
[Marker numbered E-52 in error.]

E-53   ROANOKE RIVER
Early channel of trade, its valley long an area of plantations. Frequent floods until 1952, since controlled by Kerr Dam. Old name was "Moratuck."
US 258/NC 561 at Roanoke River bridge north of Scotland Neck / 1954

E-55   ROANOKE RIVER
Early channel of trade, its valley long an area of plantations. Frequent floods until 1952, since controlled by Kerr Dam. Old name was "Moratuck."
US 158/301 at Roanoke River bridge in Weldon / 1954

E-57   JAMES HOGUN
Brigadier general in the Revolutionary War, member of Provincial Congresses. Died, 1781, as British prisoner of war. Home was 60 yds. E.
NC 125 northwest of Hobgood / 1954

**E-66   WILLIS ALSTON, JR.
1769-1837**
U.S. Congressman, 1799-1815 and 1825-1831, as a Jeffersonian Republican; N.C. Representative and Senator. Grave 4fi mi. SE.
US 158 at NC 4 in Littleton / 1960

E-67   "ENFIELD RIOT"
Here in 1759 Lord Granville's land agents were compelled to give bond to return illegal fees. This was a forerunner of Regulators.
US 301 (McDaniel Street) in Enfield / 1960

E-68   EAGLE TAVERN
Built in 1790s. Banquet for Lafayette held on February 27, 1825 when tavern was on original site 900 ft. northeast.
US 301 Business (Main Street) in Halifax / 1964

E-69   WHITAKER'S CHAPEL
Originally Anglican, 1740; later Methodist. In 1828 first annual conference of Methodist Protestant Church met here. This is third building on site.
SR 1003 (Whitaker Street) east of Enfield / 1965

E-71   KEHUKEE PRIMITIVE BAPTIST CHURCH
First church, 1742, was 2fi miles N.E. Second building is 200 feet E. Mother church of Kehukee Association begun 1765.
NC 125 at SR 1810 (Fortune Teller Road) south of Scotland Neck / 1965

E-73   EDEN CHURCH
Methodist. An active congregation by 1789. Present building, 1890-1900, is third on site.
SR 1206 (Eden Church Road) at SR 1207 (Hardy Store Road) northwest of Enfield / 1966

E-75   WILLIAM H. WILLS
Methodist Protestant minister. President of the General Conference, 1866. Head of Halifax Male Academy & Elba Female Seminary. Grave here.
NC 561 east of Brinkleyville / 1967

E-78   PERSON'S ORDINARY
In operation by 1770. Revolutionary tavern & stage stop. Named for family of Thomas Person. Restored by Littleton Woman's Club. One blk. E.
NC 4 (Mosby Avenue) at Warren Street in Littleton / 1968

**E-79   HENRY B. BRADFORD
1761-1833**
Early Methodist Protestant minister; educator; and soldier in the Revolution. Founded Bradford's Church on this site circa 1792.
NC 481 (Glenview Road) west of Enfield / 1970

E-80   ANDREW JOYNER
1786-1856
Lt. Col. in War of 1812; state senator, 1835-
52; pres. Roanoke Navigation Co. & Weldon
& Portsmouth R.R. Grave is 2 blks. S.

Tenth Street at Vance Street
in Roanoke Rapids / 1972

E-81   FIRST KRAFT PULP
IN UNITED STATES
Was made here by the sulphate process using
southern pine in 1909, by the Roanoke
Rapids Paper Manufacturing Company.

NC 48 (Roanoke Avenue) at Roanoke River
bridge in Roanoke Rapids / 1973

E-84   CONOCONNARA CHAPEL
Established as Anglican 1747; James Moir
first priest. Became Baptist 1783; inactive
since 1933. Present building, 1849, moved 1
mi. S.W. in 1878.

NC 481 southwest of Tillery / 1973

E-92   SIDNEY WELLER
1791-1854
Agricultural reformer & nurseryman. Introduced "American System" of grape culture.
His Medoc Vineyard was 1 mi. E.

SR 1002 (Ringwood Road) east of Hollister
at Medoc Mountain State Park / 1982

E-94   CALEDONIA
State prison farm since 1892. Antebellum
plantation owned by Johnston family. Name
predates 1713. Two miles N.E.

NC 561 at SR 1141 (Caledonia Road) north
of Tillery / 1987

E-98   NORTH CAROLINA
CONSTITUTION
The first constitution of the independent state
was adopted in Halifax on December 18,
1776.

US 301 Bypass at US 301 Business north
of Halifax / 1988

E-99   JOHN H. EATON
1790-1856
Secretary of War under Andrew Jackson;
U.S. Senator from Tenn.; Fla. governor; U.S.
minister to Spain. Born here.

King Street in Halifax / 1989

E-103   JAMES E. O'HARA
1844-1905
Black political leader. Member, U.S. House
of Representatives, 1883-1887. Practiced law
in Enfield. Lived 1/10 mi. S.

NC 481 (Glenview Road) at SR 1220
(Daniels Bridge Road) west
of Enfield / 1992

E-104   BARTHOLOMEW
F. MOORE
1801-1878
Noted lawyer. Attorney general of N.C.,
1848-51. Compiled *Revised Code* in 1854.
Opposed secession. Born 7/10 mile west.

NC 4/48 and NC 481 at Glenview west of
Enfield / 1993

E-105   BENJAMIN S. TURNER
1825-1894
U.S. Congressman, 1871-1873, representing
Ala.; merchant and farmer in Selma, Ala.
Born into slavery one mile south.

US 158 at SR 1641 (Country Club Road)
west of Weldon / 1995

E-106   PLUMMER BERNARD
YOUNG
1884-1962
Journalist. Publisher of *Norfolk Journal &*
Guide, 1910-1962, leading black-owned
newspaper in the South. Birthplace nearby.

US 158/NC 903 northeast of Littleton / 1995

E-108   FRANK ARMSTRONG
1898-1969
Lt. Gen., U.S. Air Force. Led first U.S.
bombing raids on Germany, 1943. Inspired
Twelve O'Clock High, novel & film. Boyhood home 200 yds. S.

NC 125 (Commerce Street)
in Hobgood / 2000

EEE-1   RAM ALBEMARLE
The Confederate ironclad Albemarle was
outfitted in Halifax with machinery and guns
before sailing down river into action, 1864.

US 301 Business (Main Street) at Dobbs
Street in Halifax / 1962

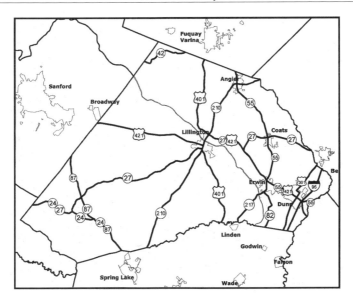

HARNETT COUNTY

H-28   SHERMAN'S MARCH
Moving on Goldsboro, Sherman's Army was temporarily checked by Hardee's Confederates, Mar. 16, 1865, in Battle of Averasboro, 3fi mi. W.

US 301 south of Dunn / 1940

Major General William C. Lee, "Father of the Airborne" (H 50)

H-40   PLANK ROAD
The route of the old Fayetteville-to-Salem plank road, a toll road 129 miles long, built 1849-54, crosses highway near this spot.

NC 87 at Spout Springs / 1948

H-42   SMILEY'S FALLS
Ruins remain of locks and dams built by the Cape Fear & Deep River Navigation Company in 1850s. Rapids extend upstream 1-1/2 miles.

*NC 217 at Cape Fear River bridge
in Erwin* / 1948

H-50   WILLIAM C. LEE
U.S. Army, 1917-1948. Pioneer in organizing Army airborne units; Major general, World War II. Home is 2 blocks, grave 1 mile, west.

Broad Street at King Avenue in Dunn / 1949

H-57   BARBECUE CHURCH
Presbyterian, founded in 1757 by Scottish Highlanders. Present building, the third, erected about 1895, is 200 yds. northeast.

*NC 27 at SR 1285 (Barbecue Church Road)
southeast of Olivia* / 1950

H-60   UNION HEADQUARTERS
Gen. H. W. Slocum, commanding the Union forces, located his headquarters in this field, March 16, 1865.

NC 82 south of Erwin / 1962

H-62   CAMPBELL UNIVERSITY

Baptist. Founded in 1887 by James A. Campbell as Buie's Creek Academy. A university since 1979.

US 421 in Buies Creek / 1952

H-83   FLORA MacDONALD

Scottish heroine, spent the winter of 1774-1775 at Mount Pleasant, the home of her half-sister, Annabella MacDonald, which stood 400 yds. S.W.

NC 24/27 southeast of Johnsonville / 1973

H-97   "LEBANON"

Farquahard Smith's home was used as Confederate hospital during the Battle of Averasboro, March 15-16, 1865.

NC 82 south of Erwin / 1961

H-98   CONFEDERATE
SECOND LINE

On the morning of March 16, 1865, Taliaferro's division fell back to earthworks which crossed the road here.

NC 82 south of Erwin / 1961

HH-2   BATTLE OF
AVERASBORO
Phase Two—March 16, 1865

You are standing at the center of the second phase of fighting in the Battle of Averasboro, March 15, 16, 1865.

On the morning of March 16th, after the fight of the preceding afternoon around John Smith's house 2 miles south of this road, Union General H. J. Kilpatrick's cavalry found a back road circled to the rear of the Confederate position. The Union cavalry attempted to use this road to flank the Confederates, but was stopped by Colonel G. P. Harrison's brigade of McLaws' division after moving only a short distance.

General W. B. Taliaferro decided to abandon the Confederate second position after finding his men in danger of being flanked. At 1:00 P.M. he withdrew to the third and final line of earthworks, where he was assisted by McLaws' division on his left and Wheeler's dismounted cavalry on his right. Rhett's disorganized brigade was held in general reserve behind the junction of this road and the Smithfield road.

The Union forces soon advanced and established a strong line immediately in front of the Confederate third line. From this new position they pressed the Confederates all afternoon and part of the evening, but were unable to break the line. At 8:00 P.M. General W. J. Hardee, commanding the Confederate forces at Averasboro, having accomplished his objectives, began withdrawing his corps along the Smithfield road. Wheeler's cavalry was left behind to cover the retreat. By 4:00 A.M. on March 17th, all Confederate units had been withdrawn leaving the Union forces in control.

General Hardee wished to accomplish two things by contesting the Union advance at Averasboro. The first objective was to determine for General Joseph E. Johnston, commander of all Confederate forces in the Carolinas, whether Sherman's army was advancing on Raleigh or Goldsboro. The Confederates learned it was moving on Goldsboro. The second objective was to stretch out the distance between Sherman's left and right wings (which were moving on parallel roads) in order to give General Johnston a chance to concentrate his smaller army and destroy the Union left wing before the right wing could come to its assistance. Both of these objectives were fully accomplished. The stage was now set for the greater Battle of Bentonville, fought 25 miles east on March 19-21, 1865.

NOTE: In order to better understand the battle it is best to read the large map-marker "Phase One" which is located two miles south of this road.

*NC 82 south of Erwin at Chicora
Cemetery* / 1961

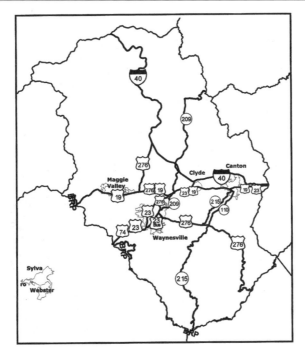

HAYWOOD COUNTY

P-7   QUALLA BOUNDARY
Soco Gap, initial point of U.S. survey, 1876, of Cherokee Reservation, created through earlier efforts of W. H. Thomas, white Cherokee chief.

US 19 at Soco Gap southwest of Maggie Valley / 1939

P-10   MARTIN'S SURRENDER
Gen. James G. Martin surrendered the army of western North Carolina, the last Confederate force in the state, in Waynesville, May 6, 1865.

US 23 Business (Main Street) in Waynesville / 1941

P-19   MORNING STAR CHURCH
Organized by German Lutherans about 1825; Methodist since 1866. Is 2fi miles south.

US 19/23/74 (Park Street) at Academy Street in Canton / 1949

P-26   FELIX WALKER
Revolutionary officer, member Congress, 1817-23, where, in "talking for Buncombe" (County), he gave new meaning to the word. Home was 1/2 mi. N.

US 19 west of Dellwood / 1950

P-40   RUTHERFORD TRACE
The expedition led by Gen. Griffith Rutherford against the Cherokee, Sept., 1776, passed nearby along Hominy Creek.

US 19/23/74 at Hominy Creek east of Canton / 1954

P-41   RUTHERFORD TRACE
The expedition led by Gen. Griffith Rutherford against the Cherokee, Sept., 1776, passed here, through Pigeon Gap.

US 276 at Pigeon Gap east of Waynesville / 1954

P-42   RUTHERFORD TRACE
The expedition led by Gen. Griffith Rutherford against the Cherokee, Sept., 1776, passed here, through Balsam Gap.

SR 1243 (Old US 19 Alternate/23) at Balsam Gap southwest of Waynesville / 1954

P-50   "CATALOOCHEE TRAIL"
An old Indian path across mountains used by early settlers and in 1810 by Bishop Asbury. Trail passed nearby.

US 19 at US 276 west of Lake Junaluska / 1959

P-51 "CATALOOCHEE TRAIL"
Indian path across the mountains used by early settlers and in 1810 by Bishop Francis Asbury. Trail passed nearby.

US 276 and I-40 at Cove Creek / 1959

P-58 N.C. EDUCATION ASSOCIATION
Organized in 1884 as N.C. Teachers Assembly in the White Sulphur Springs Hotel. Building was one mile northwest.

Depot Street in Waynesville / 1965

P-81 ARNOLD GUYOT 1807-1884
Geographer who measured elevation at sites in western N.C., 1856-1860, including Hominy Creek Gap near here & Mt. Guyot, 25 mi. N.W.

US 19/23 (Church Street) at Hampton Heights Road in Canton / 2000

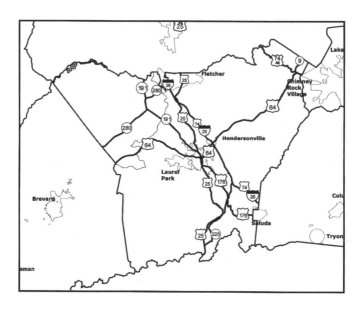

HENDERSON COUNTY

P-1 CALVARY CHURCH EPISCOPAL
Built 1859. Grave of "Bill" Nye. Memorials to many famous southerners.

US 25 at Fletcher / 1935

P-4 C. G. MEMMINGER
Secretary of the treasury of the Confederacy, from Charleston. Native of Germany. Summer home and grave nearby.

US 25 in Flat Rock / 1938

P-6 EDGAR W. ("BILL") NYE
Journalist, humorist, 1850-96. "Buck Shoals," his home, stands 3fi miles west. Grave one mile north.

US 25 at Fletcher / 1938

P-8 STONEMAN'S RAID
On a raid through western North Carolina Gen. Stoneman's U.S. Cavalry passed through Hendersonville, Apr. 23, 1865.

US 64 at I-26 northeast of Hendersonville / 1940

**P-14 NORTH CAROLINA-
SOUTH CAROLINA
NORTH CAROLINA**
Colonized, 1585-87, by first English settlers in America; permanently settled c. 1650; first to vote readiness for independence, Apr. 12, 1776.

(Reverse) SOUTH CAROLINA
Formed in 1712 from part of Carolina, which was chartered in 1663, it was first settled by the English in 1670. One of the 13 original states.

*SR 1265 (Old US 25) south of Tuxedo at
NC/SC boundary* / 1941

**P-20 FRENCH BROAD
BAPTIST CHURCH**
Organized before 1792. Present building is here. First building stood 1 mile south.

NC 191 southeast of Mills River / 1949

P-25 VANCE-CARSON DUEL
On Nov. 5, 1827, Robert B. Vance, former N.C. Congressman, was fatally wounded in a duel by Samuel P. Carson, his successor. 1/2 mile S.E.

*SR 1265 (Old US 25) south of Tuxedo at
NC/SC boundary* / 1950

P-28 GUN SHOP & FORGE
Iron works set up four mi. W. by Philip Sitton after 1804. Source for manufacture of rifles by Philip Gillespie. Both operated to 1860s.

*NC 191/280 and SR 1338 (South Mills River
Road) at Mills River* / 1951

**P-31 ST. JOHN IN THE
WILDERNESS**
Episcopal Church, built 1833-34 as a private chapel. Given to Diocese of North Carolina, 1836. Enlarged in 1852.

US 25 in Flat Rock / 1951

P-43 JUDSON COLLEGE
Baptist. Chartered in 1861 as Judson Female College; later coeducational. Operated 1882-1892 in building which stood three blocks S.W.

*US 64 (Sixth Avenue) at Fleming Street
in Hendersonville* / 1954

P-45 FLAT ROCK
Landmark for Indians and the pioneer white settlers of this area, lies nearby. Town of Flat Rock named for this natural formation.

US 25 in Flat Rock / 1954

P-52 GEORGE A. TRENHOLM
Confederate Secretary of Treasury, 1864-1865; S.C. legislator, cotton broker and financier. Summer home "Solitude" stands 1/2 mile east.

*US 25 at Highland Avenue
in Flat Rock* / 1959

**P-62 SHAWS CREEK CHURCH
AND CAMP GROUNDS**
Methodist. Congregation was organized at a camp meeting ca. 1810, on land donated by James Johnson. Church, 1905, is .3 mi. N.

*US 64 at SR 1311 (Camp Ground Road)
east of Horse Shoe* / 1974

P-65 WOLFE'S ANGEL
Marble statue from the Asheville shop of W. O. Wolfe. Inspired title of son Thomas Wolfe's *Look Homeward Angel*. Stands 150 feet south.

*US 64 (Sixth Avenue) in
Hendersonville* / 1986

**P-75 CARL SANDBURG
1878-1967**
"Poet of the People," Lincoln biographer, & Pulitzer Prize-winning author. Lived, 1945-67, at "Connemara," 1/3 mi. W.

*US 25 at Little River Road
in Flat Rock* / 1992

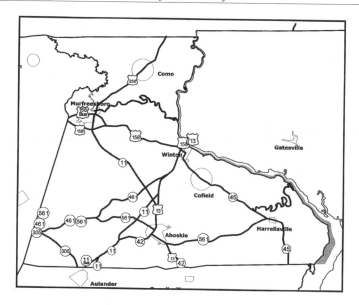

HERTFORD COUNTY

A-18   JOHN H. WHEELER

Historian, legislator, superintendent U.S. Mint at Charlotte, state treasurer, minister to Nicaragua, born 1806 in brick house 300 yds. N.

US 158/258 (Main Street)
in Murfreesboro / 1939

A-19   CHOWAN COLLEGE

Founded by the Chowan Baptist Association and opened in 1848 as the Chowan Baptist Female Institute. 2 blocks S.

US 158/258 (Main Street) at College Street
in Murfreesboro / 1939

A-20   MURFREE HOUSE

Home of William Hardy Murfree, member of U.S. Congress, 1813-1817; N.C. House, 1805 & 1812; presidential elector, 1812. House stands 1 block N.

US 158/258 (Main Street) at Wynn Street
in Murfreesboro / 1939

A-23   BURNING OF WINTON

A detachment of United States troops burned Winton on February 20, 1862. The first town in North Carolina to be burned during the war.

King Street in Winton / 1940

A-26   RICHARD J. GATLING

Inventor of the Gatling gun and of numerous agricultural implements, was born September 12, 1818, in a house which stands 400 yards north.

US 258 northeast of Murfreesboro / 1942

A-44   JOHN W. MOORE

Compiler of roster of North Carolina troops, 1861-1865, historian, novelist, Confederate major. His birthplace, "Mulberry Grove," 1fi mi. E.

NC 305 east of Mintons Store / 1954

A-45   LANE'S EXPEDITION

Ralph Lane and a group of English colonists explored the Chawanook Indian country and the Chowan River, 1586, north to this vicinity.

US 13/158 at Chowan River bridge
north of Winton / 1954

A-51   4-H CLUB

First in North Carolina, organized at Ahoskie in 1909 as the Corn Club. Beginning of present large organization of rural youth in state.

US 13/NC 561 (Academy Street)
in Ahoskie / 1955

Richard Jordan Gatling (A 26) and the weapons for which he received his fame

A-52   DR. WALTER REED
Head of U.S. Yellow Fever Commission in Cuba, 1900-01. Lived here as a young man and married Emily Lawrence of this town.

US 158/258 (Main Street) in Murfreesboro / 1959

A-56   POTECASI CREEK
Scene of minor skirmish between Confederate & Union troops driving on Richmond and Weldon Railroad, July 26, 1863. Breastworks 60 yds. SW.

US 158 at Potecasi Creek bridge southeast of Murfreesboro / 1960

A-58   CHOWAN ACADEMY
Founded for Negroes, 1886, by C. S. Brown, pastor of the Pleasant Plains Baptist Church. Since 1937, the Calvin Scott Brown High School.

Main Street in Winton / 1965

A-60   DR. WALTER REED
Head of U.S. Yellow Fever Commission in Cuba, 1900-01. Lived here as a young man. House 200 feet south.

NC 45 (Main Street) in Harrellsville / 1967

A-65   LAFAYETTE
On his American tour Lafayette spent night of Feb. 26, 1825, at Indian Queen Inn which stood two blocks north.

US 158/258 (East Main Street) at North Third Street in Murfreesboro / 1976

A-68   WESLEYAN FEMALE COLLEGE
Founded with Methodist support in 1853. Burned, 1877. Rebuilt 1881 and burned again in 1893. Site was 1 block south.

US 158/258 (Main Street) at Wynn Street in Murfreesboro / 1976

A-77   MEHERRIN TOWN
Village of the Meherrin Indians, an Iroquoian tribe, inhabited circa 1685-1727. Was located on the Meherrin River 2fi miles north.

US 158 at SR 1175 (Little Parker's Road) west of Winton / 1992

A-81   LEMUEL W. BOONE 1827-1878
Baptist leader. In 1866 he organized first black Baptist association in N.C.; trustee, Shaw University. Grave 2 mi. SE.

US 13 at SR 1457 (Old US 13) southwest of Winton / 1994

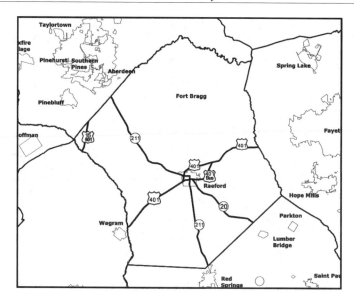

HOKE COUNTY

I-34   CAMP MACKALL
Primary training site for U.S. Army airborne troops in World War II. Established 1943; named for Private John Thomas Mackall. Two miles W.

US 15/501 at SR 1225 (Ashemont Road) west of McCain / 1996

I-41   EDENBOROUGH MEDICAL COLLEGE
Early medical school, chartered 1867, conducted by Dr. Hector McLean. Closed c. 1877. Stood one-half mile south.

US 401 Bypass in Raeford / 1954

I-43   MONROE'S CROSSROADS
Gen. Kilpatrick's Union cavalry repulsed Gen. Hampton's Confederate cavalry there, March 10, 1865, ten miles north. Now in Fort Bragg area.

US 401 Bypass in Raeford / 1954

I-45   SHERMAN'S MARCH
General Sherman, with a part of his army, on March 9-10, 1865, camped here at Bethel Presbyterian Church (organized before 1800).

US 401 at Bethel / 1955

I-47   STATE SANATORIUM
Opened in 1908. First state institution in North Carolina for treating tuberculosis. Sponsored by Dr. J. E. Brooks of Greensboro.

SR 1318 (Old NC 211) at McCain / 1957

I-50   McPHAUL'S MILL
Rendezvous point for local Tories. Near here on Sept. 1, 1781, David Fanning's men routed a Whig force under Thomas Wade. Stood 1.7 mi. W.

NC 211 and SR 1105 (Old Wire Road) at Antioch / 1959

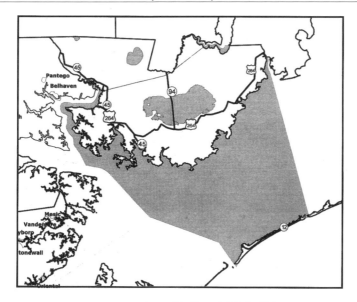

HYDE COUNTY

B-7   GRANVILLE GRANT
Formed northern half of colony of North Carolina. Survey of southern boundary began
28fi miles east across sound, 1743.

US 264 at Engelhard / 1938

B-19   BRITISH INVASION
A British force under Admiral Cockburn
occupied Portsmouth and Ocracoke, July 12-
16, 1813. S.E. 30 miles across Pamlico
Sound.

NC 45 at Swan Quarter / 1940

B-42   MATTAMUSKEET
Largest natural lake in N.C. Center of an
Indian reservation, established 1715. Twice
drained and farmed. Wildlife refuge since
1934. One mile N.

US 264 at NC 94 south of Lake
Mattamuskeet / 1965

B-43   LT. ROBERT MAYNARD
Of the Royal Navy. Sent by Gov. Spotswood
of Virginia, in the sloop "Ranger," killed the
pirate Blackbeard off shore, 1718.

NC 12 at Ocracoke ferry landing / 1965

The former pumping station and hunting lodge, today an observation tower,
at Lake Mattamuskeet (B 42 and B 58)

**B-55   OCRACOKE
              LIGHTHOUSE**

Oldest N.C. lighthouse still in service. Erected 1823 to serve Ocracoke Inlet trade. 75 ft. tall. Located 1/4 mile S.W.

*NC 12 at SR 1326 (Point Road)
on Ocracoke Island* / 1989

**B-58   MATTAMUSKEET NAT'L
         WILDLIFE REFUGE**

The refuge, observation tower, and hunting lodge were rehabilitated by Civilian Conservation Corps enrollees, 1934-42.

*US 264 and SR 1330 (CCC Road)
at New Holland* / 1994

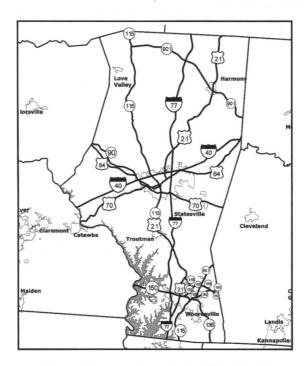

IREDELL COUNTY

M-1   FORT DOBBS

Built 1755-56 to protect western counties from Indians. Site one mile north.

*US 21 at SR 1930 (Fort Dobbs Road) north
of Statesville* / 1936

M-5   TORRENCE'S TAVERN

British cavalry led by Colonel Tarleton routed a force of American militia, Feb. 2, 1781, at Torrence's Tavern, which stood nearby.

NC 115 at Mount Mourne / 1939

M-11   STONEMAN'S RAID

On a raid through western North Carolina Gen. Stoneman's U.S. cavalry occupied Statesville, April 13, 1865.

*US 21/64 (East Front Street) at Tradd Street
in Statesville* / 1940

M-17   EBENEZER ACADEMY

Chartered in 1822. An academy to 1856; public school until 1903. This is the original building.

US 21 north of Statesville / 1948

M-18   MITCHELL COLLEGE

Founded 1856 as a college for women. Presbyterian until 1959. Granted state community college status in 1973. Is two blocks N.

*US 64 (West Front Street) at Mulberry Street
in Statesville* / 1949

M-19   J. P. CALDWELL

Editor of Statesville "Landmark" (1880-92), Charlotte "Observer" (1892-1909). His home was two blocks north.

*US 64 (West Front Street) at Mulberry Street
in Statesville* / 1949

J. P. Caldwell (M 19)

M-21   GRANVILLE GRANT
Formed northern half of the colony of North Carolina. Its southern boundary was run to a point three miles east, in the fall of 1746.

NC 115 at Iredell/Mecklenburg County line / 1950

M-22   CENTRE CHURCH
Presbyterian, organized in 1765. Synod of the Carolinas formed there, 1788. Present building, erected 1854, is 1/2 mi. W.

NC 115 at Mount Mourne / 1951

M-23   CLIO'S NURSERY
A school established about 1778 by the Rev. James Hall. Trained many prominent men. Closed about 1787. Was a few hundred yards E.

NC 115 at SR 1905 (Cowles Road) north of Statesville / 1951

M-24   JAMES HALL
Presbyterian minister, Revolutionary soldier and chaplain, educator, pioneer missionary in the Natchez country. Grave is 50 yards north.

US 21 north of Statesville / 1951

M-25   VANCE HOUSE
Now historical museum, was temporary home of Gov. Zebulon B. Vance after Sherman's capture of Raleigh, April 1865. Is 350 yards southwest.

US 64 (West Front Street) at Mulberry Street in Statesville / 1952

M-36   AGRICULTURAL EXTENSION SERVICE
First N.C. cotton & corn demonstration supervised by a county agent held here on a farm of J. F. Eagle, 1907-1908.

US 70 southeast of Statesville / 1965

M-40   NORTH CAROLINA ASSOCIATION FOR BLIND
Held first annual meeting at Vance Hotel, Sept. 26, 1934. Leader in movement for state aid to blind.

US 64 (Front Street) at Center Street in Statesville / 1967

M-45   WILLIAM SHARPE 1742-1818
Member of Continental & provincial congresses; was first legislator to advocate U.N.C., 1784. Grave is 2 miles east.

NC 115 at SR 1903 (Rickert Road) northwest of Statesville / 1977

M-46   FOURTH CREEK MEETING HOUSE
Presbyterian. Established ca. 1750; on this site by 1756. The Rev. James Hall first regular minister.

NC 90 (West End Avenue) at Meeting Street in Statesville / 1977

M-52   BARIUM SPRINGS HOME FOR CHILDREN
Formerly Presbyterian Orphans Home. Opened here in 1891 by Synod of N.C. Jethro Rumple was first chair, Board of Regents.

US 21 south of Statesville / 1998

MM-1   EARLY HISTORY
Among the original pioneers from Pennsylvania, New Jersey, and Maryland who settled on the east side of the Catawba River were George Davidson (home destroyed), Reverend John Thomson, Moses White, Hugh Lawson, John Oliphant, John Brevard, Alexander Osborne, William Morrison, and

Andrew Allison. The Thomson, White, and Lawson homesites were located on the waters of Davidson's Creek and the Catawba now under the waters of Lake Norman. John Oliphant's grist mill (underwater), located on Oliphant's Creek, served the needs of these and other early settlers. Both Davidson College (preserved) and Davidson County, North Carolina, were named for George Davidson's son, William Lee Davidson, Revolutionary officer killed while resisting Cornwallis' advance at Cowan's Ford on the Catawba River. John Thomson was a co-founder of the University of Delaware, twice moderator of the General Synod of the Presbyterian Church, contributor to Benjamin Franklin's publications, and a leading advocate of the "Old-side" Presbyterian position in the Carolina back country. Stones commemorating Lawson and Thomson may be seen in the cemetery at Centre Church (preserved, not original building), one of the oldest places of worship in western North Carolina.

Hugh Lawson White, grandson of Moses White, was born on Davidson's Creek in 1773. He later moved to Tennessee, where he became a United States senator and in 1836 presidential candidate on the Whig ticket. The homeplace of John Brevard, who migrated from Cecil County, Maryland, was known as "Purgatory" (destroyed). His tombstone may be seen at Centre Church. He was one of Rowan County's three representatives in the North Carolina Colonial Assembly and father of five sons who fought in the Revolution. Two of them, Alexander and Joseph, were officers in the Continental Line. Two miles south of Brevard lived Alexander Osborne (home destroyed), originally of New Jersey. Osborne was a colonel in the colonial militia

and aide to Governor Tryon in suppressing the Regulator movement. He, too, rests in Centre churchyard. His son Adlai Osborne, a graduate of Princeton, was one of the original trustees of the University of North Carolina. Andrew Allison (home destroyed) and William Morrison (grave preserved) received the earliest land grants issued to settlers along Fourth Creek. Morrison referred to himself as the "first Inhabitor of the country."

During the Cherokee uprising of 1755 Fort Dobbs (destroyed) named for Royal Governor Arthur Dobbs, was built under the supervision of Captain Hugh Waddell of Wilmington. The fort was 55 feet long, 40 feet wide, and 24fi feet high. There were three floors, the top two each overhanging the one below. The fort was subsequently allowed to decay.

Among the Revolutionary soldiers of the region were Robert Simonton, John Reid, Hugh Torrance, and John Davidson. Simonton (home preserved), Rufus Reid (home preserved), son of James Reid, and James G. Torrance (home preserved), son of Hugh Torrance, built interesting plantation homes. Rufus Reid, whose home "Mt. Mourne" was built in 1836 on the site of "Purgatory," was a member of the North Carolina House of Commons in 1844 and 1846. James G. Torrance was one of the original trustees of Davidson College and operated the only store in the vicinity. John Davidson, an officer in the Continental Line and a pioneer in the iron industry, lived at "Rural Hill" (destroyed).

For early history of Trans-Catawba region see marker located on N.C. 73—100 yds. west of Catawba River, Lincoln County.

NC 150 east of Lake Norman / 1964

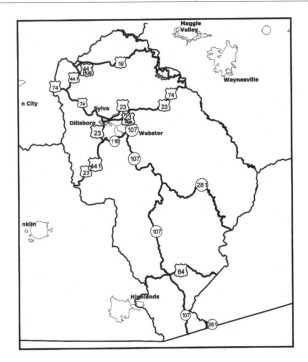

JACKSON COUNTY

Q-1   WADE HAMPTON
Confederate General, Governor of S.C., 1876-79, U.S. Senator. His summer home, "High Hampton," stood $1^1/_3$ miles southeast.

US 64 and NC 107 at Cashiers / 1936

Q-4   JUDACULLA ROCK
Large boulder covered with well-preserved Indian picture writing of unknown origin. 3fi miles southeast.

NC 107 and SR 1737 (Caney Fork Road) at East Laport / 1938

**Q-13   CHEROKEE INDIAN
RESERVATION**
Established by United States for the Eastern Band of Cherokee after the removal of 1838.

**(Reverse)   (LEAVING)
CHEROKEE RESERVATION**
Established by United States for the Eastern Band of Cherokee after the removal of 1838.

US 19 at Soco Gap / 1939

Q-16   DE SOTO
In 1540 an expedition of Spaniards led by De Soto, first Europeans to explore this area, entered North Carolina near here.

NC 107 south of Cashiers at NC/SC boundary / 1940

Q-32   INDIAN BOUNDARY
Near here the highway crosses Meigs-Freeman Line, surveyed in 1802, boundary between whites & Cherokees until 1819.

US 23/74 northeast of Sylva / 1942

**Q-38   WESTERN CAROLINA
UNIVERSITY**
Established in 1889 as a private school. Has been a state supported institution since 1893.

NC 107 at Cullowhee / 1950

Q-42   RUTHERFORD TRACE
The expedition led by Gen. Griffith Rutherford against the Cherokee, Sept., 1776, passed nearby along Savannah Creek.

US 23/441 at NC 116 southwest of Webster / 1954

Q-43   RUTHERFORD TRACE

The expedition led by Gen. Griffith Rutherford against the Cherokee, Sept., 1776,
passed here through Cowee Gap.

*US 23/441 southwest of Dillsboro at
Jackson/Macon County line* / 1954

Q-45   ECHOTA MISSION

Methodist. Maintained by Holston Conference for Cherokee c. 1840-1885. School
established 1850. Missionary's house stands
50 yards north.

*US 19 at SR 1427 (Olivet Loop Road) in
Cherokee Indian Reservation* / 1954

Q-46   WILLIAM H. THOMAS

White chief and agent of N.C. Cherokee.
Secured reservation for them. Confederate
colonel. State senator. Home "Stekoih
Fields," stood 1/4 mi. S.

US 74 at US 441 east of Whittier / 1959

Q-47   LEWIS J. SMITH
1843-1901

A founder & benefactor of Cullowhee
Academy, forerunner of Western Carolina
University. Lived 2 miles north.

NC 107 at Cullowhee / 1985

Q-48   ROBERT L. MADISON
1867-1954

Educator. A founder of present Western Carolina University. President, 1889-1912,
1920-1923. Lived 5 miles north.

NC 107 at Cullowhee / 1986

Q-51 GERTRUDE DILLS McKEE
1885-1948

First woman elected to N.C. Senate, 1930.
Civic leader and clubwoman. Home was 50
yds. west.

*US 23 East Business (Main Street)
in Sylva* / 1990

Gertrude Dills McKee (Q 51)

Q-52   JOHN R. BRINKLEY
1885-1942

Medical maverick, radio and advertising
pioneer, candidate for governor of Kansas.
Boyhood home stood across the river.

NC 107 at East Laport / 1994

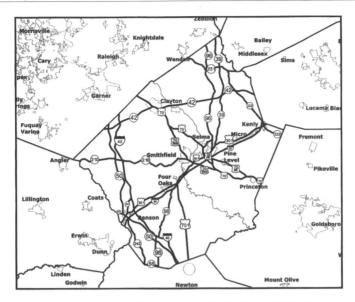

JOHNSTON COUNTY

H-1 BATTLE OF BENTONVILLE
Johnston's Confederates checked Sherman's Union army, March 19-21, 1865. Historic site 2fi mi. E.

US 701 at SR 1008 (Harper House Road)
southwest of Bentonville
Battleground / 1935

H-49   WILLIAM E. DODD
1869-1940
Ambassador to Germany, 1933-37; professor and writer of U.S. history. He was born 2 mi. N.E.

US 70 at Amelia Church Road
in Clayton / 1949

Major General William T. Sherman, left, and General Joseph E. Johnston, commanders of the armies at the Battle of Bentonville (H 1)

H-63   EDWARD W. POU

Congressman, 1901-1934, Chairman House Rules Committee during parts of administrations of Wilson, F. D. Roosevelt. Grave is 200 yds. south.

US 70 Business (Market Street) at South First Street in Smithfield / 1955

H-74   SHERMAN'S MARCH

Enroute from Goldsboro to Raleigh, Sherman's army camped 1 mile east and on April 12, 1865, celebrated the news of Lee's surrender.

US 301/NC 96 (Third Street) at Brogden Road in Smithfield / 1960

**HH-1   BATTLE OF
BENTONVILLE**

March 19, 20, and 21, 1865

At Bentonville, General William T. Sherman's Union Army, advancing from Fayetteville toward Goldsboro, met and battled the Confederate Army of General Joseph E. Johnston. General Robert E. Lee had directed the Confederates to make a stand in North Carolina to prevent Sherman from joining General U. S. Grant in front of Lee's Army at Petersburg, Virginia.

Johnston had been able to raise nearly 30,000 men from South Carolina, Alabama, Mississippi, Tennessee, and eastern North Carolina. His army included a galaxy of generals: two full generals; fourteen major generals; and many brigadier generals. Ahead of Sherman with his force, he looked for an opportunity to strike.

Sherman's Army of 60,000 men was divided into two wings: 30,000 men in the Left Wing marching via Averasboro and Bentonville, and 30,000 men in the Right Wing marching on a parallel route to the southeast. Sherman's North Carolina objective was Goldsboro, where 40,000 additional troops and fresh supplies would reinforce and nourish his weary army.

The three-day battle ended in a stalemate. After an initial success on the first day, the Confederates were unable to destroy the united Federal Left and Right Wings (60,000 men) and on the night of March 21-22 they withdrew. The Union Army, anxious to reach Goldsboro, did not pursue.

Troops involved: 85,000 to 90,000

Casualties:	Killed	Wounded	Missing
Confederate	239	1,694	673
Union	304	1,112	221
Total	543	2,806	894

Total killed, wounded, and missing: 4,243

The Battle of Bentonville was important because it was:

1. The only major Confederate attempt to stop Sherman after the Battle of Atlanta, August, 1864.

2. The last major Confederate offensive in which the Confederates chose the ground and made the initial attack.

3. The largest battle ever fought on North Carolina soil.

The Harper House, residence in which John and Amy Harper raised their 8 children, has been restored on the battleground. This home was used during the battle as a Union hospital and after the battle as a Confederate hospital.

In the Confederate Cemetery are buried 360 soldiers.

The museum and 6,000-acre battleground are open for tours on a regular schedule.

To reach the Battleground, proceed on Int. 95 nine miles to intersection of U.S. 701. Turn right and follow signs, eleven miles.

*I-95 (southbound) rest area
near Selma* / 1962

HHH-1   SHERMAN

Gen. Wm. T. Sherman camped in this area with his Left Wing on the night of March 18, 1865. The following morning, the Left wing continued along this road meeting Gen. Joseph E. Johnston's Confederates in the Battle of Bentonville, 2 miles east. Meanwhile, Sherman joined his Right Wing, marching toward Goldsboro on another road, and thus missed the first day of the battle.

*SR 1008 (Harper House Road)
at Bentonville Battleground* / 1959

HHH-2   UNION HOSPITAL

The Harper House was used as a hospital by the XIV Corps, March 19-21, 1865. About 500 Union wounded were treated here.

*SR 1008 (Harper House Road)
at Bentonville Battleground* / 1959

HHH-3 CONFEDERATE HOSPITAL

Following the battle, 45 Confederate wounded were hospitalized in the Harper House. Nineteen of these men died here. Surgeons moved the others to regular Confederate hospitals.

SR 1008 (Harper House Road)
at Bentonville Battleground / 1959

HHH-4 UNION HEADQUARTERS

Maj. Gen. A. S. Williams, commanding the XX Corps, established his headquarters here on March 19. In the woods to the north, the XX Corps erected breastworks which remain.

SR 1008 (Harper House Road)
at Bentonville Battleground / 1959

HHH-5 FEDERAL EARTHWORKS

Constructed by First Michigan Engineers and others, March 19, 1865. Occupied by Federals throughout the battle. Works begin 75 yards behind this marker.

SR 1188 (Mill Creek Road) at Bentonville Battleground / 1959

HHH-6 UNION HOSPITAL

Field Hospital of the XX Corps during the Battle of Bentonville was located here. Four hundred Union soldiers, wounded in the Battle of Averasboro (16 miles west) on March 16, were brought here for treatment.

South of SR 1008 (Harper House Road)
at Bentonville Battleground / 1959

HHH-7 CONFEDERATE CEMETERY

The remains of 360 Confederates who fell in the Battle of Bentonville lie here. They were moved to this plot from other parts of the battlefield in 1893. The monument was erected at that time.

Junction of SR 1008 (Harper House Road)
and SR 1188 (Mill Creek Road) at
Bentonville Battleground / 1959

HHH-8 UNION HEADQUARTERS

Maj. Gen. H. W. Slocum, commanding Sherman's Left Wing, had headquarters in this field, March 19-21, 1865.

SR 1008 (Harper House Road)
at Bentonville Battleground / 1959

HHH-9 FEDERAL ARTILLERY

Union batteries (26 guns) formed a line here, March 19. These guns covered retreating Federals during the Confederate charges and finally halted the advance of the Confederate Right Wing.

SR 1008 (Harper House Road)
at Bentonville Battleground / 1959

HHH-10 CONFEDERATE ATTACKS

Across the fields behind this marker the Confederate Right Wing made five attacks on Union positions to the left, March 19, 1865. They were thrown back by the XX Federal Corps.

SR 1008 (Harper House Road)
at Bentonville Battleground / 1959

HHH-11 CONFEDERATE MAIN CHARGE

After overrunning two Union lines above this road, the Confederates crossed here in the main assault of March 19, 1865. Union reinforcements halted their advance in the woods below the road.

SR 1008 (Harper House Road)
at Bentonville Battleground / 1959

HHH-12 COLE FARM HOUSE

Stood in this field. Scene of heavy fighting, March 19. Destroyed on March 20 by Confederate artillery to prevent sniping.

SR 1008 (Harper House Road)
at Bentonville Battleground / 1959

HHH-13 FIGHTING BELOW THE ROAD

One-half mile south of this point, across the road, Brig. Gen. J.D. Morgan's Union Division halted the main Confederate charge, March 19, 1865, in one of the fiercest engagements of the battle.

SR 1008 (Harper House Road)
at Bentonville Battleground / 1959

**HHH-14   FIRST UNION
ATTACK**

Brig. Gen. W. P. Carlin's Division attacked the Confederate line above the road here on March 19. Repulsed, they threw up works but were driven out by the Confederate charge.

*SR 1008 (Harper House Road)
at Bentonville Battleground* / 1959

**HHH-15   MAIN
CONFEDERATE LINE**

The Left Confederate Wing, part of a long hook-shaped line designed to trap the Union forces, extended across the road here on March 19. This sector, occupied by Maj. Gen. R. F. Hoke's Division, was evacuated on March 20. A new line parallel to the road was established 500 yards north.

*Junction of SR 1008 (Harper House Road)
and SR 1194 (Bass Road) at Bentonville
Battleground* / 1959

**HHH-16   N.C. JUNIOR
RESERVES**

Held the line along this road and repulsed the assault of Hobart's Union Brigade, March 19, 1865. This line was evacuated, March 20.

*SR 1194 (Bass Road) at Bentonville
Battleground* / 1959

**HHH-17   MAIN
CONFEDERATE LINE**

On March 19 the line extended 3/4 mile to the rear of this marker and one mile to the left, forming a strong hook-shaped position with a right angle turn here. On March 20 the Left Wing was pulled back to this point and the new Confederate line crossed the road here. Earthworks remain.

*SR 1194 (Bass Road) at Bentonville
Battleground* / 1959

**HHH-18   FEDERAL
JUNCTION**

Sherman's Left and Right Wings joined forces here during the afternoon of March 20, 1865. They constructed works across the road and skirmished with the Confederates.

*SR 1008 (Harper House Road)
at Bentonville Battleground* / 1959

HHH-19 MAIN UNION LINE

Advanced to this point during the afternoon of March 21. The XV Corps established a line of works across the road here. Earthworks remain.

*SR 1009 (Devil's Race Track)
at Bentonville Battleground* / 1959

**HHH-20   MAIN
CONFEDERATE LINE**

Crossed the road at this point, March 20-21. Gen. R. F. Hoke's Division occupied this sector. Scene of much skirmishing but no heavy fighting. Earthworks remain.

*SR 1009 (Devil's Race Track)
at Bentonville Battleground* / 1959

HHH-21   BENTONVILLE

In 1865, a local market center for naval stores (tar, pitch, & turpentine). Bentonville gives name to the battle fought nearby, March 19-21, 1865. Confederates concentrated here the day before the battle. As they retreated on March 22, they burned all stocks of naval stores. Union forces occupied the village, March 22-24.

*SR 1009 (Devil's Race Track)
at Bentonville Battleground* / 1959

**HHH-22   CONFEDERATE
WORKS**

Remains of breastworks on this hill mark a line of works built by the Confederates to protect Mill Creek Bridge.

*SR 1009 (Devil's Race Track)
at Bentonville Battleground* / 1959

HHH-23   MILL CREEK

The flooded state of this creek upstream prevented an attack by Wheeler's Confederate cavalry on the rear of Sherman's Army, March 19, 1865. A bridge here was the Confederates' sole line of retreat after the battle.

*SR 1009 (Devil's Race Track)
at Bentonville Battleground* / 1959

**HHH-24   JOHNSTON'S
HEADQUARTERS**

Established here on the night of March 18, 1865 and remained during the battle. Mower's Division came within 200 yards of this point in the Union assault of March 21.

*SR 1197 (Bentonville Road)
at Bentonville Battleground* / 1959

**HHH-25   HARDEE'S
                      CHARGE**

Near this point Gen. William J. Hardee led the charge of the 8th Texas Cavalry and other Confederates, repulsing the advance of Mower's Division, March 21, 1865.

*Junction of SR 1197 (Bentonville Road) and
SR 1199 (Scout Road) at Bentonville
Battleground / 1959*

**HHH-26   MOWER'S
                      ATTACK**

Advancing toward Mill Creek Bridge, Johnston's only line of retreat, Maj. Gen. J. A. Mower's Union Division broke the Confederate line near this point, March 21. Mower's Division reached a point 200 yards from Johnston's headquarters before it was driven back by Confederate infantry and cavalry.

*SR 1199 (Scout Road) at Bentonville
Battleground / 1959*

**HHH-27   UNION LINE
                      MARCH 21**

After withdrawing from the advance against Mill Creek Bridge, Mower's Federals reformed here and threw up works. This was the extreme right of the Union line on March 21. Earthworks remain.

*SR 1199 (Scout Road) at Bentonville
Battleground / 1959*

**HHH-28   UNION
                      HEADQUARTERS**

Sherman's headquarters were located in the field 400 yards to the rear of this marker, March 20-21, 1865. Headquarters of the XVII Corps, which included Mower's Division, were 250 yards to the left rear.

*SR 1197 (Bentonville Road) at Bentonville
Battleground / 1959*

**HHH-29   UNION LINE
                      MARCH 20**

Trenches in the woods behind this marker formed the extreme right of the Union line on March 20. This sector was occupied by the XVII Corps, commanded by Maj. Gen. F. P. Blair.

*Junction of SR 1008 (Harper House Road)
and SR 1197 (Bentonville Road) at
Bentonville Battleground / 1959*

Palmer's Brigade taking guns at Bentonville

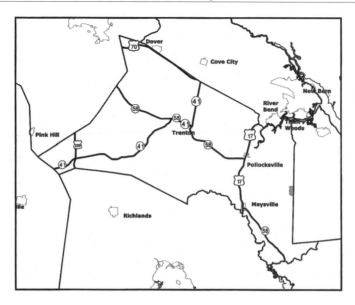

JONES COUNTY

C-15   SHINE HOME
Built about 1815-16 by James Shine. President Monroe & Secretary of War Calhoun spent the night there, April 13, 1819. Stands 1 mile S.

NC 41 at Comfort / 1939

**C-16   WASHINGTON'S
            SOUTHERN TOUR**
President Washington spent the night, April 22, 1791, at Shine's Inn which was 7 mi. S.W.

NC 58 at NC 41 west of Trenton / 1939

C-45   F. M. SIMMONS
Congressman, 1887-1889; U.S. Senator, 1901-1931; Chairman of Finance, World War I. Birthplace is one-tenth mile.

*SR 1121 (Oak Grove Road) northwest
of Pollocksville* / 1968

F. M. Simmons (C 45)

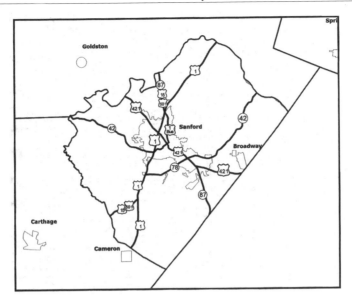

LEE COUNTY

H-19   CHARLES D. McIVER
1860-1906

Educator and first president of what is now UNC-Greensboro, 1891-1906. Boyhood home is 200 yds. W.

US 421 northwest of Sanford / 1939

H-41   EGYPT COAL MINE

Operated at intervals, 1855-1928. Supplied coal for Confederate blockade runners. Two miles north to shaft.

US 421 at SR 1400 (Cumnock Road)
northwest of Sanford / 1948

Surface plant at the Egypt Coal Mine (H 41)

H-43   A. A. F. SEAWELL
1864-1950
Justice of State Supreme Court, 1938-1950;
state legislator and attorney general. Home is
here.

NC 78 (West Main Street) in Sanford / 1975

H-44   PLANK ROAD
The Cameron-to-Gulf branch (built in 1853)
of the Fayetteville and Western Plank Road
passed near this spot.

US 15/501 at White Hill near Lee/Moore
County line / 1948

H-51   BUFFALO CHURCH
Presbyterian. Founded in 1797 by Scottish
Highlanders. Present building, the fourth,
erected 1880, stands on original site.

Carthage Street at Groce Road
in Sanford / 1949

H-102   ENDOR IRON WORKS
Large smelting furnace provided iron, 1862-
65, to Confederacy. Reopened 1870 & ceased
to operate 1896. Remains 1fi mi. NE.

US 421 at SR 1400 (Cumnock Road)
northwest of Sanford / 1991

Remains of the furnace at Endor Iron
Works (H 102)

Buffalo Church (H 51)

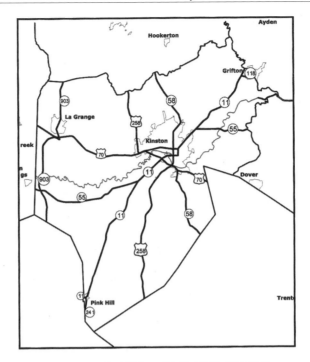

LENOIR COUNTY

F-2   RICHARD CASWELL
First governor of the State, 1776. Revolutionary statesman and soldier. Grave 166 yards south.

US 70/258 Business (Vernon Avenue)
west of Kinston / 1936

F-13   TOWER HILL
Plantation of Gov. Dobbs, selected as the colonial capital & named George City by act of assembly, 1758. Act was never executed. 1fi mi. S.

NC 55 at SR 1810 (Tower Hill Road)
east of Kinston / 1940

F-15   RAM NEUSE
Confederate ironclad, built at Whitehall and floated down the Neuse. Grounded and burned by Confederates in 1865. Remains are 250 yds. S.

US 70/258 Business (Vernon Avenue)
west of Kinston / 1940

F-20   FOSTER'S RAID
On a raid from New Bern to Goldsboro, the Union troops led by Gen. J. G. Foster passed through Kinston, Dec. 14, 1862.

US 70 at US 258 south of Kinston / 1948

F-28   LEWIS SCHOOL
A coeducational private school, conducted by Dr. and Mrs. Richard Henry Lewis, opened in 1877 and closed in 1902, was in this house.

NC 11/55 (East King Street)
in Kinston / 1950

F-40   WHEAT SWAMP CHURCH
Disciples of Christ since 1843. Organized about 1760 as Free Will Baptist. Part of present church built in 1858. One mile northwest.

US 258 at SR 1541 (Mewborn Crossroads
Road) northwest of Kinston / 1965

F-41   JAMES Y. JOYNER
1862-1954
Superintendent of Public Instruction, 1902-1919. Educator and agriculturist. Home is 3 blks. N.W.

NC 903 (South Caswell Street)
in La Grange / 1970

F-42   WILLIAM DUNN MOSELEY
Member of N.C. Senate, 1829-1836; Speaker, 1833-1835. First governor of State of Florida, 1845-1849. Home was 1 mi. N.

NC 903 (South Caswell Street)
in La Grange / 1970

The Ram *Neuse* (F 15) being raised from the Neuse River in the fall of 1961

F-49   HARMONY HALL

Office of Secretary of State during Revolution. Later owned by Richard Caswell & sons. Altered in nineteenth century.

NC 11/55 (East King Street)
in Kinston / 1972

FF-1   BATTLE OF WYSE FORK
MARCH 8-10, 1865

In the late stages of the Civil War Union forces were intent on moving up the rail line from New Bern through Kinston to Goldsboro. Their objective was to unite with Sherman and open a supply route through eastern North Carolina. Confederate troops entrenched on Southwest Creek sought to impede their progress. For three days the opposing armies clashed in the fields and woods south and east of the creek. Union Maj. Gen. Jacob D. Cox commanded over 13,000 soldiers, most belonging to the divisions of Brig. Gen. Innis N. Palmer and Brig. Gen. Samuel P. Carter. Gen. Braxton Bragg led a Confederate force of 12,500 men, organized in divisions led by fellow North Carolinians Gen. Robert F. Hoke and Gen. D. H. Hill. The Junior Reserves, mostly seventeen-year-olds mustered in only months before, came under Hill's command.

By March 6 Union troops were gathered in Gum Swamp three miles east of Wyse Fork. Travel, along the bed of the Atlantic and North Carolina Railroad and through swampy terrain, was difficult, made more so by heavy rains and a lack of wagons. Meanwhile Gen. Bragg had moved his army up from the lower Cape Fear region. On the evening of March 7 advance Union guards skirmished with Confederates at Wyse Fork as Palmer's division moved into position 800 yards east of the creek.

Friday, March 8, was the high point for the Confederates. In mid-morning Hoke's division moved down Upper Trent Road and around the head of the millpond. With whoops and yells, they "burst through like a torrent," striking the Federals' left flank. Concurrent with Hoke's move, Hill's division crossed the creek and struck the right flank. The 15th Connecticut, positioned south of Dover Road and 500 yards east of Jackson's Mill, was besieged. Col. Charles L. Upham's brigade shattered, with 890 men taken prisoner and horses and guns abandoned. By the end of the day Confederates, with the support of artillery fire, occupied a line along British Road. That evening a division led by Brig. Gen. Thomas H. Ruger arrived to offer additional Federal support.

On Gen. Cox's orders, Union forces hastily threw up a continuous line of breastworks on both sides of Lower Trent Road. Short of supplies they used boards as shovels. Confederates on March 9 tested the Union's right flank by conducting a reconnaissance survey down the Neuse Road. Artillery exchanges continued through the night of March 9. At 11:30 AM on March 10 a "vigorous assault" was made on the extreme left of the Union line. An hour later the Confederates left the field, soon thereafter returning to attack the center. Union positions were tested and driven in, but held. The 66th NC Regiment, organized in Kinston, came within 50 yards of the Federal works, withstanding a "galling fire." At 2:30 PM the Confederates made their final charge and Union skirmishers fell back to their main rifle pits. With nightfall Gen. Bragg's troops withdrew from their trenches and retired to Kinston. With the exit of Bragg's force, the crew of the ironclad Neuse burned and sank their ship.

The Battle of Wyse Fork (also known as the Battle of Kinston and the Battle of Southwest Creek) involved one of the largest concentrations of troops ever on North Carolina soil. The armies engaged were exceeded in size only by those at Bentonville. Over 225 Confederates were taken prisoner and an unknown number left dead or dying on the field. Total Union casualties for the three days were fewer, with 57 killed and 265 wounded. As a delaying maneuver the battle was a success for the Confederates. Gen. Bragg's ultimate failure to defeat Gen. Cox and his subsequent withdrawal came about in the face of rapidly mounting Federal strength. In the days thereafter forces on both sides pressed on to Goldsboro and to the last major conflict in the state, at Bentonville on March 19-21, 1865.

US 70 at SR 1821 (British Road) southeast of Kinston / 1989

Braxton Bragg, left, and Jacob C. Cox, commanders at the Battle of Wyse Fork (FF 1)

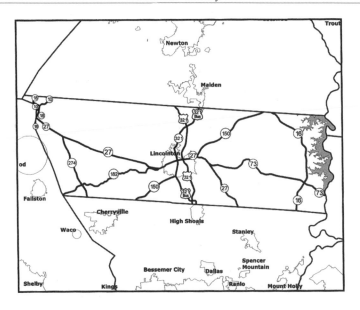

LINCOLN COUNTY

**O-3   BATTLE OF
RAMSOUR'S MILL**
Whig victory over Tories, June 20, 1780.
Scene 400 yards west.

*US 321 Business (North Aspen Street)
in Lincolnton* / 1936

O-7   SCHENCK-WARLICK MILL
First cotton mill in N.C. Built prior to 1816
by Michael Schenck and Absalom Warlick.
Mill stood one-half mile N.

NC 27/150 East at Boger City / 1939

O-8   STEPHEN D. RAMSEUR
Confederate major general at age of twenty-
seven. Mortally wounded at Cedar Creek,
Virginia, Oct. 19, 1864. Grave 2 blocks
north.

*NC 27 (East Main Street) at Cedar Street
in Lincolnton* / 1939

O-9   IRON WORKS
Many iron mines and forges were operated
within a radius of ten miles of this point
between 1790 and 1880.

NC 27 at Iron Station / 1939

**O-12   HIRAM R. REVELS
1822-1901**
First black to serve in Congress. Native of
N.C. Mississippi senator, 1870-1871. Operated own barbershop here, 1840s.

*NC 27 (West Main Street)
in Lincolnton* / 1989

O-14   INGLESIDE
Home built about 1817 by Daniel M. Forney,
major in War of 1812, congressman, 1815-
1818, legislator, and planter.

NC 73 east of Iron Station / 1942

**O-15   ROBERT F. HOKE
1837-1912**
Major general, C.S.A. Promoted after victory
at Battle of Plymouth. Led troops in Va. &
N.C. Home stands 50 yards E.

*US 321 (North Aspen Street) at Chestnut
Street in Lincolnton* / 1941

O-25   WILLIAM A. GRAHAM
Governor, 1845-1849; Secretary of the Navy;
United States Senator; Whig nominee for
Vice-President in 1852. His birthplace is
3 mi. E.

*SR 1511 (Old NC 273) at Amity Church
Road east of Lincolnton* / 1948

O-26   HUTCHINS G. BURTON
Governor, 1824-1827; Attorney General of N.C.; Congressman. Grave is 1/2 mi. E.

NC 16 and SR 1439 (Unity Church Road)
at Triangle / 1948

O-28   ANDRÉ MICHAUX
French botanist, pioneer in studying flora of western North Carolina, passed through Lincolnton, July 24, Sept. 11, 1794, and April 29, 1795.

NC 27 (West Main Street)
in Lincolnton / 1949

O-33   JAMES PINCKNEY HENDERSON 1809-1853
First governor of Texas, 1846-47; U.S. Senator; officer, Mexican War. His birthplace here.

NC 182 west of Lincolnton / 1950

O-35   CONNIE M. GUION
Pioneer female physician. Gained national reputation from work at Cornell medical clinic, 1922-1970. Born 2/10 mile N.

NC 27 at SR 1224 (Spake Road)
in Lincolnton / 2000

O-40   CONFEDERATE LABORATORY
Under Dr. A. S. Piggott, manufactured medicine for Confederacy, 1863-65. Remains are 2 mi. S.

US 321 Business (South Aspen Street) at SR 1252 (Laboratory Road)
in Lincolnton / 1952

O-41   U.D.C. MEMORIAL HALL
Building housed first the Pleasant Retreat Academy, chartered 1813. Later public library, museum. 1 block east.

US 321 Business (North Aspen Street) at Pine Street in Lincolnton / 1952

O-44   STONEWALL JACKSON
Thomas Jonathan Jackson, later a Confederate general, on July 16, 1857, married Anna Morrison in her home which stood 200 yards east.

SR 1511 (Old Plank Road) at SR 1400 (Morrison Road) east of Lincolnton / 1953

O-45   J. G. ARENDS
Native German, pioneer teacher and minister, ordained 1775, first president of the N.C. Lutheran Synod, 1803. Grave a few yds. east.

US 321 Business (South Aspen Street)
in Lincolnton / 1953

O-49   CATAWBA SPRINGS
Fashionable "watering place," a recreational and social center prior to 1861. The hotel stood five miles northeast.

NC 73 at SR 1360 (Beth Haven Church Road) east of Lincolnton / 1956

O-58   MACHPELAH CEMETERY
Presbyterian, 1801. Graves include those of Alexander Brevard, Joseph & James Graham, and Robert Hall & Joseph Graham Morrison.

SR 1511 (Old Plank Road) at SR 1360 (Brevard Place Road) east of Lincolnton / 1965

O-60   ANDREW LORETZ
Minister, 1786-1812, of German Reformed Church in the Carolinas. Home built in 1793. Located one-half mile south.

SR 1113 (Reepsville Road) northwest of Lincolnton / 1967

O-61   PETER FORNEY 1756-1834
Pioneer manufacturer of iron; Revolutionary War officer; Congressman, 1813-1815. Mt. Welcome, his home, was 3/4 mi. S.

SR 1511 (Old Plank Road) at SR 1412 (Mariposa Road) west of Lowesville / 1970

O-66   WILLIAM A. HOKE 1851-1925
Chief justice 1 year & assoc. justice 20 yrs., N.C. Supreme Court. Superior court judge 13 yrs. Birthplace stood here.

NC 27 (East Main Street) at South Cedar Street in Lincolnton / 1973

O-67   DANIELS CHURCH
Evangelical Lutheran. Organized in 1774. J. G. Arndt was first regular minister; Philip Henkel assistant. This building, 1888, is third on site.

SR 1113 (Reepsville Road) northwest of Lincolnton / 1973

O-79   MICHAEL HOKE
1874-1944

Pioneer orthopedic surgeon; founded hospitals for crippled children; chief surgeon of Warm Springs (Ga.) Foundation. Birthplace 80 yds. east.

US 321 Business (North Aspen Street)
in Lincolnton / 1995

OO-1 EARLY TRANS-CATAWBA
HISTORY

In 1747 Adam Sherrill and his 8 sons migrated from Pennsylvania and settled west of the Catawba River. By July, 1749, John Beatty had also crossed the Catawba. Sherrill's Ford (site underwater) and Beatty's Ford (underwater) were named for them. Another ford used by the original settlers was Island Ford. During the late 1740's Andreas Killen, Robert Leeper, Jacob Forney, Pieter Heyl, and John Clark settled on creeks which today bear their names. An early settler on the headwaters of Clark's Creek was Henry Weidner (home destroyed). The site of his homeplace has changed little since 1750. Remnants of Beatty's Ford and Tuckaseege roads, two of the earliest roads used by these and other early settlers, may still be seen.

During the Revolution important battles were fought at Ramsour's Mill (June 20, 1780) (destroyed) and Cowan's Ford (Feb. 1, 1781) (preserved).

During the Colonial and Early National periods it was customary to use privately-owned buildings for public purposes. Accordingly, the Tryon County Jail (partially preserved) was located in 1784 at the springhouse of Henry Dellinger, an early settler. Andrew Loretz was the first minister of the German Reformed Church in western North Carolina. His brick home (1793) is one of the oldest west of the Catawba River (preserved).

Open-hearth furnaces were established by Peter Forney, Alexander Brevard, Joseph Graham, and others between 1785 and 1800. The homeplaces of Brevard (Mt. Tirzah) (preserved) and Graham (Vesuvius Furnace) (preserved) include sites of two of these furnaces. A third furnace, built by Peter Forney, still stands. The "Ore Bank," a chief source of iron ore, was nearby (large pits to be seen).

Graham, a Revolutionary officer and leader of North Carolina troops in the Creek Indian War (1811-12); Alexander Brevard, who served under Washington at the battles of White Plains, Trenton, Brandywine, and Monmouth; and Robert H. Morrison, founder of Davidson College and father-in-law of generals D. H. Hill and "Stonewall" Jackson lie buried in Machpelah churchyard (preserved).

One of the outstanding homes of the trans-Catawba region is "Ingleside" (preserved), built by Daniel M. Forney, son of Peter Forney and grandson of the pioneer Jacob Forney who settled there.

"Mt. Welcome" (destroyed), another iron furnace built by Peter Forney, is the site of the birthplace of Robert D. Johnston, one of five Confederate generals born in Lincoln County. The others were Robert F. Hoke (home preserved), Stephen Dodson Ramseur (grave preserved), John H. Forney, and William H. Forney.

For early history of the area east of the Catawba see marker located on N.C. 150, 500 yds. east of Catawba River, Iredell County.

NC 73 west of Lake Norman
at Cowans Ford Dam / 1964

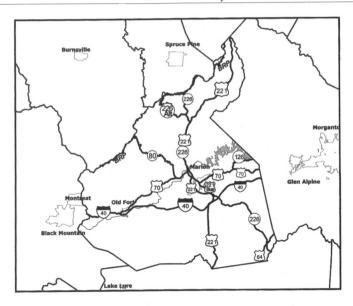

McDOWELL COUNTY

N-4   PLEASANT GARDENS
Home of Joseph McDowell (1758-1795), soldier and physician, officer at the Battle of Kings Mountain.

US 70 at Pleasant Gardens west of Marion / 1937

N-26   CATHEY'S FORT
A rendezvous for the North Carolina militia led by General Griffith Rutherford against the Cherokee in 1776, was one mile east.

US 221/NC 226 north of Woodlawn / 1950

Andrews Geyser (N 37) in postcard view

N-31   FRONTIER FORT
Early outpost against Indians. Used by Gen.
Rutherford in expedition against Cherokee,
Sept., 1776. Stood nearby and gave name to
this town.

US 70 (Main Street) in Old Fort / 1956

N-35   CARSON HOUSE
Served 1843-1845 as the seat of McDowell
County government. Home of Col. John Car-
son and his sons, Jonathan L., Samuel P.,
William, & Joseph McD. Now a historical
museum.

US 70 at Buck Creek west of Marion / 1965

N-37   ANDREWS GEYSER
Built ca. 1885 to mark railroad gateway to
the Blue Ridge Mts. Restored in 1911 &
1975. Named for A. B. Andrews of Raleigh.
Located 2.1 miles north.

SR 1400 (Old US 70) west
of Old Fort / 1976

N-41   CANE CREEK
Prelude to the Battle of Kings Mountain. Site
of a skirmish on Sept. 12, 1780, between
Loyalists and "Overmountain Men."

US 64 southeast of Dysartsville / 1991

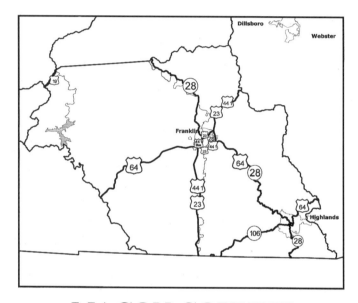

MACON COUNTY

Q-5   CHEROKEE DEFEAT
In the French and Indian War Col. Grant's
force of whites, Chickasaws, and Catawbas
defeated the Cherokee warriors near here,
June, 1761.

US 23/441 at Norton / 1939

Q-6   CHEROKEE VICTORY
In the French and Indian War, the Cherokees
defeated a colonial and British force from
N.Y. under Colonel Montgomery near here,
June, 1760.

US 23/441 south of Franklin / 1939

Q-8   CHEROKEE DEFEAT
In 1776 a force led by General Griffith
Rutherford defeated the Cherokee at Wayah
Gap, ten miles southwest.

NC 28 at SR 1434 (Old SR 1372)
north of Franklin / 1939

Q-9   NIKWASI
This mound marks the site of old Cherokee
town, Nikwasi. A council of Sir Alexander
Cuming with the Indians here led to a treaty,
1730.

US 441 Business (Main Street)
in Franklin / 1939

The Nikwasi mound (Q 9) on Main Street in Franklin

Q-17   DE SOTO
In 1540 an expedition of Spaniards led by De Soto, first Europeans to explore this area, passed near here.

*US 64/NC 28 (Main Street)
in Highlands* / 1940

Q-18   DE SOTO
In 1540 an expedition of Spaniards led by De Soto, crossed the Little Tennessee nearby, first Mississippi tributary discovered by Europeans.

*US 441 Business (Main Street)
in Franklin* / 1940

Q-24   JUAN PARDO
In 1567 an expedition of Spaniards, sent out from Florida by Pedro Menendez de Aviles and led by Juan Pardo, passed near here.

*US 64/NC 28 (Main Street) at Fourth Street
in Highlands* / 1941

Q-25   JUAN PARDO
In 1567 an expedition of Spaniards, sent out from Florida by Pedro Menendez de Aviles and led by Juan Pardo, passed near here.

NC 28 (Harrison Avenue) in Franklin / 1941

**Q-30   NORTH CAROLINA-
GEORGIA**
NORTH CAROLINA
Colonized, 1585-87, by first English settlers in America; permanently settled c. 1650; first to vote readiness for independence, Apr. 12, 1776.

(Reverse)   GEORGIA
The colony of Georgia was chartered in 1732, named for King George II of England, and settled in 1733. It was one of the 13 original states.

*US 23/441 south of Norton at NC/GA
boundary* / 1941

**Q-34   NORTH CAROLINA-
GEORGIA**
NORTH CAROLINA
Colonized, 1585-87, by first English settlers in America; permanently settled c. 1650; first to vote readiness for independence, Apr. 12, 1776.

(Reverse)   GEORGIA
The colony of Georgia was chartered in 1732, named for King George II of England, and settled in 1733. It was one of the 13 original states.

*NC 28 south of Highlands at NC/GA
boundary* / 1942

Q-36   POTTERY CLAY
Wedgwood potteries, England, used several tons of clay taken in 1767 from a nearby pit by Thomas Griffiths, a South Carolina planter.

NC 28 north of Franklin / 1950

Q-39   COWEE
The council house of Cowee, chief town of the Middle Cherokees, stood on the mound 300 yds. S. Town destroyed during the Revolution.

NC 28 northwest of Franklin / 1950

Q-44   WILLIAM BARTRAM
Philadelphia naturalist, author, exploring this area, met a Cherokee band led by their chief, Atakullakulla, in May 1776, near this spot.

US 19/74 in Nantahala National Forest at Macon/Swain County line / 1954

**Q-50   SILAS McDOWELL
1795-1879**
Botanical and historical writer; horticulturist. Originated concept of a temperate "thermal belt." Home stood 1/5 mi. W.

US 64/NC 28 at SR 1677 (Peaceful Cove Road) southeast of Franklin / 1989

QQ-1   BATTLE OF ECHOE
Beginning in 1758, South Carolina engaged in a four-year war with the Cherokee Indians, whose descendants now live in western North Carolina and eastern Tennessee. This war resulted from French efforts to incite the Southern Indians against the British in the French and Indian War (1754-63).

South Carolina Governor William H. Lyttleton in 1759 made the first effort to defeat the Indians but failed because of a smallpox epidemic which caused the abandonment of his expedition. In 1760 William Bull, Lyttleton's successor, asked British General Jeffrey Amherst to assist in a second attempt. Amherst sent Colonel Archibald Montgomery with a force of 1,200 men, composed of elements of the Royal Scottish and Highlanders regiments.

Montgomery arrived in Charleston on April 1, 1760. The troops reached Fort Prince George on June 2. Time was important since British-held Fort Loudoun, on the Tennessee River, was under close attack by the Indians. Montgomery marched on June 24, en route to the Middle Towns (situated in this valley). His force, swelled by provincial militia, numbered 1,600. Montgomery believed that the destruction of the Middle Towns would bring the Indians to terms. The expedition followed

The William Bartram marker (Q 44) stands on US 19/74 in Nantahala National Forest.

the Cherokee Trading Path across the Keowee and Oconee Rivers. At 4 A.M. on June 27 the troops crossed Rabun Gap and entered the Little Tennessee Valley. Their destination was Echoe, lowest of the Middle Towns.

At 10 A.M., June 27, the Army's advance guard entered a narrow pass between a range of mountains on the left and low hills on the right, partially encircled by the river. This was the setting for Montgomery's defeat, for the Indians led by Chief Occonostota, attacked the column on both sides, forcing it back. Montgomery sent the Provincial Rangers into the fight, while the Royal Scots moved to the hills on the right. The Highlanders went to the mountains on the left. Under this pressure the Indians withdrew to the mountains. After four hours of fighting the British continued their march, fording the river, north of the battlefield.

Montgomery's baggage train, left to shift for itself and guarded by only 100 men, was saved after heavy fighting.

The army reached Echoe, but left after a day for Fort Prince George. Montgomery's reasons for the retreat were (1) the mountains before him were "impassable," and (2) a forward movement would have forced him to abandon to the Indians his sick and wounded.

Reaching Fort Prince George on July 1, Montgomery had suffered nearly 100 casualties and had gained nothing. Fort Loudoun was surrendered to the Indians on August 9. Montgomery's Expedition provided one of the few occasions when the Cherokee were able to defeat a British Colonial army.

In the next year, June 10, 1761, the Cherokee were defeated by 2,800-man expedition under Colonel James Grant, Montgomery's second-in-command. This Second Battle of Echoe, fought two miles southeast of the 1760 battlefield, marked the beginning of a long series of reverses from which the Cherokee never recovered.

US 441 Business (Main Street)
in Franklin / 1964

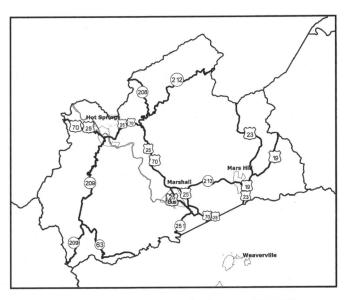

MADISON COUNTY

P-11 **NORTH CAROLINA-TENNESSEE**

NORTH CAROLINA
Colonized, 1585-87, by first English settlers in America; permanently settled c. 1650; first to vote readiness for independence, Apr. 12, 1776.

(Reverse) **TENNESSEE**
Settled before 1770 by North Carolina-Virginia pioneers, ceded by North Carolina to the United States, 1789, admitted to the Union, 1796.

US 25/70 northwest of Hot Springs at
NC/TN boundary / 1941

P-23 NORTH CAROLINA-TENNESSEE

NORTH CAROLINA
Colonized, 1585-87, by first English settlers in America; permanently settled c. 1650; first to vote readiness for independence, Apr. 12, 1776.

(Reverse) TENNESSEE
Settled before 1770 by North Carolina-Virginia pioneers, ceded by North Carolina to the United States, 1789, admitted to the Union, 1796.

US 23 at Sams Gap at NC/TN boundary / 1949

P-24 HOT SPRINGS
Health resort since 1800. Name changed from Warm Springs, 1886. Internment camp for Germans in World War I was here.

US 25/70 (Bridge Street) in Hot Springs / 1950

P-27 PAINT ROCK
Early landmark. Site of blockhouse to protect settlers from Indians, 1793. Figures on rock resemble paintings. Is 5fi miles northwest.

US 25/70 at French Broad River bridge in Hot Springs / 1950

P-34 MARS HILL COLLEGE
Baptist; coeducational. Founded 1856 as French Broad Baptist Institute. Name changed 1859. Senior college since 1962.

NC 213 (Cascade Street) in Mars Hill / 1952

P-66 BALLADRY
English folklorist Cecil Sharp in 1916 collected ballads in the "Laurel Country." Jane Gentry, who supplied many of the songs, lived here.

NC 209 (Lance Avenue) at Walnut Street in Hot Springs / 1987

P-71 "SHELTON LAUREL MASSACRE"
Thirteen men and boys, suspected of Unionism, were killed by Confederate soldiers in early 1863. Graves 8 mi. E.

NC 208 at NC 212 west of Shelton Laurel / 1988

P-73 FRANCES GOODRICH 1856-1944
Missionary and teacher. Her Allanstand Cottage Industries promoted the revival of Appalachian handicrafts. Lived here.

NC 208 at Allanstand / 1989

P-80 BASCOM LAMAR LUNSFORD 1882-1973
"Minstrel of Appalachia." Folklorist, collector, & performer. Pioneered and promoted American folk festivals. Was born here.

NC 213 (Cascade Street) in Mars Hill / 1998

Madison County native Bascom Lamar Lunsford (P 80), from 1928 until his death in 1973, presided over Asheville's Mountain Dance and Folk Festival.

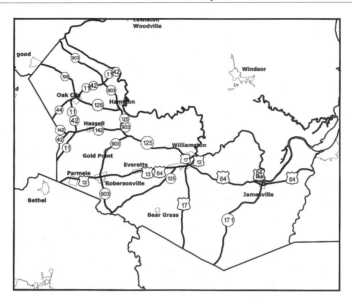

MARTIN COUNTY

B-11   ASA BIGGS
United States Senator 1855-1858, Congressman, member of state conventions, 1835 and 1861. Federal and Confederate Judge. Home is 1 block N.

US 17 Business (Main Street)
in Williamston / 1939

B-18   FORT BRANCH
Confederate fort at Rainbow Banks, built to protect railroads and the upper Roanoke River valley. Earthworks remain. 3 miles northeast.

NC 125 northwest of Williamston / 1939

B-34   ROANOKE RIVER
Early channel of trade, its valley long an area of plantations. Frequent floods until 1952, since controlled by Kerr Dam. Old name was "Moratuck."

US 13/17 at Roanoke River bridge
in Williamston / 1954

B-40   SKEWARKEY CHURCH
Baptist congregation formed about 1780. Primitive Baptist since 1830's. Church here was built in 1853.

US 17 Business (Main Street)
in Williamston / 1959

B-45   FLAT SWAMP CHURCH
Primitive Baptist. Begun in 1776. First pastor was John Page. Second building on site. Two miles S.

US 13/64 at SR 1166 (Carson Road) west of
Parmele / 1966

Asa Biggs (B 11)

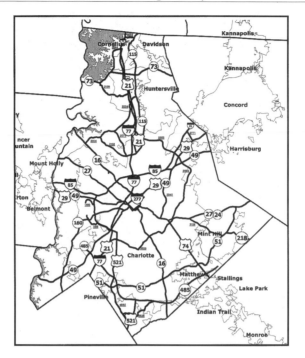

MECKLENBURG COUNTY

L-1 HEZEKIAH ALEXANDER HOUSE
Stone dwelling, built ca. 1774, by Revolutionary leader, who helped draft state constitution, 1776. Stands 400 yards S.E.
Shamrock Drive in Charlotte / 1968

L-3 CONFEDERATE CABINET
With President Davis held last full meetings April 22-26, 1865 in a house which was located here.
North Tryon Street in Charlotte / 1936

L-5 BRANCH U.S. MINT
Stood a few feet southwest. Operated 1837-61, 1867-1913. Razed, 1933, and rebuilt as art museum three miles east.
West Trade Street in Charlotte / 1936

Right: **The marker commemorating the Battle of Charlotte (L 18), which once stood on the "Square" at the junction of Trade and Tryon Streets in downtown Charlotte, has since been relocated to East Trade Street near the Civic Center.**

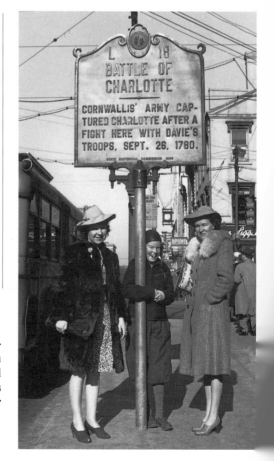

L-9 DAVIDSON COLLEGE
Founded 1837 by Presbyterians. Named for General W. L. Davidson. Woodrow Wilson studied here 1873-74.
NC 115 (North Main Street)
in Davidson / 1937

L-18 BATTLE OF CHARLOTTE
Cornwallis's army captured Charlotte after a fight here with Davie's troops, Sept. 26, 1780.
East Trade Street in Charlotte / 1938

L-19 NATHANAEL GREENE
1742-1786
Replaced Horatio Gates as leader of American army opposing Lord Cornwallis. He assumed command in Charlotte, Dec. 3, 1780.
East Trade Street in Charlotte / 1938

L-22 BATTLE OF COWAN'S
FORD
Cornwallis, pursuing Greene, crossed the Catawba, 7 mi. w., after sharp fight, Feb., 1781.
US 21/NC 73 at SR 2145 (Sam Furr Road)
northwest of Huntersville / 1939

L-23 WILLIAM LEE DAVIDSON
Whig general, was killed at Cowan's Ford, Feb. 1, 1781. Davidson College and Davidson County are named for him.
US 21/NC 73 at SR 2145 (Sam Furr Road)
northwest of Huntersville / 1939

L-25 CAMP GREENE
World War I training camp operated here on 6,000 acres, 1917-1919. Named for Revolutionary War Gen. Nat'l Greene.
NC 27 (West Morehead Street)
in Charlotte / 1940

L-31 JEFFERSON DAVIS
President Davis, moving southward after Lee's surrender, spent seven days, April 19-26, 1865, in a house which stood in this vicinity.
East Trade Street in Charlotte / 1941

L-36 TRADING PATH
Colonial trading route, dating from the seventeenth century, from Petersburg, Virginia, to the Catawba Indians in Carolina, passed nearby.
NC 49 (South Tryon Street) at NC 27
(Morehead Street) in Charlotte / 1957

L-37 TRADING PATH
Colonial trading route, dating from the seventeenth century, from Petersburg, Virginia, to the Catawba Indians in Carolina, passed here.
US 521 (Polk Street) in Pineville / 1957

Camp Greene (L 25), the massive World War I training installation in Charlotte

**L-38   NORTH CAROLINA-
SOUTH CAROLINA
NORTH CAROLINA**

Colonized, 1585-87, by first English settlers in America; permanently settled c. 1650; first to vote readiness for independence, Apr. 12, 1776.

(Reverse) SOUTH CAROLINA

Formed in 1712 from part of Carolina, which was chartered in 1663, it was first settled by the English in 1670. One of the 13 original states.

*NC 51 west of Pineville at NC/SC
boundary* / 1941

**L-39   NORTH CAROLINA-
SOUTH CAROLINA
NORTH CAROLINA**

Colonized, 1585-87, by first English settlers in America; permanently settled c. 1650; first to vote readiness for independence, Apr. 12, 1776.

(Reverse) SOUTH CAROLINA

Formed in 1712 from part of Carolina, which was chartered in 1663, it was first settled by the English in 1670. One of the 13 original states.

*US 521 (Lancaster Highway) southeast of
Pineville at NC/SC boundary* / 1941

L-40   D. H. HILL

Lieutenant general, C.S.A.; Supt. N.C. Military Institute in Charlotte; Davidson College professor; editor, "The Land We Love." Grave is here.

NC 115 (Main Street) in Davidson / 1942

L-42   S. B. ALEXANDER

First president of N.C. Farmers' Alliance, 1887-1890. State senator, advocate of good roads & agricultural education. He lived one block SE.

*Tuckaseegee Road at Parkway Avenue in
Charlotte* / 1948

L-43   J. P. CALDWELL

Editor of Statesville "Landmark" (1880-92), Charlotte "Observer" (1892-1909). His home stood at this point.

South Tryon Street in Charlotte / 1948

**L-48   D. A. TOMPKINS
1851-1914**

Crusader for southern industrial development, manufacturer, engineer, author, publisher. His grave is 1/2 mile north.

*West Trade Street at North Cedar Street
in Charlotte* / 1951

L-53   CAMERON MORRISON

Governor, 1921-1925, began state-wide paved road building program. United States Senator and Representative. His home is 1fi miles S.E.

NC 16 (Providence Road) in Charlotte /
1954

**L-56   CONFEDERATE
NAVY YARD**

Established here 1862 following its removal from Portsmouth, Va. Produced ordnance for the Confederate Navy.

East Trade Street in Charlotte / 1954

**L-69   CATAWBA INDIAN
RESERVATION**

By survey of 1772 the Catawba Indian reservation boundary in S.C. was made the N.C.-S.C. boundary in this area.

*NC 51 west of Pineville at NC/SC
boundary* / 1965

Cameron Morrison, 1920 (L 53)

L-75   QUEENS COLLEGE
Presbyterian. Organized 1857 as Charlotte Female Institute. Moved to this site, 1914. Merged with Chicora College in 1930. Coeducational since 1987.

Selwyn Avenue in Charlotte / 1970

**L-78   JAMES K. POLK
1795-1849**
U.S. President, 1845-49. Born nearby in house no longer standing. Land & reconstructed buildings now State Historic Site.

US 521 (Polk Street) in Pineville / 1936

**L-80   NORTH CAROLINA
MILITARY INSTITUTE**
Opened 1859; D. H. Hill was 1st superintendent; used as Confederate hospital; public school, 1883-1950. Stood near here.

*NC 27 (East Morehead Street) at South
Boulevard in Charlotte* / 1972

**L-86   UNIVERSITY OF N.C.
AT CHARLOTTE**
Established 1946; became Charlotte College, 1949. Moved here 1961. Campus of The University of North Carolina since 1965.

*NC 49 (University City Boulevard)
in Charlotte* / 1976

L-87   MINT MUSEUM OF ART
Operated as Branch U.S. Mint, 1837-61. Relocated to present site as art museum, 1936. Building expanded, 1968 and 1985.

Randolph Road in Charlotte / 1976

**L-92   PHILADELPHIA
PRESBYTERIAN CHURCH**
Congregation organized, 1770. David Barr, first pastor. Building, completed 1826, is 1/4 mi. E.

*NC 51 (Matthews-Mint Hill Road) at SR
1004 (Bain School Road) in Mint Hill* / 1989

L-99   GOLD MINES
Charlotte was center of region's gold rush after 1825. Rudisill & Saint Catherine, among largest mines, were near here.

*US 521 (South Boulevard) at Bland Street
in Charlotte* / 1999

**James K. Polk (L 78), the eleventh President
of the United States**

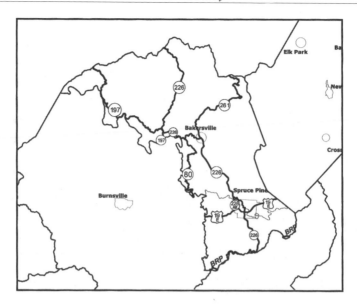

MITCHELL COUNTY

N-7   SINK HOLE MINE
Among oldest of area mica mines. Evidence indicates it was first worked by Indians. Remains 4 mi. S.W.

NC 226 at SR 1191 (Mine Creek Road) northwest of Ledger / 1939

N-19   ASA GRAY
American botanist and Harvard professor. In July, 1841, investigated flora of this region. He visited Roan Mountain, 12 miles north.

NC 226 in Bakersville / 1949

N-20   ANDRÉ MICHAUX
French botanist, pioneer in studying flora of western North Carolina, visited Roan Mountain, 12 miles north, August 16, 1794, and May 6, 1795.

NC 226 in Bakersville / 1949

Roan Mountain, visited by Asa Gray (N 19) and André Michaux (N 20)

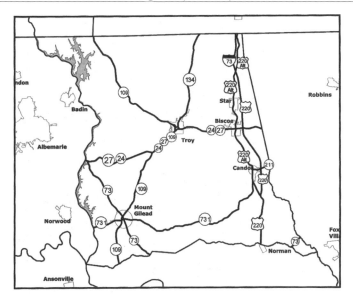

MONTGOMERY COUNTY

**K-33   EDMUND DEBERRY
1787-1859**

Member of Congress & State Senator. Planter and promoter of mining & manufacturing. Home here, grave 4/5 mi. west.

*SR 1174 (Old NC 27) southwest
of Wadeville / 1951*

K-38   FLORA MACDONALD

Scottish heroine who lived in N.C., 1774-79. Loyalist in the Revolution. Her home stood on this creek a few miles north.

NC 731 at Cheek Creek east of Pekin / 1937

**K-39   COLSON'S SUPPLY
DEPOT**

Fortified Revolutionary depot built 1781 to protect supplies and arms of Gen. Nathanael Greene. Trenches are 4fi miles W.

*NC 109 at SR 1101 (Swann Road) south
of Mount Gilead / 1962*

**K-45   ZION UNITED
METHODIST CHURCH**

Organized in 1786 by Rev. Hope Hull as Scarborough's Meeting House. The building, 4/10 mile N.E., was erected in 1854.

*NC 73 at SR 1112 (Zion Church Road)
northwest of Pee Dee / 1972*

**KK-2   TOWN CREEK
INDIAN MOUND
STATE HISTORIC SITE**

Creek Indians migrated here about 1500 A.D. and built their main village one mile south. Archeological project and restoration open to the public.

*NC 731 at SR 1542 (Indian Mound Road)
east of Mount Gilead / 1960*

Flora MacDonald (K 38)

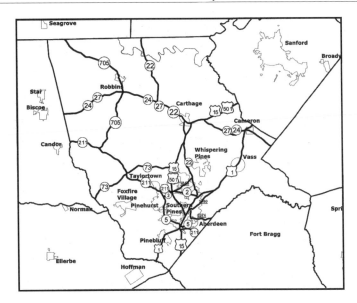

MOORE COUNTY

K-1   WALTER HINES PAGE
Ambassador to Great Britain during World
War, journalist, editor, publisher. Tomb one
mile east.

US 1/15/501/NC 211 (Sandhills Boulevard)
in Aberdeen / 1937

K-4   MECHANIC'S HILL
Site of extensive gunsmithing operations in
18th and 19th centuries. The Kennedy family
led in producing long rifles.

NC 705 (Salisbury Street) at Robbins Road
in Robbins / 1968

K-8   BENJAMIN WILLIAMS
Four times Governor; Revolutionary officer;
congressman. Grave is 9fi miles north.

US 15/501 at NC 24/27 east
of Carthage / 1939

K-9   ALSTON HOUSE
Philip Alston's Whigs were defeated there by
David Fanning's Tories, 1781. Later the
home of Benj. Williams, Governor, 1800-02.
Is 9fi mi. N.

US 15/501 at NC 24/27 east
of Carthage / 1939

K-25   PLANK ROAD
The route of the old Fayetteville-to-Salem
plank road, a toll road 129 miles long, built
1849-54, crosses the highway near this point.

US 1 northeast of Cameron at Moore/Lee
County line / 1948

K-26   PLANK ROAD
This street is the route of the Fayetteville-to-
Salem plank road, a toll road 129 miles long,
built 1849-54.

NC 24/27 (Monroe Street) at NC 22
(McNeill Street) in Carthage / 1948

K-30   JAMES BOYD
(1888-1944)
Author of "Drums" and "Marching On" &
other historical novels. His home is 3/10 mile
east.

May Street at Vermont Street
in Southern Pines / 1950

K-34   SAMARCAND
State home and industrial school for girls,
opened 1918. Academic and vocational training. Is three miles south.

NC 211 and SR 1143 (Samarcand Road)
at Samarcand / 1952

K-36   TORY RENDEZVOUS
Before going to battle of Moore's Creek Bridge, Feb., 1776, Tories of this area met in Cross Hill, at Alexander Morrison's home, 125 yards S.W.

NC 22/24/27 northwest of Carthage / 1954

K-43   JOHN MACRAE
Gaelic poet. Emigrated from Scotland in 1774. Loyalist during the Revolution. His home stood 2fi miles south.

NC 24/27 northwest of Carthage / 1970

K-47   JOHN BETHUNE
Early pastor for Scots in N.C.; chaplain for Loyalists at Battle of Moores Creek Bridge, 1776. First Presbyterian minister in Ontario. Lived 4 mi. S.

NC 24/27 southeast of Robbins / 1974

K-52   POTTERY INDUSTRY
Begun in 18th century by Chriscoe, Cole, Craven, Luck, McNeill, Owen, & Teague families living within 5 mile radius.

NC 705 at SR 1419 (Reynolds Mill Road) southwest of Jugtown / 1979

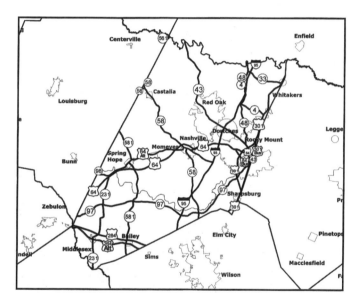

NASH COUNTY

E-7   ROCKY MOUNT MILLS
Second cotton mill in State. Building begun, 1818. Federals burned, 1863. Soon rebuilt.

NC 43/48 (Falls Road) at Tar River bridge in Rocky Mount / 1937

E-15   CORNWALLIS
On his way to Virginia, defeated the militia near here at Swift Creek and seven miles north at Fishing Creek, May 7, 1781.

NC 48 at Swift Creek south of Gold Rock / 1939

E-31   LAFAYETTE
On his American tour, Lafayette spent the night of February 28, 1825, at the home of Henry Donaldson which stood near this spot.

NC 43/48 (Falls Road) at Tar River bridge in Rocky Mount / 1941

E-59   JIM THORPE
1886-1953
Indian athlete, star of the 1912 Olympics, made his professional baseball debut with Rocky Mount Railroaders, 1909. Ball park was 300 yds. W.

US 301 Business (Church Street) in Rocky Mount / 1959

Rocky Mount Mills (E 7) on the Falls of the Tar River. The state's second oldest textile mill, founded in 1818, ceased operations in 1996.

E-61　　P. T. BARNUM

First stop of record with own circus troupe was 1/2 mile S.E., November 12-13, 1836. No show is recorded, but Barnum preached a sermon.

US 301 Bypass at Airport Road in Rocky Mount / 1956

E-72　　NORTH CAROLINA WESLEYAN COLLEGE

Methodist. Liberal arts, senior co-educational college. Chartered Oct., 1956; opened 1960.

US 301 Business (Church Street) in Rocky Mount / 1966

E-82　　COUNTRY DOCTOR MUSEUM

Chartered 1967 to honor the "old family doctor." Two doctors' offices, 1857 & 1887, restored with medical & apothecary artifacts. Two blocks south.

US 264 Alternate (Dean Street) in Bailey / 1973

E-87　　CORNWALLIS

The British Army under Gen. Cornwallis marching to Virginia camped here at Crowell's plantation on May 8, 1781.

NC 97 (Raleigh Road) in Rocky Mount / 1976

E-88　　FALLS OF THE TAR CHURCH

Constituted as Particular Baptist, 1757; Rev. John Moore & Joshua Lawrence among early ministers. Now Primitive Baptist.

NC 43/48 (Falls Road) at Hunter Hill Road in Rocky Mount / 1977

E-89　　GOLD MINES

Ore discovered at farm of Isaac Portis in 1835; mines in this area produced nearly $3 million before Civil War. Last worked in 1936.

NC 561 near Nash/Franklin County line / 1977

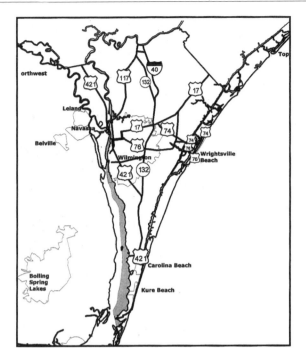

NEW HANOVER COUNTY

D-1   CORNELIUS HARNETT
(ca. 1723-1781)
Revolutionary statesman. Prominent in resistance to British rule and the creation of independent N.C. Home was 1/4 mi. N.

US 117/NC 133 (Cornelius Harnett Drive) at Fourth Street in Wilmington / 1935

D-2   OLD COURTHOUSE
Stood two blocks west. Here a stamp master, William Houston, was forced to resign, 1765, and safety committees met in 1775.

US 17 Business (Market Street) at Third Street in Wilmington / 1936

D-5   ST. JAMES CHURCH
Built 1839, near site of older church, begun about 1751. Graves of Cornelius Harnett and Thomas Godfrey.

US 17 Business (Market Street) at Fourth Street in Wilmington / 1936

D-9   WHISTLER'S MOTHER
Anna McNeill Whistler, the mother of James Whistler, artist, was born in a house which stood one block east.

US 17 Business (Third Street) at Orange Street in Wilmington / 1939

D-12   FORT FISHER
Built by Confederacy. Its fall, Jan. 15, 1865, closed Wilmington, last important southern port for blockade running.

US 421 (Fort Fisher Boulevard) at Fort Fisher State Historic Site / 1938

D-15   JOHN BURGWIN
1731-1803
Merchant, planter, and colonial official. Built this house, 1770-1771. His "Hermitage" estate was eight miles north.

US 17 Business (Third Street) at Market Street in Wilmington / 1992

D-17   EDWARD B. DUDLEY
1789-1855
Governor, 1836-41, the first in N.C. elected by popular vote; first president of Wilmington and Weldon Railroad. His home stands 2 blocks W.

US 17 Business (Third Street) at Nun Street in Wilmington / 1939

**D-19   WASHINGTON'S
SOUTHERN TOUR**
President Washington was a guest Apr. 24-25, 1791, at the Quince home which stood 2 blocks W.
US 17 Business (Third Street) at Dock Street in Wilmington / 1940

**D-20   WILMINGTON AND
WELDON RAILROAD**
Longest railroad in the world when completed in 1840. Length 161fi mi. Terminus was 4 blocks W.
Third Street at Brunswick Street in Wilmington / 1941

D-22   EARLY DRAWBRIDGE
One of the few drawbridges in the American colonies was built near here by Benjamin Heron about 1768. Destroyed by British troops, 1781.
US 117/NC 133 north of Castle Hayne / 1940

D-23   STATE SALT WORKS
The state of North Carolina to relieve a wartime scarcity, operated salt works from here to Myrtle Grove Sound, 1861-64.
NC 132 (South College Road) at Mohican Trail in Wilmington / 1940

D-31   WOODROW WILSON
President of the United States, 1913-1921. His home, 1874-1882, was the Presbyterian manse, which stood one block E.
US 17 Business (Third Street) at Orange Street in Wilmington / 1941

D-35   GEORGE DAVIS
Confederate Senator, 1862-64, and Attorney General, 1864-65. Birthplace stood 3 mi. east.
US 17 northeast of Kirkland / 1949

**D-36   GEORGE DAVIS
1820-1896**
Confederate senator, 1862-64, and attorney general, 1864-65. Home was 2 blocks E.; grave is 1/2 mile northeast.
US 17 Business (Third Street) at Orange Street in Wilmington / 1949

**D-37   CAPTAIN JOHNSTON
BLAKELEY**
After many victories, War of 1812, was lost at sea with his ship. Home was 2 blocks W.
Third Street at Princess Street in Wilmington / 1949

**D-38   MARY BAKER
GLOVER EDDY**
Founder of Christian Science Church. Spent part of 1844 at Hanover House, 2 blocks west.
Third Street at Market Street in Wilmington / 1949

D-39   THOMAS F. PRICE
Roman Catholic priest, pioneer Home Missionary of N.C. Co-founder of "Maryknoll Fathers," a foreign mission society. Birthplace (1860) 1 bl. E.
Third Street at Chestnut Street in Wilmington / 1948

D-40   EDWIN A. ALDERMAN
Crusader for education, president University of North Carolina, 1896-1900; Tulane, 1900-04; Virginia, 1904-31. This is his birthplace.
US 17 Business (Third Street) between Campbell and Red Cross Streets in Wilmington / 1949

D-41   JAMES GIBBONS
Cardinal of the Roman Catholic Church, 1886-1921. Installed as vicar apostolic of North Carolina (1868-72) at St. Thomas Church 1/2 bl. W.
US 17 Business (Third Street) at Dock Street in Wilmington / 1950

D-42   WILLIAM W. LORING
Major general in the Confederate Army, lieut. colonel in Mexican War, general in Egyptian Army, 1870-79. His birthplace was 1 bl. W.
US 17 Business (Third Street) between Orange and Ann Streets in Wilmington / 1950

D-43   JOHN A. WINSLOW
Capt. U.S.S. "Kearsarge," which sank Confederate raider "Alabama," 1864, rear admiral U.S. Navy, 1870-1873. Birthplace was one block west.
Third Street between Chestnut and Grace Streets in Wilmington / 1950

Temple of Israel (D 44), the first Jewish house of worship in North Carolina

D-44   TEMPLE OF ISRAEL
Erected 1875-6. First house of worship built in North Carolina by the Jews. Congregation established in 1867.

US 17 Business (Market Street) at Fourth Street in Wilmington / 1951

D-45   WILLIAM HOOPER
One of North Carolina's three signers of the Declaration of Independence. Home was here.

Third Street at Princess Street in Wilmington / 1951

D-47   EDWIN A. ANDERSON
Rear Admiral, U.S. Navy. Received Congressional recognition for service in War with Spain; at Vera Cruz; and in World War I. Home is 4 mi. E.

US 76 (Oleander Drive) at Masonboro Loop Road in Wilmington / 1951

D-49   THALIAN HALL
CITY HALL
Built 1855-58 as city hall and theatre for the Thalian Association (amateur), formed c. 1788.

Third Street at Princess Street in Wilmington / 1952

D-50   HENRY BACON
1866-1924
Architect of the Lincoln Memorial in Washington and many other public structures. Home is here, grave, Oakdale Cemetery.

US 17 Business (Third Street) between Dock and Orange Streets in Wilmington / 1952

D-51   JAMES SPRUNT
Author of "Chronicles of the Cape Fear River" (1914), cotton merchant, philanthropist, British vice consul. His home stands two blocks west.

US 17 Business (Third Street) at Nun Street in Wilmington / 1953

D-56   JUDAH P. BENJAMIN
United States Senator, Confederate Attorney General, Secretary of War & of State, later lawyer in England. His early home was here.

US 17 Business (Third Street) between Ann and Nun Streets in Wilmington / 1955

D-57   ROSE GREENHOW
Confederate spy and Washington society woman. Drowned near Fort Fisher in 1864, while running Federal blockade. Grave 1 m. N.E.

US 17 Business (Third Street) at Dock Street in Wilmington / 1955

D-59   ADAM EMPIE, D.D.
First chaplain of U.S. Military Academy, West Point, 1813-1817; president William and Mary College; rector St. James Church. Grave 3/4 mi. N.E.

US 17 Business (Third Street) between Market and Dock Streets in Wilmington / 1956

D-60   BEERY'S SHIPYARD
Many Confederate naval vessels, including the ironclad "North Carolina," built here. Site lies across river on Eagles Island, 1/4 mile west.

US 17 Business (Market Street) between Third and Fourth Streets in Wilmington / 1959

D-61   JOHN N. MAFFITT

Captain of Confederate cruiser "Florida" and ironclad "Albemarle." With U.S. Coast Survey, 1842-1858. Blockade-runner. Grave 14 blks. N.E.

US 17 Business (Market Street) at Fifteenth Street in Wilmington / 1959

D-64 JOHNSON JONES HOOPER

Editor and humorist, creator of "Simon Suggs" and other characters of the Southern frontier. Born in this city, 1815.

US 17 Business (Market Street) at Third Street in Wilmington / 1962

D-67   CATHERINE KENNEDY HOME

For the elderly. Grew from Ladies Benevolent Society, founded, 1845. First home, 1879, stood four blocks east.

US 17 Business (Third Street) at Orange Street in Wilmington / 1965

D-68   NICHOLAS N. NIXON 1800-1868

Planter. Developed peanut into profitable crop by scientific methods at his Porters Neck Plantation 2 miles east.

US 17 northeast of Wilmington / 1965

D-69   OAKDALE CEMETERY

Chartered, 1852. Graves of Confederate leaders, officers, & soldiers. Many yellow fever victims. Six blocks North on 15th St.

US 17 Business (Market Street) at Fifteenth Street in Wilmington / 1965

D-71   CAPE FEAR CLUB

Founded, 1866; oldest gentleman's club in South in continuous existence. Host to many famous men.

Second Street at Chestnut Street in Wilmington / 1967

D-72   JAMES HASELL

Acting governor, 1771; thrice Chief Justice, 1750-1766; President of the Council. Owned large library. Home 7 mi. S.E.

US 17 Business (Third Street) between Ann and Nun Streets in Wilmington / 1968

D-75   WILMINGTON MORNING STAR

Established Sept. 23, 1867. Oldest daily newspaper in continuous publication in North Carolina. First office was 18 blocks N.W.

Sixteenth Street in Wilmington / 1971

D-76   NORTH CAROLINA SOROSIS

Oldest Federated Women's Club in state; chartered 1896; organized in house 6fi miles southwest.

US 74 (Eastwood Road) at Cardinal Drive in Wilmington / 1972

D-77   ST. STEPHEN A.M.E. CHURCH

Congregation formed in 1865. Present church constructed 1880 on land donated by Geo. Peabody. Located 2 blocks east.

Third Street at Red Cross Street in Wilmington / 1976

D-78   ST. MARK'S

Consecrated in 1875 as first Episcopal church for colored people in North Carolina. Served by Bishop Atkinson. Is located 3 blocks east.

Third Street at Grace Street in Wilmington / 1976

D-80   UNIVERSITY OF N.C. AT WILMINGTON

Est. 1947 as Wilmington College. Moved here in 1961. A campus of The University of North Carolina since 1969.

NC 132 (College Road) in Wilmington / 1976

D-81   THOMAS F. WOOD 1841-1892

Organizer & Sec.-Treas. of State Board of Health, 1877-1892. Founded N.C. Medical Journal in 1878. Home was 1 block west.

Third Street at Chestnut Street in Wilmington / 1978

D-83   JAMES F. SHOBER 1853-1889

1st known black physician with an M.D. degree in N.C. Practiced 1878-89. Home and office stood one block north.

US 17 Business (Market Street) at Eighth Street in Wilmington / 1982

**D-84   N.C. BUILDING & LOAN
ASSOCIATION LEAGUE**
Organized on June 25, 1903, at Seashore
Hotel nearby. First president was Samuel
Wittkowsky.

*US 76 (Waynick Boulevard) at Seashore
Street in Wrightsville Beach* / 1986

D-86   USS NORTH CAROLINA
World War II battleship. Launched, June 13,
1940. Served in Pacific, 1942-1945. Decom-
missioned, 1947. Berthed here, 1961.

Battleship Avenue in Wilmington / 1987

**D-87   THOMAS ATKINSON
1807-1881**
Bishop of the Episcopal Diocese of N.C.,
1853-1881. Voice for church unity in postwar
years. Interred in the church.

*US 17 Business (Market Street) at Third
Street in Wilmington* / 1987

**D-88   GREGORY NORMAL
INSTITUTE**
School for blacks, 1868-1921. Founded by
American Missionary Assoc. Named for
benefactor James H. Gregory. Was 4 blocks
E.

*US 17 Business (Third Street) at Nun Street
in Wilmington* / 1987

**D-90   JAMES INNES
ca. 1700-1759**
Commanded N.C. troops at Cartagena, 1740;
led colonial forces, 1754-56, in French and
Indian War. Grave 4 miles W.

*US 117/NC 133 and SR 1002 (Holly Shelter
Road) at Castle Hayne* / 1989

D-94   BABIES HOSPITAL
Pioneer pediatric hospital opened here in
1920 by Dr. J. Buren Sidbury. Also provided
training of nurses. Closed 1978.

*US 74 (Eastwood Road) at Summer Street
west of Wrightsville Beach* / 1991

**D-95 JAMES BENSON DUDLEY
1859-1925**
Educator. President of what is now N.C.
A. & T. University, 1896-1925. His grave is 5
blocks N.

*US 17 Business (Market Street) at Sixteenth
Street in Wilmington* / 1991

**D-96   NORTH CAROLINA
SHIPBUILDING CO.**
Constructed 243 vessels at shipyard one mile
west, 1941-1946. Its first Liberty Ship, the
S.S. *Zebulon B. Vance*, launched Dec. 6, 1941.

*US 421 at Shipyard Boulevard
in Wilmington* / 1992

D-97   LUMINA
Built in 1905; known as "Fun Spot of the
South"; hosted big bands, other entertain-
ment. Pavilion was demolished, 1973. Stood
100 yards east.

*US 76 (Waynick Boulevard) in Wrightsville
Beach* / 1992

D-98   BROMINE EXTRACTION
Ethyl-Dow plant, which operated here, 1934-
1945, pioneered extraction of bromine from
sea water. Element used in Ethyl anti-knock
gas compound.

US 421 in Kure Beach / 1992

D-101   FALL OF WILMINGTON
Union assault on Hoke's entrenched Confed-
erates led to the city's fall, February 22, 1865.
Earthworks were nearby.

*Shipyard Boulevard at Seventeenth Street in
Wilmington* / 1993

**D-102   W. H. C. WHITING
1824-1865**
Confederate major general and engineer. He
devised the Cape Fear defense system.
Wounded nearby in fall of fort. Died in Union
hospital.

*US 421 (Fort Fisher Boulevard) at Fort
Fisher State Historic Site* / 1994

**D-103   ALEX MANLY
1866-1944**
Edited black-owned *Daily Record* four
blocks east. Mob burned his office, Nov. 10,
1898, leading to "race riot" & restrictions on
black voting in N.C.

*US 17 Business (Third Street) between Nun
and Church Streets in Wilmington* / 1994

DDD-3 CASSIDEY SHIPYARD
Confederate shipyard and outfitting station
which completed the ironclad steam sloop
Raleigh in 1863. Site is three blocks west.

*US 17 Business (Third Street) at Church
Street in Wilmington* / 1962

Katie Nixon, who is blind, is assisted by her sister Addie Dunlap, as she runs her hand across the historical marker (D 103) dedicated on October 23, 1998, as part of the centennial commemoration of the "race riot" in Wilmington.

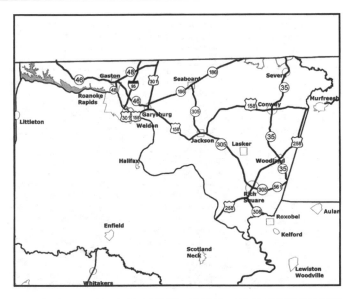

NORTHAMPTON COUNTY

E-6   THOMAS BRAGG
Attorney-General of Confederacy, Governor of N.C. 1855-59, U.S. Senator. Home stands one block north.

US 158 (Jefferson Street) in Jackson / 1936

E-10   MATT W. RANSOM
Confederate General, United States Senator, 1872-95, and Minister to Mexico. Home stands 800 yards south.

US 158 west of Jackson / 1938

Lord Charles Cornwallis (E 13)

E-13   CORNWALLIS
Ending his campaign in North Carolina, he entered Virginia near here in May, 1781, and surrendered at Yorktown on October 17, 1781.

US 301 north of Pleasant Hill at NC/VA boundary / 1938

E-29   ALLEN JONES
Brigadier General during the Revolution, member of Provincial Congress and of Continental Congress. Site of home, Mt. Gallant, 1/4 mi. S.W.

NC 46 west of Gaston / 1940

E-32   FIRST RAILROAD
The first railroad in the State was completed in 1833 from Petersburg, Va., to Blakely, on the Roanoke River, a short distance southeast.

US 158/301 at Roanoke River bridge southwest of Garysburg / 1942

E-42   LEMUEL BURKITT
Pastor Sandy Run Baptist Church, 1773-1807. A founder & historian, Kehukee Baptist Assn.; member N.C. convention, 1788. Grave 300 yds. E.

NC 308 south of Rich Square / 1950

E-45 GEORGE V. HOLLOMAN
1902-1946
Colonel U.S. Air Force, World War II. Pioneer in developing automatic devices for airplane control. Home 150 yds. W.

US 258/NC 561 (South Main Street)
in Rich Square / 1951

E-54 ROANOKE RIVER
Early channel of trade, its valley long an area of plantations. Frequent floods until 1952, since controlled by Kerr Dam. Old name was "Moratuck."

US 258 at Roanoke River bridge southwest
of Rich Square / 1954

E-56 ROANOKE RIVER
Early channel of trade, its valley long an area of plantations. Frequent floods until 1952, since controlled by Kerr Dam. Old name was "Moratuck."

US 158/301 at Roanoke River bridge south-
west of Garysburg / 1954

E-64 BOON'S MILL
Here on July 28, 1863, a Confederate force repulsed a Union march on the vital Wilmington and Weldon Railroad. Breastworks 50 yds. S.W.

US 158 west of Jackson / 1959

E-76 RICH SQUARE
MONTHLY MEETING
Society of Friends (Conservative). Meeting was organized, 1760, six mi. S. Since 1936 has met here at Cedar Grove, a Meeting established in 1868.

US 258 (Main Street) in Woodland / 1967

E-83 SIR ARCHIE
Foundation sire of American Thoroughbred race horses, including Timoleon, Boston, Lexington, & Man O'War. Died at Mowfield, one mile north, in 1833.

US 158 west of Jackson / 1967

E-91 HENRY K. BURGWYN
"Boy" Colonel 26th N.C. Regt. Killed at age 21 at Gettysburg on July 1, 1863. Home stood 4 miles south.

US 158 west of Jackson / 1961

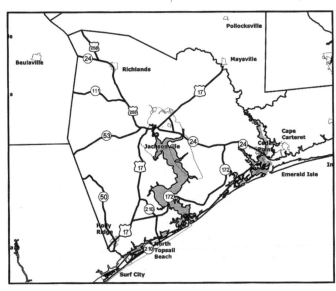

ONSLOW COUNTY

C-18 WASHINGTON'S
SOUTHERN TOUR
President Washington spent the night Apr. 23, 1791 at Sage's Inn, which stood 200 yds. E.

US 17 south of Holly Ridge / 1940

C-26 OTWAY BURNS
Privateersman, War of 1812, shipbuilder. As a State Senator he fought for the constitutional convention of 1835. His home was 3 miles south.

NC 24 west of Swansboro / 1949

C-28   FIRST POST ROAD
The road from New England to Charleston, over which mail was first carried regularly in North Carolina, 1738-39, passed near this spot.

US 17 and SR 1434 (Belgrade Road)
at Belgrade / 1949

C-29   D. L. RUSSELL
Governor, 1897-1901; member Congress 1879-1881; Superior Court judge at 23; home six, grave three miles S.

US 17 and SR 1434 (Belgrade Road)
at Belgrade / 1950

C-31   EDWARD B. DUDLEY
Governor, 1836-41, the first in N.C. elected by popular vote, first president of Wilmington and Weldon Railroad. Birthplace was 2 mi. W.

US 17 (Marine Boulevard) at Bell Fork
Road in Jacksonville / 1951

C-34   RICHLANDS OF NEW
                RIVER CHAPEL
Site of three successive Protestant congregations: Anglican until about 1758; Baptist until 1877; and Disciples of Christ since.

US 258/NC 24 south of Richlands / 1959

C-37   LOT BALLARD HOUSE
Bishop Francis Asbury stopped here many times between 1799 and 1815 on visits to New River Chapel. House was 3/4 mi. W.

US 258/NC 24 south of Richlands / 1959

C-38   ONSLOW RAID
Federal gunboat "Ellis" attacked this town Nov. 23, 1862, then ran aground downstream. It was abandoned under Confederate cross fire.

US 17 (Marine Boulevard)
in Jacksonville / 1959

C-41   HUGGINS' ISLAND FORT
Confederate 6-gun fort guarding the entrance to Bogue Inlet; burned by Union troops, Aug. 19, 1862. Remains 1 mi. S.W.

NC 24 at White Oak River bridge
in Swansboro / 1962

C-44   PORT SWANNSBOROUGH
Named for Samuel Swann. Town incorporated in 1783. Port, including area from New River to Bogue Inlet, established in 1786.

NC 24 at White Oak River bridge
in Swansboro / 1965

Training exercises on Topsail Beach conducted in 1943
by soldiers training at Camp Davis (C 65)

C-46   HOFMANN FOREST
Named for J. V. Hofmann. Research forest of
80,000 acres in Jones & Onslow counties.
Acquired, 1934, for use by North Carolina
State University.

NC 17 north of Jacksonville / 1970

C-52   COL. JOHN STARKEY
Free school advocate, 1749; Southern
District treasurer, 1750-1765; member of
assembly for 25 years. Grave located at "The
Bluff" 4 mi. N.

NC 24 at White Oak River bridge
in Swansboro / 1976

C-54   "PROMETHEUS"
First steamboat made in N.C. Built in 1818
by Otway Burns, privateer in War of 1812.
Shipyard located 350 feet S.W.

NC 24 at White Oak bridge
in Swansboro / 1976

C-65   CAMP DAVIS
Army Coast Artillery Training Center, World
War II. Named for Richmond P. Davis, native
of Statesville.

US 17 at NC 50 in Holly Ridge / 1989

C-71   CAMP LEJEUNE
Established 1 May 1941 by the U.S. Marine
Corps for amphibious training. Named for Lt.
Gen. John A. Lejeune, USMC, 13th Com-
mandant, 1920-1929.

NC 24 (Lejeune Boulevard)
in Jacksonville / 1993

C-72   CYRUS THOMPSON
1855-1930
Physician and orator. Secretary of State of
N.C., 1897-1901. Farmers' Alliance and Pop-
ulist leader. Grave 4 mi. W.

US 258/NC 24 at SR 1229 (Gregory Fork
Road) south of Richlands / 1993

C-73   MONTFORD POINT
Recruit training depot for black Marines,
1942-1949. In 1974 renamed Camp Johnson
for Sgt. Gilbert Johnson, drill instructor. One
mi. SE.

NC 24 at Montford Landing Road
in Jacksonville / 2000

Prometheus, **the first steamboat built in North Carolina (C 54)**

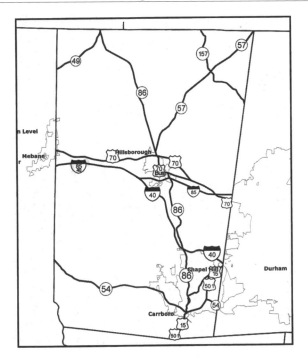

ORANGE COUNTY

G-3   THOMAS BURKE
Governor, 1781-82. Member of Revolutionary, Provincial, & Continental Congresses. Grave is 1fi miles N.E.

NC 86 at NC 57 north of Hillsborough / 1936

G-4   WILLIAM HOOPER
1742-1790
One of North Carolina's three signers of the Declaration of Independence. His home is 150 yds. W. Was buried a few yds. W.

US 70 Business/NC 86 (North Churton Street) in Hillsborough / 1936

G-9   ARCHIBALD DEBOW
MURPHEY
Champion of a new State through public schools, canals, roads, 1777-1832. Grave 50 yards west.

US 70 Business/NC 86 (North Churton Street) in Hillsborough / 1937

G-10   FRANCIS NASH
Patriot general in American Revolution, was mortally wounded at Germantown, 1777. His home is 150 yds. W.

US 70 Business/NC 86 (North Churton Street) in Hillsborough / 1938

G-11   THOMAS RUFFIN
Chief Justice of North Carolina Supreme Court, 1833-52, noted jurist, agriculturist, is buried 3/10 mi. east.

US 70 Business/NC 86 (North Churton Street) at Tryon Street in Hillsborough / 1938

Archibald DeBow Murphey (G 9)

G-16   THOMAS BURKE
Governor of N.C., was captured in Hillsboro by David Fanning and his Tories, Sept. 12, 1781, and taken to Charleston, S.C.

US 70 Business/NC 86 (South Churton Street) in Hillsborough / 1939

G-19   EDMUND FANNING
Born in New York, Yale graduate, judge. His home nearby, destroyed by Regulators, 1770. Later Loyalist, British general, governor.

US 70 Business/NC 86 (South Churton Street) in Hillsborough / 1940

G-23   REGULATORS HANGED
After the Regulators were defeated at Alamance, May 16, 1771, six of their number were hanged, 1/4 mile east, June 19, 1771.

US 70 Business/NC 86 (South Churton Street) in Hillsborough / 1939

G-26   THOMAS H. BENTON
United States Senator from Missouri, 1821-1851; Congressman; author; Jacksonian Democratic leader; was born, 1782, in this neighborhood.

US 70 at Efland / 1939

G-33   OCCANEECHI
Village of Occaneechi Indians on the Great Trading Path. Inhabited ca. 1680-1710. Visited in 1701 by the explorer John Lawson. 1/2 mi. E.

US 70 Business/NC 86 (South Churton Street) at Eno River bridge in Hillsborough / 1941

G-37   BINGHAM SCHOOL
Conducted by William J. Bingham. Moved from Mt. Repose, 1827. Removed to Oaks, 1845. Stood here.

US 70 Business in Hillsborough / 1948

G-38   BINGHAM SCHOOL
Academy under William J. Bingham. Moved from Hillsborough in 1845. Removed to Mebane, 1865. Stood near this spot.

NC 54 and SR 1007 at Oaks west of Carrboro / 1948

G-39   BINGHAM SCHOOL
Boys' military academy operated by William & Robert Bingham. Moved here from Oaks, 1865. Moved to Asheville, 1891.

US 70 east of Mebane / 1948

University of North Carolina at Chapel Hill archaeological field school excavating at the site of Occaneechi (G 33)

G-40   WILLIAM A. GRAHAM
Governor, 1845-1849; Secretary of the Navy; United States Senator; Whig nominee for Vice-President in 1852. His home stands 150 yds. W.

US 70 Business/NC 86 (North Churton Street) in Hillsborough / 1948

G-48   PAPER MILL
The first paper mill in North Carolina, built to relieve the paper shortage during the Revolution, was erected in this vicinity, 1777.

US 70 Business/NC 86 (South Churton Street) in Hillsborough / 1948

G-64   MOSES A. CURTIS
Botanist, authority on North American flora, author, and Episcopal minister. Home was two blocks east.

US 70 Business/NC 86 (North Churton Street) in Hillsborough / 1955

G-66   HUGHES ACADEMY
Classical, 1845-1884. Founded by Samuel W. Hughes. Attended by Wm. T. Dortch, David I. Craig, Geo. T. and P. H. Winston. Site is 1 mi. W.

NC 86 north of Hillsborough / 1966

**G-84   OLD ENO CHURCH
AND CEMETERY**
Presbyterian. Served by Hugh McAden, 1755-65. Henry Pattillo was first pastor. Church moved to Cedar Grove in 1893. Cemetery one mile S.

NC 86 east of Cedar Grove / 1965

**G-88   NORTH CAROLINA
SOCIETY OF THE CINCINNATI**
Formed Oct. 23, 1783, in Hillsborough, by officers of the Continental Line. First President was General Jethro Sumner.

US 70 Business/NC 86 (South Churton Street) in Hillsborough / 1970

G-90   ST. MARY'S CHAPEL
Established as Anglican chapel ca. 1759. Present building consecrated in 1859, stands 500 ft. N.

SR 1002 (Saint Mary's Road) at Pleasant Green Road east of Hillsborough / 1973

**G-92   UNIVERSITY OF N.C.
AT CHAPEL HILL**
First state university to open its doors, 1795. Chartered in 1789 under the Constitution of 1776.

East Franklin Street in Chapel Hill / 1973

**G-100   HARRIET M. BERRY
1877-1940**
Champion of good roads. Her intensive lobbying led to 1921 law creating modern state highway system. Born 8 mi. N.

NC 86 at I-40 north of Chapel Hill / 1986

**G-103   J. G. de ROULHAC
HAMILTON
1878-1961**
Historian, professor, & founder of the Southern Historical Collection at UNC. Born 1/2 block W.

US 70 Business/NC 86 (North Churton Street) in Hillsborough / 1989

**G-108   JAMES HOGG
1729-1804**
Merchant. Left native Scotland, 1774. Partner in Transylvania Company; UNC trustee. Home 1/2 mi. E.; grave 2 blks. N.

US 70 Business/NC 86 (South Churton Street) in Hillsborough / 1989

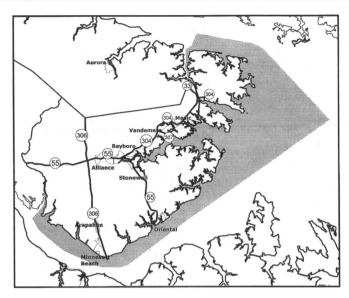

PAMLICO COUNTY

**C-47   FIRST MOTORIZED
SCHOOL BUS**
On September 5, 1917, the Pamlico Co.
School system inaugurated the first motor-

ized school bus service in North Carolina.

*NC 55 (Broad Street) at Church Street
in Oriental / 1970*

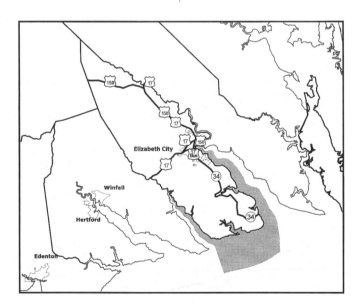

PASQUOTANK COUNTY

A-13   FIRST ASSEMBLY
The Albemarle County Assembly, initial law-
making body in Carolina, first met, 1665, in
this area.

*NC 34 (Water Street) in Elizabeth City /
1936*

A-14   FIRST SCHOOL
Charles Griffin taught in this county the first
known school in N.C. 1705-08.

*US 17 Business (Ehringhaus Street)
in Elizabeth City / 1936*

Street scene in Elizabeth City in 1949

A-21 CULPEPER'S REBELLION
Culpeper and Durant led a revolt against British trade laws, seized the government 1677, 2 mi. SE.
NC 34 (Water Street) in Elizabeth City /
1940

A-37   ELIZABETH CITY
STATE UNIVERSITY
Founded in 1891 as Negro normal school. Four-year college after 1939. Became a university in 1969.
NC 34 (Harrington Road)
in Elizabeth City / 1950

A-39   J. C. B. EHRINGHAUS
Governor, 1933-1937, friend of education, member of General Assembly, solicitor. Birthplace 1/4 mile north.
NC 34 (Water Street) in
Elizabeth City / 1951

A-40   STEPHEN B. WEEKS
Historian, bibliographer, collector of North Carolina books and manuscripts, professor at Trinity College, 1891-93. Birthplace 3/5 mi. E.
US 17 north of Little River / 1951

A-43   MOUNT LEBANON
CHURCH
A.M.E. Zion. Organized about 1850 as mission to serve black Methodists. Since 1856 congregation has met 1fi blocks N.
US 17 Business (West Ehringhaus Street) at
Culpepper Street in Elizabeth City / 1998

A-54   GEORGE W. BROOKS
Federal judge whose writ of habeas corpus, 1870, prevented arbitrary arrest of N.C. citizens during Reconstruction. Home was 1/4 mile east.
NC 34 (Water Street) in
Elizabeth City / 1959

A-61   JOSEPH C. PRICE
(1854-1893)
Negro orator and teacher. A founder and president of Livingstone College. Born in Elizabeth City. House was 2 miles S.
NC 34 (Water Street) in Elizabeth City /
1967

A-64   NATHANIEL BATTS
LAND GRANT
Sold by King Kiscutanewh on Sept. 24, 1660. From mouth of Pasquotank River to the "head of New Begin Creeke." 3fi miles southeast.
US 17 Business (Ehringhaus Street)
in Elizabeth City / 1968

A-70   SOYBEAN PROCESSING
Commercial processing of domestic soybeans in U.S. began in 1915 at a plant which was located two miles north.
US 17 Business (Ehringhaus Street)
in Elizabeth City / 1982

A-80   HUGH CALE
1835-1910
Sponsored the 1891 bill to establish present-day Elizabeth City State University; legislator, 1876-80, 1885, 1891. His grave is 6/10 mile west.
NC 34 (South Road Street) at Cale Street
in Elizabeth City / 1994

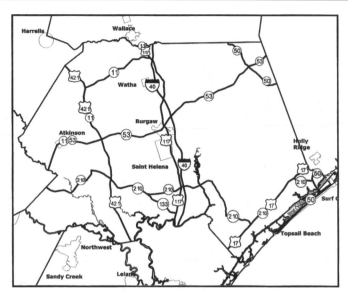

PENDER COUNTY

D-6   MOORE'S CREEK BRIDGE
First battle of the Revolution in North Carolina, Feb. 27, 1776. Tories defeated. U.S. Military Park, 5 mi. S.W.

US 421 at SR 1120 (Malpass Corner Road) northeast of Currie / 1936

**D-7   SAMUEL ASHE
1725-1813**
Governor, 1795-1798; one of the first three state judges; president, Council of Safety, 1776. His grave is 3 miles east.

US 117 at SR 1411 (Ashton Road) north of Rocky Point / 1936

The Patriot Monument at Moores Creek National Battlefield (D 6), the cornerstone for which was laid in 1857

D-10 ALEXANDER LILLINGTON
Revolutionary leader, Whig colonel in Battle of Moore's Creek Bridge, 1776. Grave 9 miles NE.
US 117 and NC 210 at Rocky Point / 1938

D-13 HINTON JAMES
First student to enter the University of North Carolina, 1795, civil engineer, state legislator. Grave 300 yards east.
US 117 north of Burgaw / 1938

D-18 S. S. SATCHWELL
A founder of State Medical Society, 1849, head of Confederate Hospital at Wilson, 1st president State Board of Health, 1879. Home stood here.
*US 117 Business (Walker Street)
in Burgaw* / 1940

D-26 JAMES MOORE
Commander of Whigs in Moore's Creek campaign, 1776, brigadier general North Carolina troops at Charleston. Died 1777. His home was 3 mi. S.E.
US 117 at Rocky Point / 1940

**D-32 GEORGE BURRINGTON
ca. 1682-1759**
Colonial governor, 1724-1725, 1731-1734; opened lower Cape Fear region to settlement. His home was 3/4 mile east.
US 117 south of Burgaw / 1948

D-33 STAG PARK
Named by Barbadian explorers, 1663. Home of Gov. George Burrington and Samuel Strudwick, colonial official. The house stood 3/4 mi. E.
US 117 south of Burgaw / 1948

D-34 WELSH TRACT
About 1730 a group of Welsh from the colony of Pennsylvania settled in this area, between the Northeast and Cape Fear rivers.
US 117 north of Burgaw / 1948

D-46 EDWARD MOSELEY
Acting governor, 1724, president of the Council, speaker of Assembly, leader of popular party. His home, "Moseley Hall," was two miles east.
US 117 south of Burgaw / 1951

D-52 SAMUEL SWANN
Speaker of assembly nearly 20 years, leader popular party, compiler first printed revisal of N.C. laws (1752). Home stood one mile south.
NC 133 southwest of Rocky Point / 1954

D-58 WILLIAM S. ASHE
Railroad president, congressman, state senator. In charge of Confederate railroad transportation, 1861-62. Home stands 1 mile W.
US 117 north of Rocky Point / 1956

D-63 MAURICE MOORE
Leader in Tuscarora and S.C. Indian Wars. One of original Cape Fear settlers. Founded Brunswick, 1726. His plantation was 3 mi. SE.
US 117 and NC 210 at Rocky Point / 1962

D-65 GENERAL JOHN ASHE
Stamp Act patriot; Speaker of the House. Colonel under Tryon in "War of Regulation." Revolutionary General. Home stood 2 mi. east.
US 117 north of Rocky Point / 1962

**D-91 PENDERLEA
HOMESTEADS**
Established in 1934 as model farm community. Planned as a New Deal homesteading project of ten thousand acres.
NC 11 at Penderlea / 1990

D-99 PRISONER EXCHANGE
Thousands of Civil War soldiers, including many held in Confederate prison at Salisbury, were exchanged here, Feb. 26-Mar. 4, 1865.
*US 117 at Northeast Cape Fear River
bridge south of Rocky Point* / 1992

D-100 TOPSAIL BATTERY
Confederate breastworks were constructed in this vicinity in 1862 to protect Wilmington from an attack from the north and for coastal defense.
US 17 south of Hampstead / 1993

D-104 MISSILE TESTS
U.S. Navy successfully tested ramjet engines in rocket flights, 1946-48. Observation towers line Topsail Island; Assembly Building 2 blocks west.
*NC 50 (Anderson Boulevard) at Flake
Avenue in Topsail Beach* / 1995

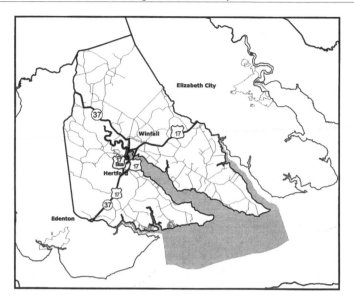

PERQUIMANS COUNTY

A-3   GEORGE DURANT
1632-1694
Pioneer settler in the Albemarle, about 1662. Speaker of Assembly. Site of home 20 miles east, at Durant's Neck.

US 17 Bypass/NC 37 at SR 1300 (Griffin Road) in Winfall / 1936

A-28   JOHN HARVEY
Five times speaker of colonial assembly, moderator of provincial congresses, 1774-1775, leader of Revolutionary movement. Lived 11 mi. S.

US 17 Business/NC 37 (Church Street) in Hertford / 1948

A-71   JOHN SKINNER
1760-1819
First U.S. marshal for District of N.C., 1790-1794. Federalist member of conventions of 1788 & 1789. Lived 12 mi. SE.

US 17 Business/NC 37 (Church Street) at Dobb Street in Hertford / 1986

A-75 ANN MARWOOD DURANT
d. 1695
First woman known to have acted as attorney in an N.C. court, 1673. Appeared before Council in Perquimans Precinct.

US 17 Bypass/NC 37 at SR 1300 (Griffin Road) in Winfall / 1990

A-79   QUAKER ACTIVITY
In 1672 missionaries William Edmundson and George Fox, founder of Society of Friends in America, held religious meetings in this area.

US 17 Bypass/NC 37 at Perquimans River bridge in Hertford / 1993

A-82   OLD NECK FRIENDS
MEETING
Quaker meeting was established by 1680. Site of Yearly Meeting, 1698-1785. Discontinued, 1797. Building was 1 mile S.E.

US 17 at SR 1301 (Old Neck Road) east of Winfall / 1994

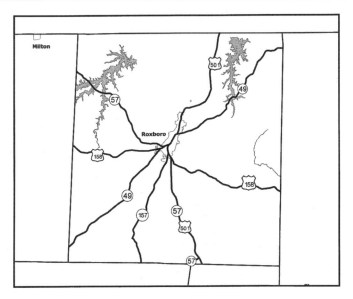

PERSON COUNTY

G-14   GREENE
Pursued by Cornwallis, crossed into Virginia and forded the Dan River northeast of here, February, 1781.

US 501 north of Bethel Hill at NC/VA boundary / 1938

G-15   CORNWALLIS
Passed a few miles west, February, 1781. Greene followed, and the Battle of Guilford Courthouse resulted, March 15, 1781.

US 501 north of Bethel Hill at NC/VA boundary / 1938

G-51   EDWIN G. READE
Member Congress, 1855-57; Confederate Senator; President State Convention, 1865; Justice N.C. Supreme Court, 1865-78. Birthplace was 2 mi. S.E.

US 501 at SR 1715 (Helena Road) west of Timberlake / 1949

G-70   ROBERT PAINE
Leader in organization of Methodist Episcopal Church, South, 1845. Bishop, president of LaGrange College, Ala., & author. Born 1 mi. E.

US 501 at SR 1703 (Garrett Road) south of Roxboro / 1957

G-72   J. G. A. WILLIAMSON
First U.S. representative to Republic of Venezuela, 1835-1840; member of N.C. General Assembly. Birthplace was 1/2 mile S.E.

NC 157 southwest of Roxboro / 1959

G-78   W. W. KITCHIN
Governor, 1909-1913; member of Congress. Moved to Roxboro from Scotland Neck in 1888. Home is 2 blocks E.

US 501/NC 49 (Madison Boulevard) in Roxboro / 1960

G-79   WILLIAM R. WEBB "SAWNEY"
Founder, 1870, of Webb School, since 1886 in Bell Buckle, Tenn. Confederate soldier, U.S. Senator, 1913. Born 1842, one mile S.

US 158 at SR 1717 (Mount Tirzah Road) at Surl southeast of Roxboro / 1962

G-87   ROBERT L. BLACKWELL
Posthumous winner of Congressional Medal of Honor. Died in battle at St. Souflet, France, Oct. 1918. Born and reared about 250 yards north.

NC 49 at SR 1166 (Whitfield Road) at Bushy Fork southwest of Roxboro / 1968

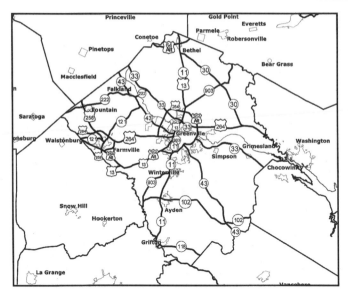

PITT COUNTY

F-3   JOHN LAWSON
Author of "History of Carolina," explorer, and Surveyor-General, was executed Sept. 20, 1711, by Tuscarora Indians at Catechna. Site 4 mi. N.

NC 118 (Queen Street) at Highland Boulevard in Grifton / 1936

F-5   BRYAN GRIMES
Major General, able Confederate leader, Yorktown to Appomattox. This is "Grimesland," his plantation.

NC 33 and SR 1569 (Grimes Farm Road) at Bryan / 1938

F-10   WASHINGTON'S SOUTHERN TOUR
President Washington spent the night, Apr. 19, 1791, at Shadrack Allen's Inn, which was 7 mi. E.

NC 102 (Third Street) at Lee Street in Ayden / 1939

F-16   PLANK ROAD
The eastern terminus of the Greenville and Raleigh Plank Road, chartered in 1850 and completed to Wilson by 1853, was nearby.

Tenth Street in Greenville / 1941

F-19   THOMAS J. JARVIS
Governor, 1879-1885; Minister to Brazil; United States Senator. Home is 3 blocks S. Grave is 1 block W.

Green Street at West Second Street in Greenville / 1948

F-23   BLOUNT HALL
Built before 1762 by Jacob Blount, member of Assembly, 1754-1762, 1764-1771, and of Provincial Congress, 1775-1776. Stood 90 Yds. N.W.

NC 11 at SR 1103 (Blount Hall Road) north of Grifton / 1949

F-36   CATECHNA
Fortified Indian town & site of the Tuscarora conspiracy of Sept., 1711. Capitulated, 1712, after a 10-day siege by Col. John Barnwell. Site is 4 mi. N.

NC 118 (Queen Street) at Highland Boulevard in Grifton / 1961

F-45   EAST CAROLINA UNIVERSITY
Established in 1907 as state-supported normal school. A campus of The University of North Carolina since 1972.

Tenth Street at College Hill Drive in Greenville / 1971

F-46   BAPTIST STATE CONVENTION

On March 26, 1830, the North Carolina Baptist State Convention was organized at the Gorham home which was near here.

Green Street in Greenville / 1971

F-57   SALLIE S. COTTEN 1846-1929

Writer and advocate of women's rights. Helped organize N.C. Federation of Women's Clubs, 1902. Lived one mile south.

NC 43 and NC 121 at Bruce northwest of Greenville / 1987

F-58   FORMER COLLEGES

Two church-affiliated schools were once located in Ayden. Carolina Christian College, founded by Disciples of Christ and a predecessor of Barton College in Wilson, operated 4/10 mile northeast from 1893 to 1903. Free Will Baptists in 1896 founded Ayden Seminary 4/10 mile southeast. Later known as Eureka College, it closed in 1929. In 1951 the Free Will Baptists established Mount Olive College in Mount Olive.

NC 102 (Third Street) at West Avenue in Ayden / 1993

F-60   ROBERT LEE HUMBER 1898-1970

Led effort in 1947 to establish N.C. Museum of Art; attorney & legislator; advocate of world federation. Lived here.

Fifth Street in Greenville / 1996

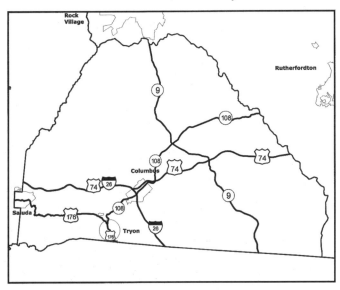

POLK COUNTY

O-2   SIDNEY LANIER

Southern poet, died in this house, September 7, 1881.

NC 108 south of Lynn / 1936

O-11   STONEMAN'S RAID

On a raid through western North Carolina Gen. Stoneman's U.S. cavalry fought southern troops at Howard's Gap, 4 mi. north, April 22, 1865.

NC 108 south of Lynn / 1940

O-19   NORTH CAROLINA-SOUTH CAROLINA

NORTH CAROLINA

Colonized, 1585-87, by first English settlers in America; permanently settled c. 1650; first to vote readiness for independence, Apr. 12, 1776.

(Reverse) SOUTH CAROLINA

Formed in 1712 from part of Carolina, which was chartered in 1663, it was first settled by the English in 1670. One of the 13 original states.

US 176 southeast of Tryon at NC/SC boundary / 1941

**O-30   NORTH CAROLINA-
SOUTH CAROLINA**

NORTH CAROLINA

Colonized, 1585-87, by first English settlers in America; permanently settled c. 1650; first to vote readiness for independence, Apr. 12, 1776.

(Reverse) SOUTH CAROLINA

Formed in 1712 from part of Carolina, which was chartered in 1663, it was first settled by the English in 1670. One of the 13 original states.

*NC 9 southeast of Sandy Plains at NC/SC
boundary* / 1949

O-34   TRYON'S MARCH

Governor William Tryon, with a body of militia en route to survey the Cherokee boundary line, camped near this spot, June 7, 1767.

*NC 9 southeast of Sandy Plains at NC/SC
boundary* / 1951

O-38   THE BLOCK HOUSE

Early landmark, western terminus of the 1772 boundary survey between North and South Carolina. Stood 1/2 mile east.

*US 176 southeast of Tryon at NC/SC
boundary* / 1951

O-52   "OLD BILL" WILLIAMS

Well-known guide and trapper. Helped survey Santa Fé Trail. Guided the ill-fated Frémont expedition of 1848. Was born near here in 1787.

NC 108 (Mills Street) in Columbus / 1959

O-73   SALUDA GRADE

The steepest, standard gauge, mainline railway grade in the U.S. Opened in 1878; three mi. long. Crests here.

US 176 (Main Street) in Saluda / 1987

O-77   TRYON MOUNTAIN

Landmark on Cherokee boundary, negotiated by Gov. William Tryon and Cherokee chiefs, 1767. Elevation 3,231 feet.

NC 108 (Mills Street) in Columbus / 1989

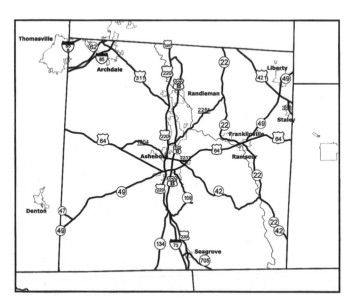

RANDOLPH COUNTY

K-2   JONATHAN WORTH

Governor, 1865-1868. State Treasurer, 1862-1865. Home stood one block south.

*NC 42 (East Salisbury Street)
in Asheboro* / 1936

K-3   TRINITY COLLEGE

Stood here. Union Institute, 1839; Normal College, 1851; Trinity, 1859; Duke University, 1924. Moved to Durham, 1892.

*NC 62 and SR 1603 (Johnson Road)
at Trinity* / 1937

K-5 SANDY CREEK BAPTIST CHURCH
Mother of Southern Baptist churches. Founded, 1755 by Rev. Shubael Stearns, whose grave is there. Two mi. South.

SR 2442 (Old Liberty Road) and SR 2261 (Ramseur-Julian Road) at Melancton / 1938

K-10 COX'S MILL
Headquarters of David Fanning, noted leader of North Carolina Tories, 1781-82, stood 4fi mi. southeast, near site of present "Bean's Mill."

NC 22 (Coleridge Road) in Ramseur / 1939

K-18 TRADING PATH
Colonial trading route, dating from 17th century, from Petersburg, Virginia, to Catawba and Waxhaw Indians in Carolina, passed nearby.

SR 1006 (Old US 421) at Julian / 1941

K-19 TRADING PATH
Colonial trading route, dating from 17th century, from Petersburg Virginia, to Catawba and Waxhaw Indians in Carolina, passed nearby.

US 311 at US 220 southwest of Randleman / 1941

K-27 PLANK ROAD
This street is the route of the Fayetteville-to-Salem plank road, a toll road 129 miles long, built 1849-54.

US 220 Business (Fayetteville Street) at Atlantic Avenue in Asheboro / 1948

K-54 CEDAR FALLS MILL
Chartered 1828; opened 1836. Jonathan Worth, N.C. governor (1865-68), its president. Supplied clothing for Confederate war effort. 2 mi. N.

US 64/NC 49 at SR 2221 (Trogdon Pond Road) east of Asheboro / 1989

KKK-1 MUSTERING OUT OF CONFEDERATE ARMY
General Johnston's men paid off and mustered out near here, May 1-2, 1865, after surrender near Durham, April 26.

NC 62 (Liberty Road) and US 311 (Main Street) in Archdale / 1962

Trinity College, 1882 (K 3)

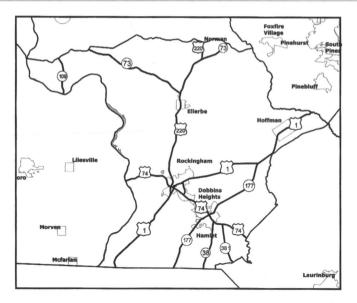

RICHMOND COUNTY

K-12   SHERMAN'S MARCH
Kilpatrick's Cavalry, a part of Sherman's Army, marching from Savannah to Goldsboro, passed through Rockingham on March 7-8, 1865.

US 1 in Rockingham / 1940

K-13   SHERMAN'S MARCH
As Sherman's army moved north from Georgia on its path of destruction, one part entered North Carolina near here, March 4-7, 1865.

US 1 south of Everetts Mill at NC/SC boundary / 1940

**K-23   NORTH CAROLINA-
SOUTH CAROLINA

NORTH CAROLINA**
Colonized, 1585-87, by first English settlers in America; permanently settled c. 1650; first to vote readiness for independence, Apr. 12, 1776.
(Reverse) SOUTH CAROLINA
Formed in 1712 from part of Carolina, which was chartered in 1663, it was first settled by the English in 1670. One of the 13 original states.

US 1 south of Everetts Mill at NC/SC boundary / 1941

**K-28   HENRY WILLIAM
HARRINGTON**
Brigadier general of militia, 1776-81, State senator, a commissioner to locate State capital. Grave is five miles S.

*US 1 North (Franklin Street)
in Rockingham* / 1948

**K-31   JOHN COLTRANE
1926-1967**
Jazz saxophonist and composer; influential stylist. Work spanned bebop to avant garde. Born one block S.W.

*US 74 (Hamlet Avenue) at Bridges Street
in Hamlet* / 1992

**Plaque at the birthplace of John Coltrane
(K 31)**

**Cameron Morrison (K 50), governor
(1921-1925)**

K-37　CAMERON MORRISON
SCHOOL

State home and school for boys, opened 1925. Gives academic, vocational, and agricultural training. Three miles W.

US 1 (Main Street) in Hoffman / 1954

K-42　CARTLEDGE CREEK
BAPTIST CHURCH

Originally Dockery's Meeting House, about 1774. Baptist State Convention, 1833, voted here to found Wake Forest Institute. About 4 miles North.

*US 74 at SR 1005 (Prison Camp Road)
northwest of Rockingham* / 1968

K-46　HAMLET STATION

Built in 1900 to serve Seaboard Air Line Railroad. Depot was major stop for passengers on east-west & north-south rail lines. About 2 blocks east.

*US 74 (Hamlet Avenue) at Wilmington Street
in Hamlet* / 1974

K-48　ALFRED DOCKERY
1797-1875

U.S. Congressman; state legislator for 10 years. A founder of the state Republican party, 1867. Home is 6 mi. northwest.

*US 1 North (Franklin Street)
in Rockingham* / 1974

K-50　CAMERON MORRISON
1869-1953

Governor, 1921-1925; State legislator; U.S. Senator & Congressman; mayor of Rockingham. Birthplace was 6 mi. S.

*US 1 North (Franklin Street)
in Rockingham* / 1975

K-53　N.C. FARMER'S
ALLIANCE

Organized by statewide convention of delegates in Rockingham, Oct. 4, 1887. Leonidas L. Polk elected first secretary.

*US 220 at Green Street
in Rockingham* / 1988

K-58　PEE DEE MEETING

Quaker meeting organized, 1755. Westward migration led to decline by the 1840s. Cemetery located 1fi mi. west.

*US 1 at SR 1108 (Klopman Mill Road
southeast of Rockingham* / 2000

KK-3　TOWN CREEK
INDIAN MOUND
STATE HISTORIC SITE

Pee Dee Indians migrated here during the 11th century A.D. and built their main village around 1300 A.D. Their reconstructed civic-ceremonial center, a site worked by archaeologists since 1937, is two miles north.

*NC 73 at SR 1160 (Indian Mound Road)
southeast of Mount Gilead* / 1960

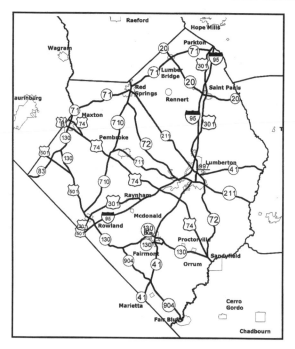

ROBESON COUNTY

I-20   ANGUS W. McLEAN
Governor, 1925-1929, assistant secretary of the United States Treasury, 1920-1921. His birthplace stood four miles north.

NC 71 northeast of Maxton / 1940

I-23   NORTH CAROLINA-
          SOUTH CAROLINA
          NORTH CAROLINA
Colonized, 1585-87, by first English settlers in America; permanently settled c. 1650; first to vote readiness for independence, Apr. 12, 1776.

(Reverse) SOUTH CAROLINA
Formed, 1712, from part of Carolina, which was chartered in 1663, it was first settled by the English in 1670. One of the 13 original states.

US 301/501 south of Rowland at NC/SC boundary / 1941

I-24   FLORA MacDONALD
          COLLEGE
Presbyterian. Founded in 1896. Closed 1961. Merged to create St. Andrews College. Was located 1 mi. east.

NC 71 (Third Avenue) at NC 211 (Main Street) in Red Springs / 1941

I-25   FLORAL COLLEGE
One of earliest colleges for women in the South, 1841-78. Centre Presbyterian Church, formerly the college chapel, is 150 yards north.

NC 71 northeast of Maxton / 1941

I-27   CAROLINA COLLEGE
          1911-1926
Site used by Presbyterian Jr. College 1929-60; Carolina Military Academy 1962-1972. One blk. south.

US 74 Business (Saunders Street) at Austin Street in Maxton / 1949

I-30   UNIVERSITY OF N.C.
          AT PEMBROKE
Established 1887 as the State Normal School for Indians. Since 1972 a campus of The University of North Carolina.

NC 711 (Third Street) in Pembroke / 1950

I-38   JOHN WILLIS
Founder of Lumberton, captain in Revolution, later brigadier general; member of legislature, conventions of 1788, '89. Plantation was here.

Pine Street, Cedar Street, and Godwin Avenue in Lumberton / 1953

I-39   ANGUS W. McLEAN
Governor, 1925-1929, Assistant Secretary of the United States Treasury, 1920-1921. Home is 1 mile south, grave 100 yards N.W.

Pine Street, Cedar Street, and Godwin Street in Lumberton / 1953

I-49   ASHPOLE CHURCH
Union center of worship, originally 2fi miles N.W. Presbyterians withdrew in 1796 and organized their own church here. 1860 building, 300 yds. W.

US 501/NC 130 at NC 710 northwest of Rowland / 1959

I-51   RAFT SWAMP
After the Tory victory at McPhaul's Mill, the Whigs routed the Tories near here on Oct. 15, 1781, and broke their resistance in this area.

NC 211 southeast of Red Springs / 1959

I-67   FIRST RURAL HEALTH DEPARTMENT
In 1912 Robeson County established first rural health department in U.S. three blocks N.

NC 72 (Second Street) between Elm and Chestnut Streets in Lumberton / 1986

I-68   CROATAN NORMAL SCHOOL
Est. in 1887 to educate teachers of Indian youth. Forerunner of Pembroke State University. Building was 2/10 mile east.

NC 710 at SR 1351 (Tucker Road) northwest of Pembroke / 1987

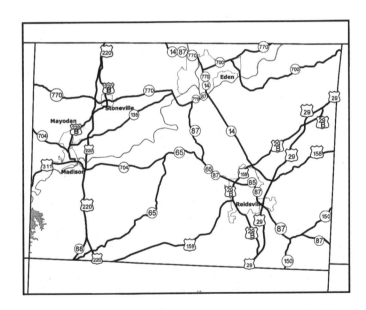

ROCKINGHAM COUNTY

J-7   "LAND OF EDEN"
20,000-acre estate of William Byrd, Virginia planter, author, surveyor of Va.-N.C. line, 1728. S.W. corner here.

NC 87 (South Hamilton Street) at Early Avenue in Eden / 1936

J-8   SPEEDWELL CHURCH
Presbyterian. Organized ca. 1759. James McCready first regular minister, 1793. Present building erected about 1844.

SR 2406 (Iron Works Road) at SR 2409 (Boyd Road) southwest of Reidsville / 1972

J-13   DAVID S. REID
Governor, 1851-54, U.S. Senator, Congressman, member of peace conference, 1861, and of state conventions, 1861, 1875. Home stands 2 blocks E.

Scales Street south of Settle Street
in Reidsville / 1939

J-14   STEPHEN A. DOUGLAS
Presidential nominee, 1860, United States Senator from Illinois, was married to Martha Martin, 1847, in house standing 2 miles N.E.

NC 704 east of Madison / 1939

J-15   ALEXANDER MARTIN
1738-1807
Governor, 1782-85 and 1789-92, officer in the Revolution, member Federal Convention of 1787, United States Senator. Home stood 1/2 mile N.

NC 704 east of Madison / 1939

J-16   TROUBLESOME IRON
WORKS
Used in the Revolution. Greene's army camped there after Battle of Guilford Courthouse, 1781. Washington was there, 1791. 1fi mi. north.

US 158 and SR 2422 (Monroeton Road)
at Monroeton / 1939

J-17   THOMAS SETTLE, JR.
1831-1888
Justice N.C. Supreme Court, served in N.C. House & Senate, Confederate captain, minister to Peru. Home is 2 mi. W.

SR 2150 (Settles Bridge Road) at SR 2145
(River Road) north of Dan River southwest
of Eden / 1970

J-25   "LAND OF EDEN"
Near here ran southern line of estate of Wm. Byrd, Virginia planter, author, and surveyor of Va.-N.C. boundary line, 1728.

NC 770 (Washington Street) east of NC 87
(Hamilton Street) in Eden / 1948

J-26   WRIGHT TAVERN
Built in 1816. Rare example of dog-run building. Operated by Wrights and Reids. Birthplace and home of Congressman J. W. Reid.

NC 65 at Wentworth / 1973

J-44   LOWER SAURA TOWN
A village of the Saura Indians, abandoned by that tribe in the early 18th century, was on Dan River, 2fi mi. N.E.

NC 14 southeast of Eden / 1955

J-45   ALFRED M. SCALES
1827-1892
Governor, 1885-1889, Confederate general, state legislator, and Congressman. Birthplace stood 3fi mi. E.

NC 87 at US 29 in Reidsville / 1955

J-47   O. P. FITZGERALD
Bishop of the Methodist Episcopal Church, South, 1890-1911; editor; author; Superintendent of Public Instruction, California. Born near here, 1829.

US 29 Business at Ruffin / 1956

J-56   JAMES HUNTER
Militant leader of the Regulators and their commander at the Battle of Alamance, 1771. Member N.C. Legislature, 1772-82. His grave is 8 mi. N.

NC 704 at US 220 southeast
of Madison / 1963

J-59   LENOX CASTLE
Also called Rockingham Springs. Council of State met here, 1790. Owned by John Lenox, Archibald D. Murphey, & Thomas Ruffin. Famous health resort.

NC 150 at Lenox Castle / 1970

J-60   HIGH ROCK FORD
Gen. Nathanael Greene maintained headquarters here, Feb. 28-Mar. 12, 1781, before meeting Cornwallis at Guilford Courthouse. Ford is 100 feet west.

SR 2614 (High Rock Road) at Haw River
bridge southeast of Reidsville / 1970

J-67   LUTHER H. HODGES
1898-1974
Governor, 1954-1961; U.S. Secretary of Commerce, 1961-1965. A founder of Research Triangle Park. Home is 100 yards east.

Boone Road at Highland Drive
in Eden / 1976

J-82   CALCIUM CARBIDE
Industrial experiment nearby in 1892 led to discovery of process for its manufacture. First produced commercially by James T. Morehead.

Church Street in Eden / 1985

J-88   BARNETT CANAL
Built near here by James Barnett in 1813. Later powered largest continuously operating textile complex in the northern piedmont.

NC 770 (Boone Road) at Church Street in Eden / 1989

J-90   SLINK SHOAL SLUICE
Dan River improvements built 1820s by Roanoke Navigation Co. include sluice & wing dams 1/4 mi. E. Rebuilt, 1880s.

US 220 Bypass at Dan River bridge east of Madison / 1989

J-91   LEAKSVILLE LANDING
Port for bateau trade on Dan River. Improved by Roanoke Navigation Company, 1820s. Ruins visible at low water. 200 yards west.

NC 87 (South Hamilton Street) at Dan River bridge in Eden / 1990

J-93   CHARLIE POOLE
1892-1931
Pioneer country music recording artist. With N.C. Ramblers, 1918-31, popularized old-time music. Grave 1/2 mi. SW.

NC 14 at SR 1700 (Fisher Hill Road) northwest of Eden / 1990

J-94   FIRST PUBLIC SCHOOL
IN N.C.
First free school in the state, established under Common School Law of 1839, opened January 20, 1840, in this vicinity.

NC 87 at SR 2598 (Cook Florist Road) southeast of Reidsville / 1990

Charlie Poole (J 93), left, and his fellow North Carolina Ramblers, Posey Rorrer and Norman Woodlieff

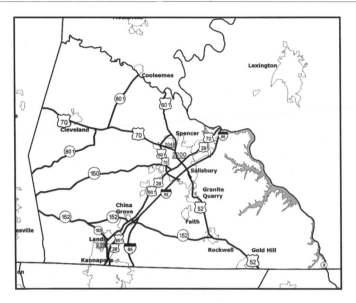

ROWAN COUNTY

L-2   CONFEDERATE PRISON
Enclosure, 16 acres. Once held 10,000 men.
Destroyed by Federals, 1865. Site one block
south.

East Innes Street at Long Street
in Salisbury / 1936

L-10   THYATIRA
Presbyterian Church. Founded about 1753.
Present building completed 1860. Grave of
Sam'l E. McCorkle. 600 yards north.

NC 150 and SR 1737 (White Road)
at Millbridge / 1937

Birdseye view of the Confederate Prison (L 2) at Salisbury

L-12   JOHN W. ELLIS
Governor, 1859-61. A leader of the secession movement in N.C. Died July, 1861, aged 40. Home stands 1fi blocks south.

West Innes Street at Ellis Street in Salisbury / 1938

L-14   "CHRISTIAN REID"
Mrs. Frances Fisher Tiernan, 1864-1920, author of "Land of the Sky" and other novels, is buried 200 yards northwest.

US 29/70/NC 150 (Main Street) in Salisbury / 1939

L-15   JOHN STEELE
Congressman, 1789-93, Comptroller of the United States Treasury, Federalist party leader. Home stands 2 blocks east.

US 29/70/NC 150 (Main Street) at Steele Street in Salisbury / 1939

L-17   RURAL FREE DELIVERY
The first mail over an R.F.D. route in N.C. was carried out of China Grove, October 23, 1896.

US 29 Alternate (Main Street) in China Grove / 1939

L-20   SAM'L E. McCORKLE
Presbyterian preacher and educator. The site of his famous academy, Zion Parnassus (about 1794 to 1798) is 3/4 of a mile north.

NC 150 west of Salisbury / 1939

L-21   GRIFFITH RUTHERFORD
Indian fighter, member provincial congresses, Revolutionary general. Home stood a few mi. W.

US 29 at US 29 Alternate northeast of China Grove / 1939

L-24   TRADING FORD
On famous trading path used by Indians and early settlers. There Greene, retreating from Cornwallis, crossed on Feb. 2, 1781. East 1 mi.

US 29/70/NC 150 at Yadkin River bridge northeast of Spencer / 1939

L-26   KNOX HOME
Home of the Knox family since colonial days. James Knox, grandfather of President James Knox Polk, lived there. House stood 4 miles west.

US 70 at SR 1001 (Amity Hill Road) in Cleveland / 1940

L-27   LEE S. OVERMAN
United States Senator, 1903-30, a leading supporter of Wilson's war policies, Speaker of House of Representatives. His home is here.

West Innes Street at Ellis Street in Salisbury / 1940

L-28   STONEMAN'S RAID
On a raid through western North Carolina Gen. Stoneman's U.S. cavalry fought a skirmish with southern troops near here, April 12, 1865.

US 70/601 (Jake Alexander Boulevard) at Grants Creek in Salisbury / 1940

L-29   STONEMAN'S RAID
Stoneman's U.S. cavalry occupied the town of Salisbury, Apr. 12, 1865, and destroyed the Confederate warehouses, supplies, and prison.

US 29/70/NC 150 (Main Street) at Liberty Street in Salisbury / 1940

L-30   TRADING PATH
Colonial trading route dating from 17th century, from Petersburg, Virginia, to Catawba and Waxhaw Indians in Carolina, passed nearby.

US 29/70/NC 150 (Main Street) at Seventeenth Street in Salisbury / 1941

L-41   THIRD CREEK CHURCH
Presbyterian. Founded before 1789. Present building erected 1835. Stands 2 miles north.

US 70 in Cleveland / 1948

L-44   ST. LUKE'S EPISCOPAL CHURCH
Parish established in 1753. Present building constructed in 1828, stands one block west.

US 29/70/NC 150 (Main Street) at Council Street in Salisbury / 1949

Grace or Lower Stone Church and Cemetery (L 45)

**L-45   GRACE OR LOWER
              STONE CHURCH**
Evangelical and Reformed. Organized by
early German settlers. Building erected 1795
is 2fi miles south.

US 52 (Main Street) in Rockwell / 1950

L-46 ORGAN OR ZION CHURCH
Lutheran. Organized by early German settlers. The building erected in 1794 is 1fi mi.
south.

NC 152 west of Rockwell / 1950

L-47   ANDREW JACKSON
Studied law under Spruce Macay, 1784-85, at
an office which stood 1 bl. W. Admitted to
the bar in Rowan County, Nov. 6, 1787.

*US 29/70/NC 150 (Main Street) at Fisher
Street in Salisbury* / 1951

L-59   CATAWBA COLLEGE
Coeducational, liberal arts. Affiliated with
Evangelical & Reformed Church. Opened at
Newton, 1851. Moved here, 1925, and
enlarged.

West Innes Street in Salisbury / 1956

L-60   OLD STONE HOUSE
Built 1766 by Michael Bräun. One of the few
remaining Pennsylvania German stone houses in North Carolina. Stands 1/2 mile N.E.

*US 52 at Old Stone House Road in
Granite Quarry* / 1959

L-61   FRANCIS LOCKE
Colonel of Whig force which routed Tories at
Battle of Ramsour's Mill, June 20, 1780.
Home stood nearby.

*NC 150 at SR 1728 (Briggs Road) west
of Salisbury* / 1959

L-62   MATTHEW LOCKE

Brigadier-General in the American Revolution. Member of the Provincial Congress. U.S. Congress, 1793-1799. Grave 1/4 mi. N.

NC 150 and SR 1737 (White Road) at Mill-bridge / 1959

L-63   MAXWELL CHAMBERS
HOUSE

A good example of the larger homes built about 1820. Now used by the Rowan Museum. Located 1/2 block south.

West Innes Street at Jackson Street in Salisbury / 1959

L-64   WASHINGTON'S
SOUTHERN TOUR

President Washington was a visitor in the town of Salisbury, May 30-31, 1791.

US 29/70/NC 150 (Main Street) at Council Street in Salisbury / 1962

L-70   SETZER SCHOOL

Restored one-room log school of 1840's. Now located at the Knox Junior High School, 1/4 mile east.

West Innes Street at Mahaley Avenue in Salisbury / 1965

L-71 OLD ENGLISH CEMETERY

Cornwallis' men buried here in 1781. Granted to city in 1770 by British government. Grave of Gov. John W. Ellis is here.

North Church Street in Salisbury / 1966

L-79   OLD STONE HOUSE

Home of Michael Braun. Built 1766; restored 1966 by Rowan Museum, Inc. Family burial ground 100 yards South.

Old Stone House Road in Granite Quarry / 1967

L-81   GOLD HILL MINING
DISTRICT

Gold discovered here by 1824. Extensive mining begun 1843, creating a boom town. Copper mined in district until 1907.

US 52 at Gold Hill / 1972

L-85   LIVINGSTONE COLLEGE

Founded as Zion Wesley Institute, 1879. Became College in 1885. Rev. J. C. Price president 1882-93. Named for British missionary. 5 blocks west.

US 29/70/150 (Main Street) at Monroe Street in Salisbury / 1975

L-89   JOSEPH C. PRICE
1854-1893

Minister, teacher, and founder of Livingstone College. Home stands here. Grave 700 ft. E.

West Monroe Street in Salisbury / 1978

M-35   PROSPECT CHURCH
AND ACADEMY

Presbyterian. Both founded in 1824. Plans for Davidson College adopted here in 1835.

NC 152 west of China Grove near Rowan/Iredell County line / 1965
[Numbered M-35 in error; should be in the L district.]

M-39   AUGUSTUS LEAZER

Introduced bill, 1885, for industrial school, now N.C. State University. Speaker of House, 1889; prison reformer. Taught at academy here.

NC 152 west of China Grove near Rowan/Iredell County line / 1967
[Numbered M-39 in error; should be in the L district.]

Joseph C. Price (L 89)

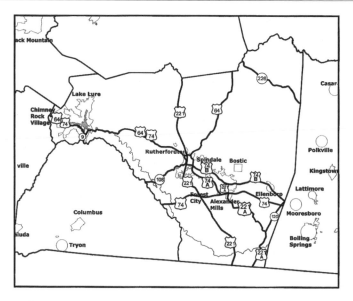

RUTHERFORD COUNTY

O-4   GILBERT TOWN
Rutherford County seat, 1781-85, stood here-
about. Before Battle of Kings Mountain both
armies camped nearby.

*US 221 at Hollands Creek in
Rutherfordton / 1938*

Christopher Bechtler (O 16 and O 17)

O-10   STONEMAN'S RAID
On a raid through western North Carolina
Gen. Stoneman's U.S. cavalry passed
through Rutherfordton, April 21, 1865.

*US 221 (Main Street) in Rutherfordton /
1940*

O-16   BECHTLER'S MINT
Established 1831, four miles N., by Christopher Bechtler. Later stood at this point.
Minted more than $2/million in gold. Closed
about 1849.

*US 74 Business (Washington Street) at Sixth
Street in Rutherfordton / 1941*

O-17   BECHTLER'S MINT
Established near here by Christopher
Bechtler in 1831. Later moved to Rutherfordton. Minted over $2/million in gold. Closed
about 1849.

*US 221 at Hollands Creek in
Rutherfordton / 1941*

**O-20   NORTH CAROLINA-
        SOUTH CAROLINA**
NORTH CAROLINA
Colonized, 1585-87, by first English settlers
in America; permanently settled c. 1650; first
to vote readiness for independence, Apr. 12,
1776.
(Reverse) SOUTH CAROLINA
Formed in 1712 from part of Carolina, which
was chartered in 1663, it was first settled by
the English in 1670. One of the 13 original
states.

*US 221 southeast of Harris at NC/SC
boundary* / 1941

**O-21   NORTH CAROLINA-
        SOUTH CAROLINA**
NORTH CAROLINA
Colonized, 1585-87, by first English settlers
in America; permanently settled c. 1650; first
to vote readiness for independence, Apr. 12,
1776.
(Reverse) SOUTH CAROLINA
Formed in 1712 from part of Carolina, which
was chartered in 1663, it was first settled by
the English in 1670. One of the 13 original
states.

*US 221 Alternate southwest of Cliffside at
NC/SC boundary* / 1941

O-31   ELISHA BAXTER
Governor of Arkansas, 1873-74; Union
colonel in Civil War; elected to U.S. Senate,
1864, but not seated. Birthplace stood 4⁄
miles S.E.

*US 74 Business (East Main Street) at US
221 Alternate (Broadway Street)
in Forest City* / 1950

O-36   BRITTAIN CHURCH
Presbyterian, organized 1768. Present building, the third, erected 1852, brick-veneered
1940.

US 64 northeast of Rutherfordton / 1951

O-37   JOSHUA FORMAN
Founder of Syracuse, N.Y., early advocate of
Erie Canal. Moved to N. Carolina, 1829.
Land and mining speculator. Grave is 50 yds.
east.

*US 221 (Main Street) in
Rutherfordton* / 1951

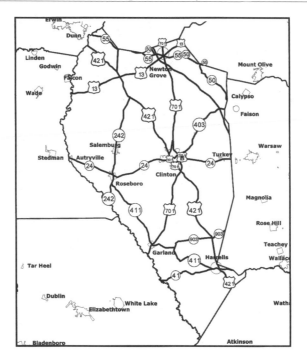

SAMPSON COUNTY

I-5   WILLIAM RUFUS KING
Congressman from N.C., 1811-16; Senator from Alabama for 29 years. Vice-President of the United States, 1853. Born six miles east.

US 701 and SR 1845 (Rosin Hill Road) at Monks Crossroads / 1936

I-6   GABRIEL HOLMES
1769-1829
Governor, 1821-1824; Congressman. His son, Theophilus Holmes, a Confederate general. Home stood 2 mi. SE.

US 701 north of Clinton / 1936

I-35   RICHARD CLINTON
Lieut. colonel militia, member Provincial Congress, 1775, legislature, conventions 1788, 1789. This town named for him. Home was nearby.

Main Street in Clinton / 1951

I-36   MARION BUTLER
United States Senator, 1896-1901. Populist-Republican. Supporter of education, sponsor of rural free delivery act. Birthplace is here.

NC 242 north of Salemburg / 1951

I-40   THOMAS O. MOORE
1804-1876
Governor of Louisiana, 1860-1864; a leader of the secession movement. His birthplace stood 4fi miles northwest.

NC 24 in Turkey / 1953

I-44   GUN FACTORY
A Revolutionary arms manufactory in this vicinity was operated by Richard Herring and John Devane until destroyed by the Tories.

NC 41 at Black River bridge west of Harrells / 1954

I-53   PINELAND COLLEGE -
EDWARDS MILITARY INSTITUTE
Founded 1875. Includes kindergarten through junior college. Campus is 250 yards west.

NC 242 (Main Street)in Salemburg / 1960

I-58   BLACK RIVER CHURCH
Presbyterian. Organized 1740. Present building constructed 1859. First regular pastor was the Rev. Colin Lindsay.

SR 1100 (Ivanhoe Road) at SR 1102 (Eddie L. Jones Road) south of Ivanhoe / 1968

I-69 STEAMBOAT TRADE
Naval stores and lumber were primary cargo on vessels navigating Black River, ca. 1875-

1914. Remains of the steamer *A. J. Johnson* 60 yds. S.

NC 411 at Black River bridge at Clear Run / 1988

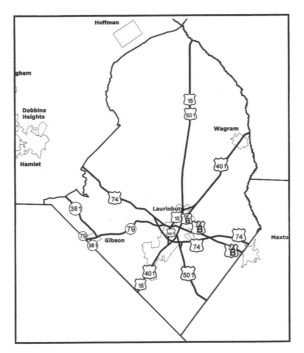

SCOTLAND COUNTY

I-3 JOHN CHARLES McNEILL
Notable North Carolina poet, 1874-1907. House in which he was born restored at his burial site 1fi miles west.

US 401 (Main Street) in Wagram / 1936

I-15 SHERMAN'S MARCH
As Sherman's army moved north from Georgia on its path of destruction, one part entered North Carolina near here, March 4-7, 1865.

US 15/401 southwest of Laurinburg at NC/SC boundary / 1940

I-16 SHERMAN'S MARCH
As Sherman's army moved north from Georgia, several units passed through Laurel Hill and camped in this vicinity, March 8-9, 1865.

US 74 near Laurel Hill / 1940

John Charles McNeill (I 3)

I-19   SHERMAN'S MARCH
A part of Sherman's army, marching from Savannah to Goldsboro, camped at Laurel Hill Presbyterian Church, 2/3 mi. SW, Mar. 8-9, 1865.

US 15/501 at SR 1319 (Wire Road) north of Laurinburg / 1940

**I-22   NORTH CAROLINA-
SOUTH CAROLINA
NORTH CAROLINA**
Colonized, 1585-87, by first English settlers in America; permanently settled c. 1650; first to vote readiness for independence, Apr. 12, 1776.

(Reverse) SOUTH CAROLINA
Formed in 1712 from part of Carolina, which was chartered in 1663, it was first settled by the English in 1670. One of the 13 original states.

US 15/401 southwest of Laurinburg at NC/SC boundary / 1941

I-46   JAMES LYTCH
Invented Lytch cotton planter (patented 1878), a favorite in the South, and other implements. Shops were 1/4 mile S.W. This was his home.

SR 1108 (West Boulevard) southeast of Gibson / 1957

I-48   TEMPERANCE HALL
Meeting hall of the Richmond Temperance and Literary Society, 1860 to 1890's. Sacked by Sherman's army in 1865. Stands 1fi mi. W.

US 401 (Main Street) in Wagram / 1959

**I-56   ST. ANDREWS
PRESBYTERIAN COLLEGE**
Chartered 1958; opened 1961. Formed by merger of colleges dating from 1858. Coeducational, four-year liberal arts college.

US 15/401 in Laurinburg / 1966

**I-57   STEWARTSVILLE
CEMETERY**
Begun 1785. Congressman James Stewart gave land. J. C. McLaurin, who founded Laurinburg, and many Scots buried here. Two miles southeast.

US 74 Business at SR 1611 (South Rocky Ford Road) east of Laurinburg / 1967

Temperance Hall (I 48)

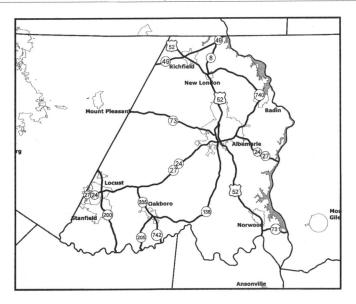

STANLY COUNTY

L-51 FIGHT AT COLSON'S

Colonel William Lee Davidson's Whig militia defeated Colonel Samuel Bryan's Tories, in July, 1780, a few miles S.E.

*US 52 at Rocky River bridge south
of Norwood* / 1952

L-73 PFEIFFER UNIVERSITY

Methodist. Founded as Oberlin Home & School near Lenoir, 1885. Moved here 1910. Renamed for Pfeiffer family, 1935.

US 52 at Misenheimer / 1962

**L'Aluminium Français (L 95), a French manufacturer of aluminum, financed construction
of the Narrows Dam, shown here around 1915.**

L-83   RANDALL'S UNITED METHODIST CHURCH

First services held ca. 1785 by Jesse Lee & Bishop Asbury in home of John Randle. Fifth building, 1974, 3/4 mile East.

SR 1743 (Randall's Church Road) at SR 1740 (Indian Mound Road) north of Norwood / 1974

L-95   L'ALUMINIUM FRANÇAIS

French company in 1913 began Narrows Dam and town named for Adrien Badin, president Southern Aluminum, a subsidiary. Office stood 1/2 mi. N.W.

NC 740 at SR 1719 (Falls Road) in Badin / 1995

L-97   HARDAWAY SITE

Archaeological site key to understanding earliest native population. Its occupation dates to ca. 10,000 B.C. One mi. N.E.

NC 740 in Badin / 1998

L-98   BARRINGER MINE

Gold discovery in 1825 by Mathias Barringer launched the state's subsurface gold mining industry. Site 2 mi. W.

NC 49 at US 52 (Church Street) in Richfield / 1999

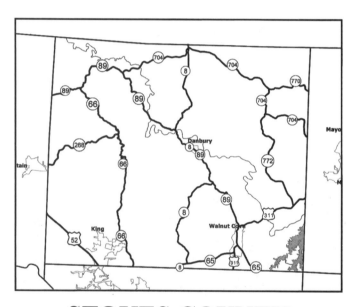

STOKES COUNTY

J-12   BENJAMIN FORSYTH

Officer in the War of 1812. Mortally wounded in Canada, 1814. Forsyth County named for him. Home stood a few feet north of this spot.

NC 8/65 at Germantown / 1939

J-18   STONEMAN'S RAID

On a raid through western North Carolina Gen. Stoneman's U.S. cavalry passed through Danbury, April 9, 1865.

NC 8/89 (Main Street) in Danbury / 1940

J-28   NORTH CAROLINA-VIRGINIA

NORTH CAROLINA

Colonized, 1585-87, by first English settlers in America; permanently settled c. 1650; first to vote readiness for independence, Apr. 12, 1776.

(Reverse)   VIRGINIA

First permanent English colony in America, 1607, one of thirteen original states. Richmond, the capital, was seat of Confederate government.

NC 8 north of Lawsonville at NC/VA boundary / 1949

J-39　JOSEPH WINSTON
Major in Revolution, a commander at Kings Mountain, Congressman, state legislator. Town of Winston named for him. Home was 4 mi. W.

NC 65 at US 311 (Stokesbury Road) southwest in Walnut Cove / 1954

J-43　UPPER SAURA TOWN
A village of the Saura Indians, abandoned by that tribe in the early 18th century, was on Dan River, two mi. S.

US 311 at Dan River bridge northeast of Walnut Cove / 1955

J-53　GABRIEL MOORE
Governor of Alabama, 1829-1831. Served in U.S. House and Senate. Official of Mississippi and Alabama Territories. Born near here, 1785.

NC 8/89 (Main Street) in Danbury / 1962

J-68　BEAN SHOALS CANAL
Attempted ca. 1820-25 by Hiram Jennings for Yadkin Navigation Co. Hamilton Fulton was consultant. Never completed. Ruins located 5 miles S.W.

SR 1147 (Perch Road) at US 52 south of Pinnacle / 1976

J-76　LEWIS DAVID von SCHWEINITZ 1780-1834
Moravian administrator. Botanist and pioneer in American mycology. Discovered falls 3 mi. SW.

NC 8/89 and SR 1001 (Moores Springs Road) at Hanging Rock State Park / 1979

J-98　MORATOCK FURNACE
Smelting furnace built by Nathaniel Moody in 1843. It supplied iron to Confederacy, 1862-1865. Stands 3/10 mi. NE.

NC 8/89 (Main Street) at Shepard Mill Road in Danbury / 1992

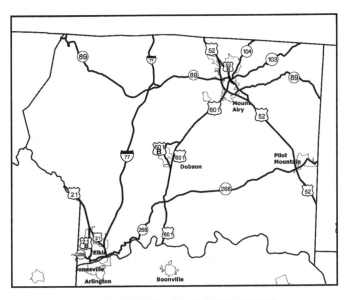

SURRY COUNTY

M-6　JESSE FRANKLIN
Governor 1820-21; state & U.S. Senator and representative; officer in Revolution. His home stood 1/4 mile south.

NC 89 at Low Gap / 1940

M-7　SIAMESE TWINS
Eng and Chang, the Siamese twins, born in 1811 in Siam, settled as farmers in this neighborhood. Died 1874. Grave 100 yards west.

SR 2258 (Old US 601) at White Plains / 1940

Chang and Eng Bunker (M 7)

M-8   STONEMAN'S RAID
On a raid through western North Carolina
Gen. Stoneman's U.S. cavalry passed
through Mount Airy, April 2-3, 1865.

*Main Street at West Oak Street
in Mount Airy* / 1940

M-9   STONEMAN'S RAID
On a raid through western North Carolina
Gen. Stoneman's U.S. cavalry passed
through Dobson, April 2, 1865.

*US 601 Business (Main Street)
in Dobson* / 1940

M-26   PILOT MOUNTAIN
Landmark for Indians and pioneer settlers.
Elevation 2,420 feet. State park since 1968.
Stands 3 miles west.

*SR 2053 (Pilot Mountain Park Road) at
Pilot Mountain State Park* / 1951

**M-50   TABITHA A. HOLTON
1854-1886**
First woman licensed to practice law in North
Carolina, 1878. Lived thirty yards northwest.

*US 601 Business (Main Street) at Kapp
Street in Dobson* / 1993

**M-51   HARDIN TALIAFERRO
1811-1875**
Humorist, minister, and editor. Wrote *Fisher's River Scenes* (1859), a collection of folk
tales with local settings. He was born 2 miles
N.W.

*NC 89 and SR 1396 (Pine Ridge Road)
at Pine Ridge* / 1993

Pilot Mountain (M 26)

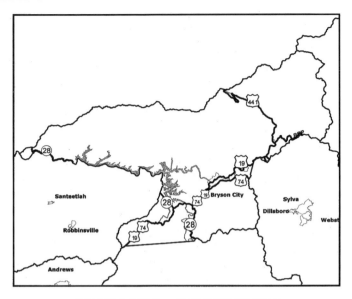

SWAIN COUNTY

Q-3 TSALI
Cherokee brave, surrendered to Gen'l Scott to be shot near here, 1838, that remnant of tribe might remain in N.C.

US 19 (Main Street) in Bryson City / 1937

Q-7 CHEROKEE DEFEAT
During the American Revolution a South Carolina force under Col. Andrew Williamson defeated the Cherokees near here, Sept., 1776.

NC 28 north of Swain/Macon County line / 1939

Q-12 YONAGUSKA
ca. 1760-1839
Chief of Oconaluftee Cherokee. He advocated temperance and opposed removal of his people from their homeland. Lived in this vicinity.

US 19 northeast of Bryson City / 1939

Q-14 CHEROKEE INDIAN RESERVATION
Established by United States for the Eastern Band of Cherokee after the removal of 1838.

(Reverse) (LEAVING)
CHEROKEE INDIAN RESERVATION
Established by United States for the Eastern Band of Cherokee after the removal of 1838.

US 19 southwest of Cherokee / 1939

Q-28 NORTH CAROLINA-
TENNESSEE
NORTH CAROLINA
Colonized, 1585-87, by first English settlers in America; permanently settled c. 1650; first to vote readiness for independence, Apr. 12, 1776.

(Reverse) TENNESSEE
Settled before 1770 by North Carolina-Virginia pioneers, ceded by North Carolina to the United States, 1789, admitted to the Union, 1796.

US 129 at Deals Gap at NC/TN boundary / 1941

Q-41 HORACE KEPHART
Author of "Our Southern Highlanders" (1913) and other works, naturalist, librarian. Grave 3/10 mi. S.W. Mt. Kephart, 30 mi. N., is named for him.

US 19 (Main Street) in Bryson City / 1951

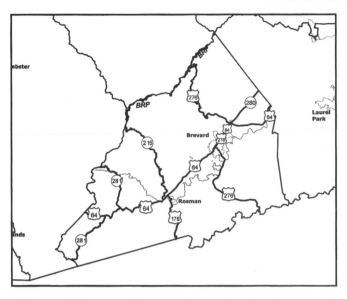

TRANSYLVANIA COUNTY

**P-12 NORTH CAROLINA-
SOUTH CAROLINA**

NORTH CAROLINA

Colonized, 1585-87, by first English settlers in America; permanently settled c. 1650; first to vote readiness for independence, Apr. 12, 1776.

(Reverse) SOUTH CAROLINA

Formed in 1712 from part of Carolina, which was chartered in 1663, it was first settled by the English in 1670. One of the 13 original states.

*US 178 south of Rosman at NC/SC
boundary* / 1941

**P-13 NORTH CAROLINA-
SOUTH CAROLINA**

NORTH CAROLINA

Colonized, 1585-87, by first English settlers in America; permanently settled c. 1650; first to vote readiness for independence, Apr. 12, 1776.

(Reverse) SOUTH CAROLINA

Formed in 1712 from part of Carolina, which was chartered in 1663, it was first settled by the English in 1670. One of the 13 original states.

*NC 276 south of Cedar Mountain at NC/SC
boundary* / 1941

**P-15 A. S. MERRIMON
1830-1892**

U.S. Senator, 1873-79; Chief Justice of State Supreme Court, 1889-92. Birthplace was 1 mi. E.

*US 64 at SR 1331 (Whitmire Road)
southwest of Brevard* / 1948

P-47 ESTATOE PATH

Trading route between mountain settlements of the Cherokee and their town Estatoe, in what is now South Carolina, passed nearby.

*US 178 at French Broad River bridge in
Rosman* / 1956

A. S. Merrimon (P 15)

The 1908 graduating class of the Biltmore Forestry School (P 59), often called the "Cradle of Forestry." Founder C. A. Schenck is in the center framed by the door.

P-48   ESTATOE PATH

Trading route between mountain settlements of the Cherokee and their town, Estatoe, in what is now South Carolina, passed nearby.

US 64/276 at Davidson River bridge north-east of Brevard / 1956

P-59   FORESTRY SCHOOL

First U.S. school of forestry. Established 1898 by Dr. C. A. Schenck, chief forester, Biltmore estate. Location until 1909 was nearby.

US 276 in Pisgah National Forest / 1965

P-67 CIVILIAN CONSERVATION CORPS

CCC camps were established as a New Deal relief measure. Camp John Rock, among first, opened here, 1933-36.

US 276 in Pisgah National Forest / 1986

P-70   BREVARD COLLEGE

Methodist. Opened 1934 on campus of Brevard Institute after merger of Rutherford College (est. 1853) and Weaver College (est. 1873).

US 64 Bypass (Broad Street) in Brevard / 1988

P-76   "WALTON WAR"

A boundary dispute in 1804 between N.C. & Ga. led to armed conflict. Militia called out after constable John Havner was killed 1/2 mile E.

US 276 southeast of Brevard / 1992

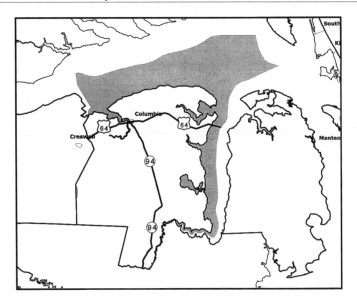

TYRRELL COUNTY

B-20   EDWARD WARREN
Born in Tyrrell County, 1828, Surgeon General of N.C., 1862-65, Professor of Surgery in Maryland, Chief Surgeon of Egypt, died in Paris.

US 64 Business (Main Street)
in Columbia / 1941

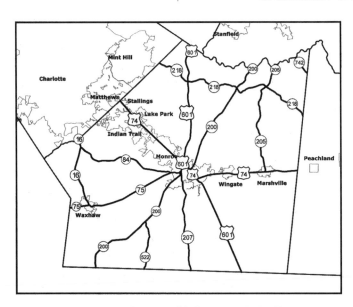

UNION COUNTY

L-6   WM. HENRY BELK
1862-1952
Merchant, philanthropist, and Presbyterian layman. Opened first store, May 29, 1888, two blocks east.

NC 200 (Charlotte Avenue) at NC 75/84
(Franklin Street) in Monroe / 1988

L-11   ANDREW JACKSON
Seventh president of the United States, was born a few miles southwest of this spot, March 15, 1767.

NC 75 (South Main Street) at Rehobeth
Road in Waxhaw / 1938

L-16   CORNWALLIS
First led his army into North Carolina near here, Sept. 1780. After Battle of Kings Mountain, Oct. 7, he returned to S.C.

NC 200 south of Waxhaw at NC/SC boundary / 1939

L-32   FERDINAND FOCH
Commander-in-chief of Allied armies, 1918, made a speech at the Union County Court-house, on December 9, 1921.

NC 200 (South Hayne Street) at Jefferson Street in Monroe / 1941

L-34   TRADING PATH
Colonial trading route, dating from the seventeenth century, from Petersburg, Virginia, to the Waxhaw Indians in Carolina, passed nearby.

US 74 at SR 1008 (Indian Trail Road) in Indian Trail / 1941

L-35   TRADING PATH
Colonial trading route, dating from the seventeenth century, from Petersburg, Virginia, to the Waxhaw Indians in Carolina, passed nearby.

NC 75 (Main Street) at NC 16 (Broom Street) in Waxhaw / 1941

L-54   DAVID F. HOUSTON
Secretary of Agriculture and later of the Treasury under Wilson. College president and author. His birthplace stood 60 yards north.

Stewart Street at Jefferson Street in Monroe / 1954

L-57   T. WALTER BICKETT
Governor, 1917-21, first in state nominated by a Democratic primary. N.C. Attorney General, state legislator. Birthplace was 50 ft. north.

Jefferson Street at Beasley Street in Monroe / 1955

L-58   WINGATE UNIVERSITY
Baptist. Est. as Wingate School in 1896; a junior college, 1923; became a senior college in 1977. University since 1995. Campus one block north.

US 74 (Monroe Street) in Wingate / 1955

L-67   CAMP SUTTON
World War II army camp, trained 13,000 engineers. Named for R.C.A.F. pilot Frank Sutton of Monroe, killed December 7, 1941. Camp was here.

US 74 in Monroe / 1965

**L-68   PLEASANT GROVE
          CAMP GROUND**
Methodist. Established before 1830 and still in use. Noted for unusual "arbor" and "tents." 1/ miles northwest.

NC 75 and SR 1327 (Pleasant Grove Road) at Mineral Springs / 1962

**L-88   A. R. NEWSOME
          1894-1951**
Educator, author, editor; Sec'y of N.C. Historical Commission, 1926-35. Birthplace 1 block east.

NC 205 (North Elm Street) in Marshville / 1977

**L-90   JOHN J. PARKER
          1885-1958**
Chief judge, U.S. Fourth Circuit, 1931-58; alternate member, Nuremberg tribunal, 1945-46. He was born one block SE.

Franklin Street at Houston Street in Monroe / 1987

L-94   DAVIE'S ATTACK
Cavalry led by William R. Davie attacked and dispersed band of Tories, September 20, 1780, at the plantation of James Wauchope, 3fi mi. NW.

NC 200 at SR 1100 (Tirzah Church Road) south of Waxhaw / 1991

**L-100   SAMUEL I. PARKER
           1891-1975**
One of two North Carolinians awarded Medal of Honor for service in World War I (France, 1917-18). Born 1 blk. SE.

Franklin Street at Houston Street in Monroe / 2000

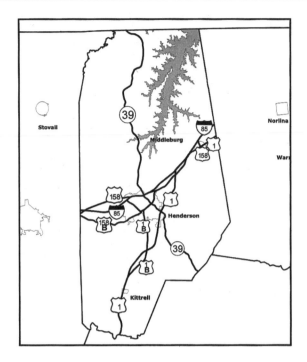

VANCE COUNTY

G-20 WILLIAMSBOROUGH
Eighteenth century town, named for John Williams, judge, state legislator, congressman, who lived nearby. Old St. John's Church is here.

NC 39 and SR 1329 (Boyd Road) at Williamsboro / 1939

G-42 KITTRELL'S SPRINGS
Health resort, social and recreational center in nineteenth century. Springs are 1/2 mi. W.

US 1 in Kittrell / 1948

G-44 WILLIAM HAWKINS 1777-1819
Governor, 1811-1814; speaker, State House of Commons, 1810-1811. His home, Pleasant Hill, stands one mile N.W.

US 1/158 in Middleburg / 1948

G-46 JAMES TURNER
Governor, 1802-1805, United States Senator, 1805-1816, and State legislator. Oakland, his home, stood 1 mile E.

NC 39 and SR 1329 (Boyd Road) at Williamsboro / 1948

G-47 BINGHAM SCHOOL
First military school in North Carolina, was founded in 1826 by D. H. Bingham. Moved to Littleton in 1829. Stood nearby.

NC 39 and SR 1329 (Boyd Road) at Williamsboro / 1948

G-49 ST. JOHN'S EPISCOPAL CHURCH
Parish established in 1746. Present building, constructed in 1757, stands 200 yds. west.

NC 39 and SR 1329 (Boyd Road) at Williamsboro / 1949

G-62 RICHARD HENDERSON
Founder of Transylvania Colony (Ky.) & Nashville (Tenn.), author Cumberland Compact (1780), judge, member of N.C. Council of State. Grave 1 mi. N.

SR 1319 (Satterwhite Road) north of Henderson / 1954

G-74 THE GLASS HOUSE
Noted winter health resort patronized by Northern hunters and tuberculosis patients. Opened 1871; burned 1893. Site is 1/2 mi. W.

US 1 in Kittrell / 1959

St. John's Episcopal Church (G 49) at Williamsboro

G-99 LEONARD HENDERSON
1772-1833

Jurist and educator. Member of first N.C. Supreme Court; Chief Justice, 1829-1833. His grave is 1/2 mi. W.

NC 39 south of Williamsboro / 1986

G-106 NUTBUSH ADDRESS

Document issued June 6, 1765, protesting abuses by local officials. Later spurred the Regulator movement. Author, George Sims, lived nearby.

NC 39 at Townsville / 1989

G-107 MARY L. WYCHE
1858-1936

A pioneer in field of organized nursing. In 1902 she founded the N.C. Nurses' Association. Home was 7/10 mile W.

NC 39 at SR 1308 (Harris Road) south of Williamsboro / 1989

GGG-1 CONFEDERATE CEMETERY

Graves of 52 soldiers individually marked, who died in the Kittrell Springs Hotel hospital 1864-65, are 1/2 mi. NE.

US 1 north of Kittrell / 1962

Mary L. Wyche (G 107)

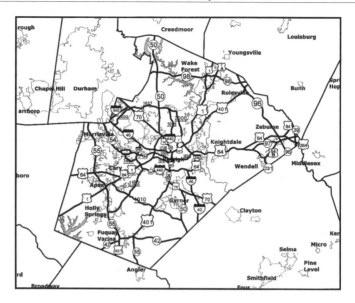

WAKE COUNTY

H-2   JOEL LANE HOUSE
Built prior to 1770 and often site of political meetings. Decision to locate Raleigh on Lane's land made there, 1792. Stands 2 blocks south.

Hillsborough Street at Saint Mary's Street
in Raleigh / 1935

H-3   ISAAC HUNTER'S TAVERN
Stood nearby. State Capital located within 10 miles by order N.C. Convention, 1788.
Wake Forest Road in Raleigh / 1935

H-4   STATE CAPITOL
Built 1833-40. Ithiel Towne, A. J. Davis and David Paton, architects. First State House built here, 1796; burned, 1831.
Morgan Street in Raleigh / 1936

H-5   STATE BANK BUILDING
Built about 1813 for State Bank; used 1873-1951 as Christ Church Rectory; moved and re-opened as bank, 1969.
New Bern Avenue in Raleigh / 1936

Dorothea Dix Hospital (H 7), authorized in 1849 and completed in 1854

H-6   ANDREW JOHNSON
1808-1875

President of the United States, 1865-69. Born near here in a kitchen now located 1 mile N.E.

Morgan Street at Wilmington Street
in Raleigh / 1936

H-7 DOROTHEA DIX HOSPITAL

Authorized 1849, largely through work of Dorothea L. Dix, crusader for better care of the mentally ill. 500 yards southwest.

South Boylan Avenue in Raleigh / 1936

H-8   GOVERNOR'S PALACE

Completed 1816. Vance was the last governor to reside there, 1862-5. Stood 50 yards south.

South Street in Raleigh / 1936

H-9   PEACE COLLEGE

Founded by Presbyterian elder Wm. Peace 1857 as school for women; opened 1872. Main building used as Confederate hospital & by Freedmen's Bureau.

Peace Street in Raleigh / 1961

H-11   ANDREW JOHNSON
1808-1875

The small kitchen in which the seventeenth President of the United States was born stands 64 yards west.

Wake Forest Road in Raleigh / 1938

H-13   JOHN CHAVIS

Early 19th century free Negro preacher and teacher of both races in North Carolina. Memorial park 200 yards east.

East Street at Worth Street in Raleigh / 1938

H-20   WALTER HINES PAGE
1855-1918

Journalist, editor, and publisher. Ambassador to Great Britain, 1913-1918. His birthplace stood 400 yards north.

East Chatham Street in Cary / 1939

H-21   GEORGE E. BADGER

Secretary of the Navy, 1841; United States Senator, 1846-55; judge of the superior court; staunch nationalist. Grave 1/3 mile north.

New Bern Avenue at Seawell Street
in Raleigh / 1939

H-22   EXPERIMENTAL
RAILROAD

Est. 1833. Horses hauled granite for the Capitol over a railroad from a quarry 1/ miles S.E.

Wilmington Street in Raleigh / 1939

H-23   RALEIGH AND GASTON
RAILROAD

Chartered in 1835 and completed in 1840. Length 85 miles. Its southern terminus was 400 ft. W.

Wilmington Street at North Street
in Raleigh / 1939

H-25 NORTH CAROLINA STATE
UNIVERSITY AT RALEIGH

Chartered 1887. Opened 1889 as a land grant college. Since 1931 campus of Consolidated University.

Hillsborough Street in Raleigh / 1939

H-26   CAMP BRYAN GRIMES

Spanish-American War camp, 95 acres, named for the Confederate general, was located here. Only U.S. Army camp in the state, 1898.

Hillsborough Street in Raleigh / 1939

H-27   LEONIDAS L. POLK

President Nat'l Farmers' Alliance 1889-92; founder Progressive Farmer; a founder of N.C.S.U. and Meredith College. Home stands 75 yds. West.

North Person Street in Raleigh / 1939

H-29   FALL OF RALEIGH

Commissioners of North Carolina's capital met officers of Sherman's army near this spot, on April 13, 1865, and surrendered the city.

Garner Road in Raleigh / 1940

H-30   OLD BREASTWORKS

Breastworks were thrown up around Raleigh, 1863, by order of Governor Vance, for protection against Federal raids. Remains are 1/3 mile W.

Wake Forest Road at Poplar Street in
Raleigh / 1940

H-31   GENERAL GRANT
In the Governor's Palace April 24-27, 1865, Grant conferred with Sherman and approved new terms for surrender of Johnston's Confederate Army.
South Street in Raleigh / 1940

H-32   SHAW UNIVERSITY
Founded 1865 by Baptist missionary Henry Martin Tupper. Chartered 1875; named for benefactor Elijah Shaw of Mass.
South Street in Raleigh / 1940

H-33   PETTIGREW HOSPITAL
Site of Confederate hospital, U.S. Army barracks, Confederate Soldiers' Home, 1891-1938.
New Bern Avenue in Raleigh / 1940

H-34 N.C. STATE FAIR, 1873-1925
STATE EXPOSITION OF 1884
CAMP POLK
The area across Hillsborough Street from this site, today combining commercial and residential use, has a varied history with particular significance to the development of North Carolina State University. Extending from Brooks Avenue to Horne Street, the tract was from 1873 to 1925 the second site of the North Carolina State Fair. In October 1884 the fairgrounds hosted the State Exposition which promoted agriculture and mechanic arts, thereby boosting the state's industrial growth. Exposition president William S. Primrose served as first chairman of the trustees of the North Carolina College of Agriculture and Mechanic Arts (present-day N.C. State University), founded in 1887. The site in 1918 was part of Camp Polk, a World War I tank training facility.
Hillsborough Street in Raleigh / 1940
(revised 1994)

H-35   STATE MUSEUM
OF NATURAL HISTORY
Begun about 1851 by the State Geologist. Administered since 1879 by Dept. of Agriculture. Entrance 150 feet north.
Edenton Street in Raleigh / 1941

H-36   SAINT MARY'S
Episcopal School for girls, established 1842 by Rev. Aldert Smedes on site of an earlier Episcopal School for boys, which opened 1834.
Hillsborough Street in Raleigh / 1941

H-37   HAYWOOD HALL
Built 1800-1801 by John Haywood, N.C. treasurer, 1787-1827. Operated now by the National Society of the Colonial Dames of America in State of N.C.
New Bern Place in Raleigh / 1952

H-38   MEREDITH COLLEGE
A Baptist College for women, chartered 1891, opened 1899, named for Thomas Meredith, the founder of the *Biblical Recorder*, 1835.
Hillsborough Street in Raleigh / 1942

H-39   JOSEPHUS DANIELS
Secretary of the Navy, 1913-21; ambassador to Mexico; author; editor, *News and Observer*. His home was here.
Glenwood Avenue north of intersection with Wade Avenue in Raleigh / 1948

H-45   FIRST N.C. STATE FAIR
Sponsored by the State Agricultural Society, the fair was held here, October 18-21, 1853.
New Bern Avenue in Raleigh / 1948

H-46   THE GOVERNOR
MOREHEAD SCHOOL
Established for visually impaired students in 1845 under leadership of John Motley Morehead. Present plant is 500 yards north.
Western Boulevard in Raleigh / 1949

H-47   THE GOVERNOR
MOREHEAD SCHOOL
Established for visually impaired students in 1845 under leadership of John Motley Morehead. Present plant is 3 blocks south.
Hillsborough Street at Ashe Avenue in Raleigh / 1949

H-52   L. O'B. BRANCH
Confederate brigadier general; president of Raleigh and Gaston Railroad, 1852-55; member of Congress, 1855-61. Home here, grave 2/3 mi. east.
Hillsborough Street at Dawson Street in Raleigh / 1949

H-53   J. MELVILLE BROUGHTON 1888-1949

Governor, 1941-45; U.S. Senator, 1948-49. Member, General Assembly, 1927, 1929. Home was two blocks west.

Glenwood Avenue in Raleigh / 1950

H-54   "ELMWOOD"

Home of chief justices John L. Taylor & Thos. Ruffin; of Wm. Gaston, Romulus M. Saunders, & Samuel A. Ashe. Built about 1813. Is 70 yds. N.

Hillsborough Street in Raleigh / 1950

H-55   JOHN L. TAYLOR 1769-1829

First Chief Justice of N.C. Supreme Court, 1819-1829; author of numerous legal works. Grave is 1/2 mi. E. Home is 1 mi. S.W.

North Person Street at Oakwood Avenue in Raleigh / 1950

H-56   THE GOVERNOR MOREHEAD SCHOOL

This branch of the school was established in 1869 for visually or aurally impaired students. Located on this site in 1929.

Old Garner Road in Raleigh / 1950

H-58   MANGUM TERRACE

Early erosion-checking terrace, constructed by Priestly H. Mangum about 1885, widely copied in other parts of the U.S. Remains are 2 mi. N.

NC 98 west of Wake Forest / 1950

H-59   JOSIAH W. BAILEY

United States Senator, 1931-1946. A Baptist leader and editor of "The Biblical Recorder." Home was here.

North Blount Street in Raleigh / 1951

H-64   WILLIS SMITH

United States Senator, 1950-53, speaker N.C. House of Representatives, president American Bar Assn. Home is 100 yds. W., grave is two miles S.E.

Glenwood Avenue at Saint Mary's Street in Raleigh / 1955

H-65   NORTH CAROLINA DENTAL SOCIETY

Organized in 1856 in the Guion Hotel, which stood here. Dr. W. F. Bason, Haw River, first president.

Edenton Street in Raleigh / 1956

H-66   CENTRAL PRISON

State prison site since 1869. Original buildings completed in 1884. First supt., W. J. Hicks. New facility finished 1983.

Western Boulevard in Raleigh / 1959

H-67   OAKWOOD CEMETERY

Governors Aycock, Bragg, Fowle, Holden, Swain, and Worth, other notables and Confederates buried there. 3 blocks E.

North Person Street at Oakwood Avenue in Raleigh / 1959

H-68   WAKE FOREST UNIVERSITY

Baptist; coeducational. Opened as Wake Forest College, 1834. Moved to Winston-Salem, 1956. University since 1967.

US 1 Alternate (South Main Street) in Wake Forest / 1936

H-69   WILLIAM BOYLAN

President of Raleigh and Gaston Railroad; president of the State Bank; publisher of the Raleigh "Minerva" 1803-1810. Home is 3 blks. S.W.

Hillsborough Street in Raleigh / 1959

H-70   MEDICAL SOCIETY OF NORTH CAROLINA

Successor to earlier group founded in 1799. Formed here in 1849. Dr. Edmund Strudwick was first president.

Edenton Street in Raleigh / 1959

H-71   JOHN S. RAVENSCROFT

First Episcopal Bishop of the Diocese of N.C., 1823-1830. Active in the revival of the Church. Interred in church 50 yds. south.

Edenton Street in Raleigh / 1959

**H-75   WAKE FOREST
COLLEGE BIRTHPLACE**

This simple provincial house was built before 1820. For some years it was the home of Dr. Calvin Jones, a founder of the North Carolina Medical Society, major-general in the War of 1812 and Grand Master of the Masonic Order in North Carolina. He was for 30 years a trustee of the University of North Carolina.

In 1832 Dr. Jones sold his home and plantation at Wake Forest to the Baptist State Convention. On February 3, 1834, Wake Forest Institute, as it was called until 1838, was opened in the building with an enrollment of 16 students. The dwelling house was used as the residence of the first President of the College, Samuel Wait, and for classroom purposes. The carriage house was used as a chapel. The seven "good substantial log cabins" were used as dormitories.

The house, now on its fourth site, was moved from its original location in the center of the campus in 1835 to make way for "The College Building," and later to a third location on Wingate Street. It is now restored to the 1830 period.

*US 1 Alternate (North Main Street)
in Wake Forest* / 1963

**H-76   NORTH CAROLINA
MUSEUM OF ART**

Outgrowth of N.C. Art Society. In 1947 state funded purchase of art. Museum opened, 1956. Moved here, 1983.

Blue Ridge Road in Raleigh / 1965

H-77 BERRY O'KELLY SCHOOL

Begun 1910. Early Negro teacher training school. Named for benefactor. Later used as elementary school. Closed in 1966.

Method Road in Raleigh / 1968

**H-79   THOMAS R. JERNIGAN
1847-1920**

U.S. negotiator in China for 30 years. Consul in Japan and China. Editor, author, and lawyer. His home was 2 blocks E.

*US 70/401/NC 50 (McDowell Street) at
Cabarrus Street in Raleigh* / 1968

**H-80 ALEXANDER B. ANDREWS
1841-1915**

Railroad builder and financier. Vice-president, Southern Railroad; superintendent, North Carolina Railroad. Home is here.

North Blount Street in Raleigh / 1971

H-81   W. N. H. SMITH

N.C. Chief Justice, 1878-1889; state legislator; U.S. & Confederate Congressman. Home was one blk. W.; grave 3/4 mi. E.

*Wilmington Street at Polk Street
in Raleigh* / 1972

**H-82   N.C. DIVISION OF
ARCHIVES & HISTORY**

Organized as the N.C. Historical Commission in 1903; R. D. W. Connor, first secretary. Moved to this building, 1968.

East Jones Street in Raleigh / 1993

**H-85   NORTH CAROLINA
STATE LIBRARY**

Established 1812 under Wm. Hill, Sec. of State; James F. Taylor first state librarian, 1843. Moved here in 1968.

East Jones Street in Raleigh / 1975

**H-86   JAMES H. HARRIS
1832-1891**

Union colonel; legislator; member 1868 convention; a founder of Republican Party & Union League in N.C. Home was 1 block W.

*Person Street at Davie Street
in Raleigh* / 1975

Alexander B. Andrews (H 80)

H-87   JAMES H. YOUNG
1860-1921
Colonel of black N.C. regiment in war with Spain; edited *Raleigh Gazette*; legislator. Home was 25 ft. W.

Person Street at Lenoir Street
in Raleigh / 1975

H-89   N.C. PHARMACEUTICAL
ASSOCIATION
Organized in 1880 at a meeting held in the Senate Chamber. E. M. Nadal of Wilson was the first president.

Wilmington Street in Raleigh / 1979

H-90   EDWARD A. JOHNSON
1860-1944
Politician, businessman, philanthropist, author, and educator. First black to publish a N.C. textbook. Home was here.

West Street at Lenoir Street
in Raleigh / 1982

H-91   R. STANHOPE PULLEN
1822-1895
Businessman. Benefactor of NCSU, UNC-G, and Peace College. Gifts included land for Pullen Park. Birthplace here.

Falls of the Neuse Road at Durant Road
in Raleigh / 1985

H-92   WILLIAM W. HOLDEN
1818-1892
Editor. Appointed provisional governor, 1865. Elected governor, 1868; impeached and removed, 1871. Home stood here.

US 70/401/NC 50 (McDowell Street) at
Hargett Street in Raleigh / 1986

H-93   NORTH CAROLINA
STATE FAIR
Agricultural fair. Was first held in 1853 and moved to this location, its third, in 1928.

Hillsborough Street at Blue Ridge Road
in Raleigh / 1987

H-94   LAMAR STRINGFIELD
1897-1959
Musician and composer. First conductor of the N.C. Symphony, 1932-38. Boyhood home 3 blks. E.

North Person Street in Raleigh / 1988

H-95   JANE McKIMMON
1867-1957
Home economist. From 1911 to 1937 she organized and led N.C.'s home demonstration program. Lived here.

North Blount Street at Polk Street
in Raleigh / 1988

H-96   ST. AUGUSTINE'S
COLLEGE
Founded in 1867 by the Episcopal Church as a normal school for freedmen. Since 1928 a four-year college. 4 blocks N.

Edenton Street at Tarboro Road
in Raleigh / 1988

H-99   GALES FAMILY
Joseph, *Raleigh Register* founder, 1799; his wife Winifred, early novelist; sons Joseph and Weston, editors, lived 2 blks. E.

McDowell Street at Davie Street
in Raleigh / 1990

H-100   FIRST PRESBYTERIAN
CHURCH
Organized 1816. Site of Constitutional Convention of 1835. State Supreme Court met here, 1831-40, after Capitol fire. This building completed 1900.

Salisbury Street at Morgan Street
in Raleigh / 1990

Lamar Stringfield (H 94)

H-101   CLARENCE POE
1881-1964
Editor and publisher of *The Progressive Farmer*, 1903-1954. Social and agricultural reformer. Lived 400 yards S.E.

New Bern Avenue at Peartree Lane in Raleigh / 1990

H-103   CHARLES N. HUNTER
1852-1931
Black teacher, writer, & reformer. Principal, Berry O'Kelly School; a founder, N.C. Industrial Assoc. Lived 1 block S.

New Bern Avenue in Raleigh / 1991

H-104   WILLIAM POLK
1758-1834
Revolutionary War officer; first president of State Bank, 1811-19. In 1825 hosted Lafayette in house that stood here.

Blount Street at North Street in Raleigh / 1992

H-105   C. C. CRITTENDEN
1902-1969
Historian, archivist, & editor. Promoted "History for all the people" as head of N.C.'s state historical agency, 1935-1968. Boyhood home was here.

US 1 Alternate (Main Street) in Wake Forest / 1995

H-106   NORTH CAROLINA BAR ASSOCIATION
Organized here, Feb. 10, 1899, in room then used by N.C. Supreme Court. Platt Walker of Charlotte, group's first president.

Edenton Street at Salisbury Street in Raleigh / 1998

H-107 STUDENT NONVIOLENT COORDINATING COMMITTEE
Civil rights organization, an outgrowth of sit-in movement, had origins in conference at Shaw University, Apr. 15-17, 1960.

Wilmington Street in Raleigh / 1998

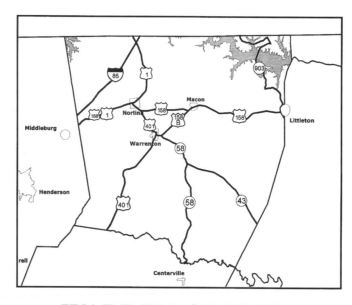

WARREN COUNTY

E-2   NATHANIEL MACON
Speaker of U.S. House of Representatives and U.S. Senator. Lived 1758-1837. Home 4 miles northwest.

US 158 at Vaughan / 1935

E-5   ANNIE CARTER LEE
1839-1862
Daughter of Robert E. Lee & Mary Custis Lee. Was buried 1/2 mile W. General Lee visited her grave in 1870.

US 401 north of Warren/Franklin County line / 1936

E-14   HORACE GREELEY
1811-1872

Journalist & politician was married in Emmanuel Church on July 5, 1836, to Mary Youngs Cheney.

US 401/158 Business (Main Street)
in Warrenton / 1938

E-17   JETHRO SUMNER

General in the American Revolution, officer in the French and Indian War. His famous inn stood in this vicinity.

US 401 southwest of Warrenton / 1939

E-19   BUTE COUNTY

Formed 1764. Named for the Earl of Bute. Divided, 1779, into Warren and Franklin counties. Courthouse stood nearby.

US 401 southwest of Warrenton / 1939

E-21   SHOCCO SPRINGS

Famous health resort, social and recreational center, in nineteenth century. 4fi miles southeast.

NC 401 at Afton / 1939

E-30   TRADING PATH

Colonial trading route, dating from 17th century, from Petersburg, Virginia, to Catawba and Waxhaw Indians in Carolina, passed nearby.

US 1 (Hyco Street) in Norlina / 1941

E-36   WARRENTON MALE
ACADEMY

Stood here. Chartered 1787, named Warrenton High School, 1898. Since 1923 a public school.

US 158 Business (Macon Street)
in Warrenton / 1948

E-37   WILLIAM MILLER

Governor, 1814-1817; state legislator and attorney general; U.S. Charge d'Affaires to Central America. Lived three miles north.

US 158 at SR 1335 (Church Hill Road) east
of Macon / 1948

E-38   BRAGG HOME

Boyhood home of Bragg brothers, Thomas, governor, 1855-9; Braxton, Confederate general, and John, U.S. Congressman. One block east.

North Main Street in Warrenton / 1948

E-44   BENJAMIN HAWKINS

Member Continental Congress, United States Senator, 1789-1795, U.S. Indian Agent to the Creek Nation, 1796-1816. Home was 5fi mi. S.W.

US 401 (South Main Street) at Franklin
Street in Warrenton / 1950

Jacob W. Holt House (E 86) in Warrenton

E-58   JAMES TURNER
Governor, 1802-1805, United States Senator and state legislator. "Bloomsbury," his home, stood 2 miles north.

US 1/158 east of Manson / 1955

E-60   JOHN WHITE
N.C. commissioner to buy ships and supplies in England during the Civil War. Gen. R. E. Lee visited in his home, 1870, standing 1 block E.

US 401 (South Main Street) in Warrenton / 1956

E-63   "BRIDLE CREEK"
The birthplace of two Confederate major generals: Matt W. and Robert Ransom, brothers. House stood 1/4 mile W.

US 401 southwest of Warrenton / 1959

E-86   JACOB W. HOLT
1811-1880
A chief architect-builder in town's 1845-61 boom era; worked in Greek Revival & Italianate styles. Home stands 1 block east.

US 401 (South Main Street) at Franklin Street in Warrenton / 1976

E-93   JOHN HALL
1767-1833
One of three original justices of the N.C. Supreme Court, 1819-1832. Grave 1 block S.

NC 158 (Macon Street) at Hall Street in Warrenton / 1985

E-100   WELDON EDWARDS
1788-1873
President, N.C. Secession Convention, 1861-1862; Congressman, 1816-1827; legislator. His grave is three miles north.

US 1/158 and SR 1224 (Ridgeway Road) at Ridgeway / 1989

E-101   JOHN A. HYMAN
1840-1891
First black to represent N.C. in U.S. Congress, 1875-1877; state senator, 1868-1874. Home is one block west.

US 401 (South Main Street) at Franklin Street in Warrenton / 1989

E-102   JOHN H. KERR
1873-1958
Congressman, 1923-1952; jurist. Sponsored bills to create tobacco price supports and Kerr Lake. He lived 2 blocks east.

US 401 (Main Street) at Church Street in Warrenton / 1991

John H. Kerr (E 102)

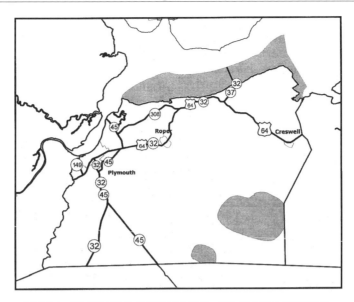

WASHINGTON COUNTY

B-9   BATTLE OF PLYMOUTH
Confederates under Gen. Robert F. Hoke, aided by the ram "Albemarle," took the town, April 17-20, 1864.

Main Street in Plymouth / 1938

B-10   RAM ALBEMARLE
Confederate ironclad, winner of notable victories under Capt. J. W. Cooke, was sunk 600 feet north, night of Oct. 27, 1864.

Main Street in Plymouth / 1938

B-12   JAMES JOHNSTON PETTIGREW
Confederate General, famed for charge at Gettysburg. His grave is 8 miles south.

US 64 at Sixth Street in Creswell / 1939

B-13   AUGUSTIN DALY
Playwright, dramatic critic, theatrical producer, and actor, was born, July 20, 1838, in a house which stood 300 feet north.

Main Street in Plymouth / 1939

Street scene in Plymouth, 1949

B-22　　MACKEYS FERRY
Established 1735 over Albemarle Sound, succeeding Bells Ferry. Discontinued in 1938. Southern terminus was 3 miles northwest.

US 64 and SR 1300 (Mackeys Road)
at Pleasant Grove / 1942

B-23　　BUNCOMBE HALL
The home of Col. Edward Buncombe of the Continental Line, who was captured at Germantown and died a prisoner in 1778, stood one mi. N.

Old US 64 in Roper / 1942

B-29　　CHARLES PETTIGREW
First Bishop-elect of Episcopal Church in N.C., 1794. St. David's Church, erected 1803 at his expense, and his home are 1/2 mile southeast.

US 64 at Sixth Street in Creswell / 1951

B-35　　LAKE COMPANY
Josiah Collins, Sr., and partners drained part of 100,000-acre tract near Lake Phelps with 6-mile canal, completed 1788; mouth 2 mi. southeast.

US 64 at Sixth Street in Creswell / 1955

B-49　　REHOBOTH CHURCH
Colonial Anglican congregation known as Skinners Chapel. Present church constructed 1850-1853. Now United Methodist.

US 64 east of Skinnersville / 1975

B-57　　SOMERSET PLACE
Antebellum plantation of Josiah Collins III, who grew rice & corn. Home in 1860 to 328 slaves. Located six miles south.

US 64 at Sixth Street in Creswell / 1990

BB-6　BATTLE OF PLYMOUTH
At 4 P.M. on April 17, 1864, an advanced Union patrol on the Washington Road was captured by Confederate cavalry. A company of the 12th N. Y. Cavalry attacked the Confederates, but was repulsed. Soon a large force of Confederate infantry appeared on the Washington Road, and at the same time Fort Gray, two miles above Plymouth on the river bank, was attacked by advanced Confederate infantry. During the evening skirmishing continued from the Washington Road to the Acre Road. Union General Henry W. Wessells' garrison of about 3,000, which had held

Plymouth since December, 1862, was under attack by General Robert F. Hoke's Division of over 5,000 men.

At 5:30 A.M. on April 18, a heavy Confederate artillery fire was directed against Fort Gray. Both Fort Gray and Battery Worth in Plymouth returned the fire. Soon a Union gunboat, the *Bombshell*, was disabled by the Confederate barrage.

At 6:30 P.M. on the 18th the Confederates advanced their line and began an infantry assault upon the Union position; but this attack was abandoned at 8 P.M. The 85th Redoubt was then attacked and captured at 11 P.M.

At 3 A.M. on April 19, the Confederates again attacked Fort Gray. Soon the Confederate iron-clad ram *Albemarle,* aiding the army, passed undetected down the river. The *Albemarle* engaged the *Southfield* and the *Miami* at 3:30 A.M., sinking the former and driving the latter away. The *Albemarle* then began to shell the Union defenses.

On April 19 the Confederates opened fire on the Union line from the 85th Redoubt. Fort Williams and Battery Worth returned the fire. Heavy skirmishing continued all day. At 6:30 P.M. the Confederates crossed Coneby Creek in an unexpected advance. Their infantry were now in an important position east of Plymouth.

At 5 A.M. on April 20, the Confederates under General Matt W. Ransom assaulted the Union line east of Plymouth, while General Hoke, with two brigades, demonstrated against the Union right. After capturing the Union defenses east of Plymouth, the Confederates halted their advance and re-formed. Union infantry counter-attacked, but were repulsed by a renewed Confederate advance. In spite of determined resistance by the garrison of Fort Williams, the town was surrendered by General Wessells at 10 A.M.

The capture of Plymouth by the Confederates was significant because it returned two rich eastern North Carolina counties to the Confederacy; it supplied "immense ordnance stores" to the Southern war effort; and the Roanoke River was reopened to Confederate commerce and military operations.

Washington Street in Plymouth / 1962

BBB-4   HOKE'S FINAL LINE
The extreme left flank of Confederate General Robt. F. Hoke's brigade was formed a few yds. N. just before the final attack, April 20, 1864.

West Main Street at Alden Road
in Plymouth / 1961

BBB-5   RANSOM'S ASSAULT
General Matt Ransom's brigade formed in line of battle near here in the final Confederate attack, April 20, 1864.

East Main Street west of Conaby Creek
in Plymouth / 1961

BBB-6   85th REDOUBT
Union fort built by the 85th New York Regiment. It was taken on April 18, 1864, in one of the heaviest assaults of the siege.

Campbell Street at Winston Street
in Plymouth / 1961

BBB-7   UNION EARTHWORKS
The main line of Union defenses during the Battle of Plymouth, April 17-20, 1864, was built across the road at this point.

Fort Williams Street in Plymouth / 1961

BBB-8   NAVAL ACTION
The Confederate ironclad ram "Albemarle" sank the Union gunboat "Southfield," April 19, 1864, one mile N.E. in the Roanoke River.

East Main Street in Plymouth / 1961

BBB-9   FORT WILLIAMS
Principal Union fort at Plymouth, named for Gen. Thomas Williams, stood here. It was the last fort to fall, April 20, 1864.

Jefferson Street at Fort Williams Street
in Plymouth / 1961

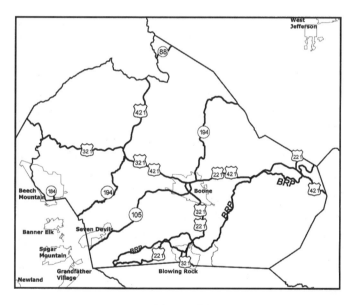

WATAUGA COUNTY

N-9   VALLE CRUCIS
EPISCOPAL MISSION
Established in 1842 by Bishop Levi S. Ives. Reorganized in 1895 by Bishop J. B. Cheshire.

NC 194 at Valle Crucis / 1939

N-10   STONEMAN'S RAID
On a raid through western North Carolina Gen. Stoneman's U.S. cavalry passed through Blowing Rock, March 28, 1865.

US 321 Business (Lenoir Turnpike)
in Blowing Rock / 1940

N-12   STONEMAN'S RAID
On a raid through western North Carolina
Gen. Stoneman's U.S. cavalry fought a skirmish with the home guard at Boone, March
28, 1865.

US 321/421 (King Street) in Boone / 1940

**N-14   NORTH CAROLINA-
                   TENNESSEE**

NORTH CAROLINA
Colonized, 1585-87, by first English settlers
in America; permanently settled c. 1650; first
to vote readiness for independence, Apr. 12,
1776.

(Reverse)   TENNESSEE
Settled before 1770 by North Carolina-
Virginia pioneers, ceded by North Carolina to
the United States, 1789, admitted to the
Union, 1796.

*US 421 north of Zionville at NC/TN
boundary* / 1941

**N-23   APPALACHIAN STATE
                   UNIVERSITY**
Founded as Watauga Academy. State-
supported since 1903. A part of The University of North Carolina since 1972.

US 321 (Hardin Street) in Boone / 1950

**N-25 ELLIOTT DAINGERFIELD
                   1859-1932**
Artist, teacher, author. His paintings hang in
the National Gallery, Metropolitan Museum,
and other galleries. His home is here.

*US 221 (Yonahlossee Road) northwest of
Blowing Rock* / 1951

N-33   STONEMAN'S RAID
On raid through western North Carolina Federal forces under Gen. George Stoneman
erected a palisaded fort here in April 1865.

*US 421 at Blue Ridge Parkway east
of Deep Gap* / 1959

**N-42   EMILY PRUDDEN
                   1832-1917**
Missionary. Founded 15 western N.C.
schools including Pfeiffer College forerunner. Her Skyland Institute stood here.

*US 321 Bypass (Valley Boulevard) at Main
Street in Blowing Rock* / 1991

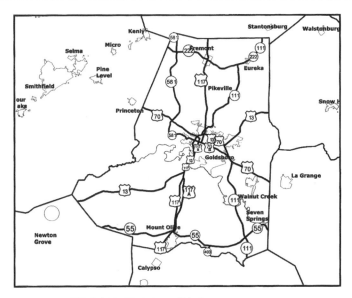

WAYNE COUNTY

F-1   CHARLES B. AYCOCK
Governor, 1901-1905. Crusader for public education. Birthplace stands 2/3 mi. east.
US 117 at SR 1542 (Governor Aycock Road) south of Fremont / 1936

F-9   WAYNESBOROUGH
First seat of Wayne County, incorporated 1787. The town died after the county seat was moved to Goldsboro in 1850. Site is here.
US 117 Bypass in Goldsboro / 1939

F-11   SHERMAN'S MARCH
Sherman's army, on its march from Savannah, entered Goldsboro, its chief North Carolina objective, Mar. 21, 1865.
NC 581 (West Ash Street) in Goldsboro / 1940

Inauguration of Governor Charles B. Aycock (F 1) at the State Capitol, 1901

**F-12   NORTH CAROLINA
               RAILROAD**
Built by the State, 1851-56, from Goldsboro
to Charlotte. Eastern terminus a few yards N.

*NC 581 (West Ash Street) in
Goldsboro* / 1940

F-18   CURTIS H. BROGDEN
Governor, 1874-1877; congressman; legislator; and major-general of State militia. His
home was 2 miles northwest.

US 13 southwest of Goldsboro / 1948

F-21   FOSTER'S RAID
On a raid from New Bern Union troops led
by Gen. J. G. Foster attacked Goldsboro,
December 17, 1862.

*NC 581 (West Ash Street)
in Goldsboro* / 1948

F-24   WM. T. DORTCH
Confederate Senator, Speaker State House of
Representatives, head of commission to cod-
ify State laws, 1883. Home is 1, grave 6,
blocks S.

*US 70 Business (Ashe Street) at US 117
Business (William Street)
in Goldsboro* /1949

F-25   DOBBS COUNTY
Formed 1758 & named for Gov. Arthur
Dobbs. From it were formed Wayne, 1779,
Lenoir and Glasgow (now Greene), 1791.
Courthouse was 3 miles S.

*US 70 at SR 1719 (Best Station Road)
northeast of Walnut Creek* / 1949

F-35   CHARLES B. AYCOCK
Governor of North Carolina, 1901-1905.
Crusader for universal education. His law
office is 2 blocks S.W.

*US 70 Business (Ash Street)
in Goldsboro* / 1960

F-38   TORHUNTA
Large Indian farming community before the
Tuscarora War. Destroyed in 1712 by Col.
John Barnwell. Site 3 mi. NE.

*US 13 at SR 1572 (Saulston-Patetown Road)
northeast of Goldsboro* / 1961

F-43 MOUNT OLIVE COLLEGE
Original Free Will Baptist. Chartered in 1951
as junior college. Moved here, 1953. Senior
college charter granted in 1982.

*US 117 Alternate (North Breazeale Avenue)
in Mount Olive* / 1970

Cherry Hospital (F 61) as it appeared in 1895

F-44 BATTLE OF WHITEHALL
On December 15-16, 1862, on a raid at Whitehall, Union troops led by Gen. J. G. Foster damaged the Confederate Ram "Neuse."
NC 55 at Main Street in Seven Springs / 1970

F-51 NORTH CAROLINA PRESS ASSOCIATION
Organized May 14, 1873. J. A. Engelhard elected first president at meeting held near this spot.
Walnut Street in Goldsboro / 1973

F-52 KENNETH C. ROYALL
Last Sec'y of War & first Sec'y of Army, 1947-49. Attorney; state senator; brig. gen., 1943-45. Led military justice reform. Home was here.
NC 581 (West Ash Street) in Goldsboro / 1973

F-53 ODD FELLOWS HOME
Orphanage and school opened in 1892. Provided for 960 children before closing in 1971. The original 20-acre tract is now a city park.
US 70 Business (East Ash Street) at Herman Street in Goldsboro / 1974

F-59 SEYMOUR JOHNSON AIR FORCE BASE
Field used, 1942-46, for flight training by Army Air Forces; reopened in 1956. Named for Seymour Johnson, naval aviator and Goldsboro native.
Berkeley Boulevard at Elm Street in Goldsboro / 1995

F-61 CHERRY HOSPITAL
Opened by state in 1880 for black citizens with mental illness. Named in 1959 for R. Gregg Cherry, governor, 1945-49. Open to all races since 1965.
NC 581 at SR 1008 (Stevens Mill Road) in Goldsboro / 1997

F-62 GENERAL BAPTIST STATE CONVENTION
Statewide association of black Baptists organized, Oct. 18, 1867, at First African Baptist Church, then located 2/10 mi. W.
US 117 Business (George Street) at Pine Street in Goldsboro / 1997

Kenneth C. Royall (F 52), center, with President Harry S. Truman and Governor R. Gregg Cherry

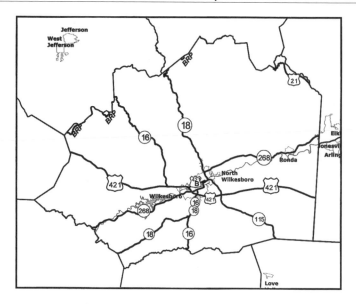

WILKES COUNTY

M-2   MONTFORT STOKES
1762-1842
Governor, 1830-1832; U.S. Senator; Federal Indian Commissioner. Home stood 1 mi. N.
NC 268 at Wilkesboro / 1938

M-10   STONEMAN'S RAID
On a raid through western North Carolina Gen. Stoneman's U.S. cavalry occupied Wilkesboro, March 29, 1865.
NC 18/268 (East Main Street)
in Wilkesboro / 1940

M-13   JAMES B. GORDON
Brigadier general in the Confederate States Army. Mortally wounded near Richmond, Virginia, May 12, 1864. Birthplace stands 300 yards north.
US 421 Business in North Wilkesboro / 1940

M-30   BENJAMIN CLEVELAND
Colonel in Revolution, Whig leader in battle of Kings Mountain, state legislator. Home was on "The Round About," one mile southwest.
NC 268 at Chatham Street in Ronda / 1955

M-31   "FORT HAMBY"
Fortified stronghold of band of robbers & army deserters, was captured by force of citizens in May, 1865. Stood one mile north.
NC 268 east of Goshen / 1956

M-38   WILKESBORO
PRESBYTERIAN CHURCH
Established in 1837; present church built in 1849-50. The first Presbyterian church in Wilkes County.
NC 18/268 (Main Street)
in Wilkesboro / 1967

M-42   JAMES WELLBORN
1767-1854
Served 27 years as state senator; colonel in War of 1812; delegate to the Constitutional Convention 1835. Grave is 1/5 mi. N.
NC 268 in Wilkesboro / 1972

M-43   RICHARD ALLEN, SR.
Colonel of N.C. Militia at Battle of King's Mountain. Delegate to the Hillsborough Convention, 1788; in General Assembly, 1793. Grave is 4 mi. N.
NC 268 at Roaring River / 1972

M-48   THOMAS C. DULA
1844-1868
"Tom Dooley" of popular legend and song. Hanged in Statesville for murder of Laura Foster. Grave is 1fi mi. S.W.
NC 268 and SR 1134 (Dula Road)
at Ferguson / 1986

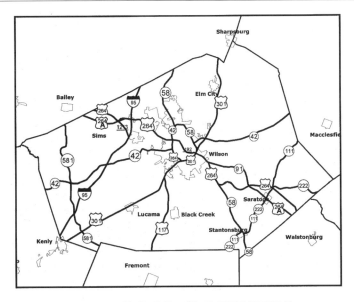

WILSON COUNTY

F-17   PLANK ROAD
The western terminus of the Greenville and Raleigh Plank Road, chartered in 1850 and completed to Wilson by 1853, was nearby.

Pender Street at East Nash Street in Wilson / 1941

F-30   BARTON COLLEGE
Founded in 1902 by the Christian Church of N.C. as Atlantic Christian College. Renamed 1990 for a church founder, Barton W. Stone.

Vance Street at Rountree Street in Wilson / 1953

F-31   PEACOCK'S BRIDGE
Here Lt. Col. Tarleton's British dragoons and Colonel James Gorham's militia engaged in a skirmish, May, 1781.

NC 58 at Contentnea Creek bridge southeast of Stantonsburg / 1953

F-32   MILITARY HOSPITAL
Confederate. Headed by Dr. S. S. Satchwell in building of the Wilson Female Seminary, which was chartered in 1859. Stood 1fi blocks S.E.

Herring Avenue at Gold Street in Wilson / 1954

F-33   TOISNOT CHURCH
Baptist. Founded 1756. Was moved 3fi miles west in 1803. Early church site and graveyard are 350 yards south.

NC 42 east of Wilson / 1959

F-34   GEN. W. D. PENDER
Confederate Major-General. Mortally wounded at Gettysburg. His birthplace stood 1.4 miles north.

NC 42 east of Wilson / 1959

P. D. Gold (F 54)

F-39   R. D. W. CONNOR
First Archivist of the U.S., 1934-41. Secretary of the N.C. Historical Commission, historian, author, and teacher. His birthplace stood here.

NC 58/US 264 (East Nash Street)
in Wilson / 1965

F-54   P. D. GOLD
1833-1920
Primitive Baptist leader & for 50 years editor of Zion's Landmark. Office & home was 1/2 blk. NE.

Vance Street at Maplewood Avenue
in Wilson / 1979

F-55   CHARLES LEE COON
1868-1927
Educational reformer, historian and author. Secty. of Child Labor Committee, 1904-1916. Home was 1/2 blk. west.

Vance Street at Rountree Street
in Wilson / 1979

F-56   HENRY G. CONNOR
1852-1924
Justice of N.C. Supreme Court; Federal District Judge; state legislator. Grave is 3/5 mi. west.

Whitehead Avenue at Raleigh Road
in Wilson / 1979

F-64   OWEN L. W. SMITH
1851-1926
U.S. minister to Liberia, 1898-1902; born into slavery. Pastor, St. John A.M.E. Zion Church in Wilson. Lived 1/10 mi. N.

Nash Street at Pender Street
in Wilson / 2000

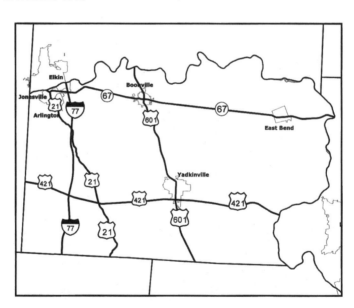

YADKIN COUNTY

M-4   THOMAS L. CLINGMAN
United States Senator, Confederate General, born at Huntsville, 9 mi. east, 1812. Clingman's Dome, 160 miles west, is named for him.

US 601 at SR 1001 (Courtney-Huntsville
Road) south of Yadkinville / 1939

M-12   RICHMOND PEARSON
1805-1878
Chief Justice, State Supreme Court, 1859-78. Conducted law school at Richmond Hill, his home, located five miles N.W.

NC 67 at SR 1570 (Nebo Road) east of
Boonville / 1940

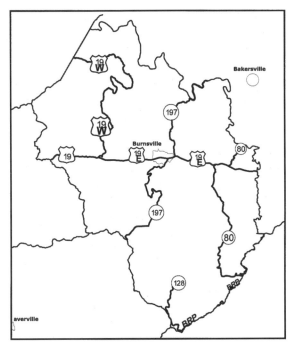

YANCEY COUNTY

**N-16   NORTH CAROLINA-
TENNESSEE**

NORTH CAROLINA
Colonized, 1585-87, by first English settlers in America; permanently settled c. 1650; first to vote readiness for independence, Apr. 12, 1776.

(Reverse)   TENNESSEE
Settled before 1770 by North Carolina-Virginia pioneers, ceded by North Carolina to the United States, 1789, admitted to the Union, 1796.

US 19 West at NC/TN boundary / 1941

**N-27   YANCEY COLLEGIATE
INSTITUTE**
A Baptist preparatory school, 1901-1926. Two of the buildings later used by public schools. 1/2 mile northeast.

Main Street in Burnsville / 1952

**N-38   ELISHA MITCHELL
1793-1857**
Scientist and professor. Died in attempt to prove this mountain highest in eastern U.S. Grave is at the summit, 285 yds. S.

NC 128 at Mount Mitchell State Park / 1988

Elisha Mitchell (N 38)

Subject-Title Index

A